The Eighth Situpa on the Third Karmapa's Mahāmudrā Prayer

The Eighth Situpa on the Third Karmapa's Mahāmudrā Prayer

Introduction by
Venerable Khenchen Trangu Rinpoche

Translation by
Lama Sherab Dorje

Snow Lion
Boulder

Snow Lion
An imprint of Shambhala Publications, Inc.
4720 Walnut Street
Boulder, Colorado 80301
www.shambhala.com

Drawing of the Third Karmapa Rangjung Dorje on page 20 by Robert Beer.

Printed in the United States of America

♾ This edition is printed on acid-free paper that meets the American National Standards Institute Z39.48 Standard.
♻ Shambhala Publications makes every effort to print on recycled paper. For more information please visit www.shambhala.com.
Shambhala Publications is distributed worldwide by Penguin Random House, Inc., and its subsidiaries.

The Library of Congress catalogues the previous edition of this book as follows:

Si-tu Paṇ-chen Chos-kyi-'byuṅ-gnas, 1699 or 1700–1774.
[Ṅes don phyag rgya chen po'i smon lam gyi 'grel pa grub pa mchog gi źal luṅ. English]
Mahāmudrā Teachings of the Supreme Siddhas / The Eighth Situpa, Tenpa'i Nyinchay on "The aspiration prayer of Mahāmudrā of definitive meaning" by the Third Karmapa, Rangjung Dorje; introduction by Venerable Trangu Rinpoche; translated by Sherab Dorje. — First edition.
p. cm.
ISBN 978-1-55939-025-5 (first edition)
ISBN 978-1-55939-213-6 (second edition)
1. Raṅ-byuṅ-rdo-rje, Karma-pa III, 1284–1339. Ṅes don phyag rgya chen po'i smon lam. 2. Karma-pa (Sect)—Prayer-books and devotions—Tibetan—History and criticism. 3. Mahāmudrā (Tantric rite). I. Raṅ-byuṅ-rdo-rje, Karma-pa III, 1284–1339. Ṅes don phyag rgya chen po'i smon lam. II. Sherab Dorje.
BQ7682.6.R363S5 1994
294.3'443—dc20
93-40280
CIP

Contents

Foreword

All students of the Kagyu traditions of Tibetan Buddhism are familiar with Karmapa III Rangjung Dorje's beautiful prayer, known in brief simply as the *Aspiration of Mahāmudrā,* and recited daily in countless Tibetan temples, retreats and homes. The depth of the significance this short litany holds for those practicing within the tradition first became clear to me some twenty years ago, when I had the good fortune to read, under the guidance of the late Kalu Rinpoche, the great commentary that Situ Paṇchen composed to explain Rangjung Dorje's words. Hearing the actual phrases once spoken by Rangjung Dorje and Situ Paṇchen expounded by perhaps the greatest contemporary representative of the Mahāmudrā approach to meditation came with the force of a revelation, pointing the way to a transition from treating Mahāmudrā as an object of study, to the possibility of comprehending it as the very texture of experience, defying all prospects of objectification.

In the present volume Lama Sherab Dorje offers us an accurate and highly readable translation of this masterwork of Kagyu Buddhism, a work that is sure to be read with profit both by those who wish to learn something about the system of Mahāmudrā, and by those practicing within the tradition. The latter, in particular, will find here a text that deserves to be studied in depth, until, in the words of the tradition, the intentions of the author have become fully integrated with one's own meditations.

Matthew Kapstein
Department of Religion
Columbia University
July 1994

Preface

The title of the eighth Tai Situpa Tenpa'i Nyinchay's work translated in this book, *Teachings of the Supreme Siddhas*, is apt. The eighth Tai Situpa Rinpoche, Tenpa'i Nyinchay, more commonly known by the name Chokyi Jungnay (or Situ Paṇchen— "Situ the great paṇḍita"), undoubtedly chose this title to highlight the fact that he draws abundant supporting testimony from sources in sūtras, tantras, treatises, and Indian and Tibetan commentaries for his interpretations of the aspiration prayer and his explication of the view of mahāmudrā. The list of paṇḍitas and siddhas whom he quotes is impressive, and since, in most cases, he assumes his source materials to be self-explanatory, the task of translating these profound and at times arcane statements proved formidable.

I have therefore carefully reviewed the more difficult passages in this text with three different master khenpos of the Kagyu lineage, and have often supplemented terse or difficult passages with their comments, placed in the footnotes or, in some instances, in square brackets in the text. Because I have relied on the wisdom of these great contemporary scholars and siddhas, this book is also properly titled *Mahāmudrā Teachings of the Supreme Siddhas*.

Here, "supreme siddhas" are those who have realized mahāmudrā, and "definitive meaning" is the final meaning of the ultimate nature.

Despite its obvious weightiness as a scholarly text, I have not translated this book as an academic exercise, but with the wish that dharma students everywhere might appreciate Situ Rinpoche's presentation of how the mantra practice of mahāmudrā rests on a sound scriptural and philosophical basis within the Buddhist tradition. It has also been my hope that the reader will discover how complete and beautiful are Karmapa Rangjung Dorje's words of advice and instruction on the ground, path, fruition, view, meditation and action of mahamudra.

There are many technical terms that come into play in any discussion of philosophical view. I have chosen not to be overly technical and rigid in my use of English words to translate dharma terms, but instead have attempted to convey the fullest range of meanings by varying and altering these words according to context. I hope therefore to have avoided creating a lot of formalistic jargon. The reader may find one Tibetan word translated four or five different ways in different contexts and at different points in the text. However, none of these divergences should prove confusing.

I have translated the text titles of the many scriptural sources cited in the commentary. Proper Tibetan and Sanskrit titles for these works are given in the bibliography. I have also added words in square brackets to fill out the outline within the body of the text. Finally, as I have always been dissatisfied by efforts to translate the Sanskrit term *prajñā* into English, I have decided to allow the definition proffered in the text ("Prajñā is that faculty of mind which finely distinguishes among dharmas") to speak for itself.

Every word in the aspiration has great significance, and it seems to me that the more precisely we understand the author's intention when he wrote these verses, the more powerful and valuable our recitation of them will be. As thorough as Situ Rinpoche's treatment is, I would still advise anyone studying this text to approach a reliable teacher in person with the questions that will undoubtedly remain after studying this commentary. Many of the explanations found in the commentary themselves require some degree of elucidation or elaboration. Indeed the author himself often points the reader in the direction of further research.

Because we foreign students of the Kagyu lineage have been graced with so much direct and profound instruction on mantra mahāmudrā practice, yet in many cases lack the background knowledge and experience that would help us understand its place and function within the overall teachings of the lineage (such as might be obtained in a tantric college or practice seminary), we may retain doubts and uncertainty about the rigorous foundations and precise nature of this approach to practice, especially in comparison with the very systematic teachings and logical arguments found in other schools.

It is therefore with the aspiration that Tenpa'i Nyinchay's teachings might help remedy these doubts and supply vital background information to those who lack it that I undertook this translation. I beg the forgiveness of scholars in the academic community for any defects they may perceive in my work, and in particular I supplicate the lineage masters to look kindly and forgivingly upon whatever I have been unable to communicate of their profound intentions due to my own ignorance or lack of understanding. May they look beyond my shortcomings to see my honest intentions, and may future practitioners and scholars be kind enough to repair any errors I have unknowingly made.

I must thank Lama Norlha and the kind saṅgha members of Kagyu Thubten Choling for creating the supportive circumstances for Khenpo Tsultrim Gyatso Rinpoche's seminar of teachings on this text in the Autumn of 1989, from which some of the footnote references and comments have been drawn. I also wish to thank Khenchen Trangu Rinpoche for encouraging me to translate several commentaries on the aspiration prayer, including a briefer presentation of Situ Rinpoche's words arranged by Mendong Tshampa, and an even briefer work by Karma'i Khenpo, Rinchen Darjay, and for his introduction to the text and many insightful comments on difficult passages. I would also like to thank Riwoche Khenpo Sonam Topgyal Rinpoche for offering his help with many passages.

I finally would like to thank Richard Marshall and my parents, Jacob and Rita Posel, for the ongoing encouragement they gave to my work on this project, Lama Yeshe Gyatso for offering a number of valuable suggestions, and Sidney Piburn and the people at Snow Lion for enabling it to reach a wide audience.

May the glorious teachings of the succession of Gyalwa Karmapas spread;
may the masters of their lineage enjoy long and productive lives;
may all practitioners discover these teachings and practice them with no obstacles; and
may the profound doctrine of mahāmudrā always flourish in this world.

Lama Sherab Dorje
Kathmandu, Nepal
Montreal, Canada
New York, USA
Spring 1993 to Winter 1994

Introduction

The succession of incarnations of the single being named Karmapa, from Dusum Kyenpa until the current seventeenth, Orgyen Trinley, have all manifested their own unique qualities and activities. The first, Dusum Kyenpa, was a great meditation master who founded the Karma Kamtsang lineage and established the great monastic seats of his lineage at Karma Gon, Tsurphu and Gampo Naynang. The next incarnation, Karma Pakshi, was an extremely powerful and realized practitioner who trained all manner of beings through his overwhelming display of power and majesty.

The third incarnation, Rangjung Dorje (1284-1339), never displayed powers on the order of his predecessor, yet was nonetheless a great paṇḍita and siddha in his own right. In terms of his scholarship, we see that he composed many important treatises summarizing and explicating the meanings of, on the one hand, profound tantras, such as "The Profound Inner Meaning" (*Zab mo nang don*), and on the other hand, vast sūtras, such as "Distinguishing Primordial Wisdom and Consciousness" (*Ye shes rnam shes che ba*) and "Treatise that Points Out the Essence" (*sNying po ten pa'i bstan bcos*). As a siddha, he accomplished such feats as appearing to beings even after he had departed from his body to the pure realms. He also left a legacy of many treatises and compositions on the subjects of mahāmudrā and the six doctrines of Nāropa, among others.

His main concern as both a scholar and realized master was with the view that unites mahāmudrā and great perfection. Although these two are explained using different linguistic devices and appear to be distinct from each other, they are essentially the same. Even though their lineages of transmission and provisional methods differ slightly, ultimately they are identical. What do instruction manuals in the mahāmudrā tradition offer? Instructions on the nature of mind. What is it that is taught when the great perfection tradition is presented? The nature of mind. These instructions are more or less the same. That is how we can speak of a view of unified mahāmudrā and great perfection.

In particular, Karmapa Rangjung Dorje composed, out of his own realization, this *Aspiration Prayer of Mahāmudrā* as a concise yet complete set of formal instructions on the ground, path and fruition of mahāmudrā practice. This prayer came to be highly regarded at all the monastic seats of the Kagyu lineage. Why is that? It is because all of the stages of instruction on the path of mahāmudrā are incorporated in the prayer and can therefore be learned from it. But not only is this a concise and complete teaching on mahāmudrā, it is also a set of aspiration prayers. One recites "May I realize this!" "May perfect serene abiding arise in my mindstream!" "After that, may exceptional higher insight arise in my mind!" "May I correctly realize the view!" "May perfect compassion be born in my heart!" and so forth. Aspiring in this way creates tremendous benefit for the practitioner, and that is why, out of his aspiration to benefit beings and with the fervent wish that the teachings of mahāmudrā spread far and wide and continue to benefit beings far into the future, Rangjung Dorje composed this teaching in the form of a prayer of aspiration. And so it came to pass that this prayer became extremely famous throughout Tibet and was practiced in all the various dharma lineages.

No actual commentary explicating the vast and profound meaning contained within these poetic verses existed until the time of the eighth Situpa, who was himself a remarkable scholar, the greatest among all of the succession of Tai Situpas. In general he wrote many commentaries and annotated guidebooks, and among them, this commentary on Lord Rangjung Dorje's extraordinary *Aspiration Prayer of Mahāmudrā* in particular achieved great renown. Later, abbreviated commentaries on the same prayer were composed by Mendong Tshampa Rinpoche and Karma'i Khenpo Rinchen Darjay which were based on Situ Rinpoche's authoritative work.

The seventh Situ Rinpoche, Lekshay Maway Nyima (1683-1698), spent most of his brief life at Karma Gon Monastery, the seat of his five preceding incarnations, where his activities on behalf of the dharma were very extensive. The eighth Situ Rinpoche was born in 1700 and recognized by the eighth Shamar, Chokyi Dondrup, who gave him the name Chokyi Jungnay Trinlay Kunkyab Yeshe Pal Zangpo, and later gave him his novice ordination name, Karma Tenpa'i Nyinchay Tsuglag Chokyi Nangwa. Situ Rinpoche used these names interchangeably throughout his life.

In 1724 Situ Rinpoche went to Penjor Monastery in the Alok Valley in the kingdom of Derge after years of study in Kham and Central Tibet and a year-long visit to Nepal in the company of both Karmapa Changchub Dorje and Shamar Rinpoche. The king of Derge, Tenpa Tsering, encouraged him to establish a new monastic seat, funding the construction of Palpung, completed in 1727.

Situ Rinpoche was influential in the formation of the famous Derge printing house, overseeing and editing the first (1741) editions of the Derge Kangyur and Tangyur and creating the index (*dkar chag*). He travelled far and wide across Tibet, in the east, in the central region, and in the south, and also spent many years pursuing his grammatical and philological studies of Sanskrit in Nepal. He established many new monasteries in different regions, and when he visited established monasteries, he corrected and advanced their understanding of custom and ritual. His autobiography acknowledges that he also excelled in the studies of composition, medicine, Chinese astronomy and the arts. His fame as a Sanskrit scholar exceeded that of the Indian paṇḍitas of his day. He met Jayamangala, a pandit from Benares, in the Gurkha kingdom in Nepal, who praised his erudition and suggested he would be honored with a high throne covered by seven parasols were he in India.

This most influential Kagyu lama of his era passed away in 1774, entrusting the many volumes of his writings to his disciple Belu Tsewang Kunkyab. This commentary of his on the *Aspiration Prayer of Mahāmudrā* is most excellent because it is neither too brief nor too extensive, and is therefore very easy to work with as an aid to fully understanding the prayer itself.[1]

With regard to the view Karmapa Rangjung Dorje sets forth in this aspiration prayer, we need to consider first that there are two types of view: the view of Sūtrayāna, and the view of Mantrayāna.

One arrives at the view of sūtrayāna through application of valid inferential reasoning. Of the two types of Madhyamaka view, empty of self and empty of other, the empty of self approach regards all things as essentially lacking any true self-identity, and therefore to be empty. Through examination and analysis using the various forms of Madhyamaka reasoning one sees that things are not established in and of themselves. This investigation and conclusion applies both to the self-identity of persons and the self-identity of phenomena. The truth of emptiness is something to be understood through applying arguments and reasons, whereby one attains complete certainty that it is so. This approach can be called "making inference the path."

The view of the Mantrayāna system, however, is not just inferential, but "makes direct perception the path," that is, makes direct experience itself, unmediated by abstract reasoning, the path that is practiced. By being made directly aware of the fundamental enduring condition of one's own mind, one directly experiences the essential emptiness of one's mind in a manner that is not merely inferential.

Accordingly, this view is not the intellectual ascertainment of an abstraction that approximates the true nature of mind, but rather a direct glimpse of the final fruition. That is why in Secret Mantra the view must be introduced through what are called "mind instructions" which directly point out the nature of mind. This is true regardless of whether we are speaking of the mahāmudrā or great perfection dharma traditions.

Karmapa Rangjung Dorje's insight was that this direct, nonconceptual "view" of the enduring condition of mind must always be the same, for there is only one ultimate nature. That is why he is said to have combined the views of mahāmudrā, great perfection and Madhyamaka. Although technically, if we compare definitions and terms, we can isolate differences among these views, from an experiential point of view there is little or no difference. That is why, for example, echoing the verse in this aspiration prayer that says:

Free from being mind-made, this is mahāmudrā;
free of extremes, it is mahāmadhyamaka;
this contains all, and so is "mahāsaṃdhi" too.
Through knowing one, may I gain firm realization of the meaning of all.

the omnsicient teacher Jigme Lingpa, in the aspiration prayer that he composed for the practice of great perfection, said:

Fully nonabiding, the meaning of mahāmadhyamaka;
all encompassing and universally present, the sphere of mahāmudrā;
measureless expanse without any limits, the pith of mahāsaṃdhi....

Parallel to the verse that says:

It is not existent, for even Buddhas have never seen it.
It is not nonexistent, for it is the basis of all saṃsāra and nirvāṇa.
This is the unified central course, not a paradox.
May I realize the unlimited dharmatā of mind.

Jigme Lingpa wrote:

It is not existent, for Buddhas have never seen it.
It is not nonexistent, for it is the basis of both saṃsāra and nirvāṇa.
This is not a paradox, for it transcends what can be articulated.
May I realize great perfection, the enduring condition of the fundamental ground.

May these teachings be of benefit to all who come into contact with them.

Ven. Khenchen Trangu Rinpoche
Boudhanath, Nepal
March 1993

Third Karmapa Rangjung Dorje

The Aspiration Prayer of Mahāmudrā

by His Holiness the Third Gyalwa Karmapa Rangjung Dorje

1. Homage to the guru! Lamas and yidam maṇḍala deities,
   Victors of the three times and ten directions, and your
   offspring,
   lovingly consider me and bless my aspiration prayers
   that they may turn out exactly as intended.

2. May the streams of accumulated virtue, uncontaminated
   by the three concerns,
   that spring from the snow mountain of my own
   and countless other sentient beings' totally pure
   intentions and actions
   flow into the ocean of the four kāyas of the Victors.

3. For however long that may take to accomplish,
   in all lifetimes through my succession of lives,
   may even the sounds "nonvirtue" and "suffering"
   be unknown,
   and may I enjoy the wealth of oceanic virtue and
   happiness.

4. Possessing the greatest leisure and endowments,
   with faith, industry and prajñā,
   serving an excellent spiritual advisor, may I obtain
   quintessential instructions,
   and with no hindrance to their proper implementation,
   may I practice superb dharma in all my lifetimes.

5. Study of scripture and reasoning delivers one from the pall of nescience.
Reflection on the oral instructions vanquishes the darkness of uncertainty.
The light cast by meditation vividly illuminates the enduring condition.
May the radiance of the three prajñās intensify.

6. The meaning of "ground" is the two truths, beyond the polarity of existence and nonexistence.
Through the supreme path of two accumulations, beyond the extremes of embellishment and discredit,
the fruition of the two purposes, beyond the limits of conditioned existence and serenity, is attained.
May I encounter the dharma that neither errs nor misleads.

7. The ground of purification is mind nature, unified cognizance and emptiness.
Through the purifying agency of the great vajra yoga of mahāmudrā,
may delusory incidental stains be purified
and the result of purification, stainless dharmakāya, become manifest.

8. Cutting off embellishments of the ground, the view is assured.
Sustaining that without distraction is the point of meditation.
Gaining full proficiency in meditation is the finest activity.
May I have confident view, meditation and activity.

9. All phenomena are apparitions of mind.
Yet mind is not there, for mind is essentially empty,
and while empty, unimpeded, displayed any way at all—
examining well, may I sever the underlying root.

10. Self-display with no existence is mistaken for an object.
Out of ignorance, self-awareness is mistaken for one's self.
Driven by dualistic clinging, one wanders the vastness of creation.
May I strip away ignorance, the source of confusion.

11. It is not existent, for even Buddhas have never seen it.
It is not nonexistent, for it is the basis of all saṃsāra and nirvāṇa.
This is the unified central course, not a paradox.
May I realize the unlimited dharmatā of mind.

12. There is nothing to indicate that "it is this."
There is no refutation to show "it is not this."
Unfabricated dharmatā that defies the intellect
is the perfect, ultimate limit —may I be certain of it.

13. Simply not realizing this stirs the ocean of conditioned existence;
just realizing this, there is no enlightenment elsewhere.
Being all, it is never "this but not that."
May I discover the hidden dimensions of the universal ground, dharmatā.

14. Since appearance is mind, and emptiness also is mind,
realization is mind, and confusion also is my own mind,
arising is mind and cessation, too, is just mind,
may I sever all embellished claims within my mind.

15. Without being corrupted by deliberate, fabricated meditation,
and without being disturbed by the commotion of common affairs,
knowing how to settle into what is natural and uncontrived,
may I expertly sustain practice of the vital point of mind.

16. May the waves of coarse and subtle thoughts subside on their own
and the placid river of mind gently come to rest.
May the ocean of serene abiding, without the silt and mire
of torpor and dullness, remain steady and unperturbed.

17. When invisible mind is looked at again and again,
the unglimpsed meaning is beheld distinctly, just as it is.
With the severing of all doubts about what is and is not,
may the non-mistaken inner essence reveal itself.

18. Looking at an object, there is none; I see it is mind.
Looking for mind, mind is not there; it lacks any essence.
Looking at both, dualistic clinging is freed on its own.
May I realize luminosity, the enduring condition of mind.

19. Free from being mind-made, this is mahāmudrā;
free of extremes, it is mahāmadhyamaka;
this contains all, and so is "mahāsaṃdhi" too.
Through knowing one, may I gain firm realization of the meaning of all.

20. Great bliss with no attachment is continuous.
Luminosity without grasping at characteristics is unobscured.
Nonconceptuality that goes beyond intellect is spontaneous.
May unsought experiences occur without interruption.

21. Preferential grasping at experiences is liberated on the spot.
The confusion of negative thoughts is purified in the natural expanse.
Natural cognizance adopts and discards nothing, has nothing added or removed.
May I realize what is beyond limiting constructs, the truth of dharmatā.

22. The nature of beings is ever enlightened,
    yet not realizing this, they wander endlessly in saṃsāra.
    May intense compassion arise within me
    for sentient beings, whose suffering knows no bounds.

23. In the moment of love, when the vibrant power of intense compassion
    is uncontained, the empty essence shines forth nakedly.
    May I never step off this supreme path of unity that never goes awry,
    and practice it at all times, day and night.

24. With eyes and paranormal powers that arise from potent meditation,
    sentient beings are matured and buddha fields well cleansed.
    Aspirations to accomplish buddha dharmas are fulfilled.
    May I complete fulfillment, maturation and cleansing, and attain enlightenment.

25. Through the compassion of Victors and their offspring everywhere
    and the power of all the immaculate virtue there is,
    may my own and all countless sentient beings'
    totally pure aspirations be accomplished exactly as we intend.

nges don phyag rgya chen po'i smon lam gyi 'grel pa grub pa mchog gi zhal lung zhes bya ba bzhug so

Teachings of the Supreme Siddhas

Teachings of the Supreme Siddhas

I bow before Karmapa, master of the world,[1]
whose activity to rescue mother beings from oceanic suffering
and harbor them on the shore of liberation
is not surpassed even by the Victors of the three times.

This *Aspiration Prayer of Mahāmudrā of Definitive Meaning,* bestowed upon us by the supreme personage, the guide of all creatures, glorious Rangjung Gyalwa,[2] is concise and yet inclusive of all the stages of the path for great individuals.[3] Although we, his followers, should be generally familiar with its contents, since the prayer consists of the foremost, central instructions for newly generating realization and for progressively improving such realization, and is clearly also an indispensable teaching for practitioners of mahāmudrā, I will endeavor to explain the meaning of the words of the text to the best of my ability.

This explanation will be grouped into three main sections:

I. Preparation for Engaging in the Aspiration Prayer
II. The Main Body of the Prayer
III. A Concluding Summary of the Prayer

[I]
PREPARATION FOR THE ASPIRATION PRAYER

For the aspiration prayer to be performed, a consummate support should be solicited to act as a witness and the prayer should be made wholeheartedly in its presence. As is stated:

> *Before a stūpa containing relics, through acclaim for the Sugatas [aspirations are] accomplished.*

and

> *As all dharmas are conditioned, they rest on the acuity of intention.*
> *Whatever aspiration one makes, just so will its result transpire.*

Therefore, keeping in mind the importance of single-minded intent, request the support[4] to serve witness as follows:

1. **Homage to the guru! Lamas[5] and yidam maṇḍala deities,**
   Victors of the three times and ten directions, and your offspring,
   lovingly consider me and bless my aspiration prayers
   that they may turn out exactly as intended.

The phrase "and your offspring" is used to also include hearers and solitary realizers. In "Embarking on the Central Course":[6]

> *Hearers and intermediate Buddhas are born of the Mighty One.*[7]

The remainder of the verse is easy to understand.

[II]
THE MAIN BODY OF THE PRAYER

[This section has two parts:] a general dedication of merit towards perfect enlightenment; and the specific components of the aspiration prayer.

[II.A]
GENERAL DEDICATION OF MERIT TOWARDS PERFECT ENLIGHTENMENT

2. May the streams of accumulated virtue, uncontaminated by the three concerns,
that spring from the snow mountain of my own
and countless other sentient beings' totally pure intentions and actions
flow into the ocean of the four kāyas of the Victors.

"My" refers to the individual who is performing the aspiration prayer. All sentient beings are mentioned because this is the inclination of excellent individuals. In the "Concise Versified Prajñāpāramitā":

> *Without acting for the benefit of others there can be no enlightenment.*

And, as is said in the sūtra "Requested by Madröpa,"

> *When a bodhisattva possesses a single dharma, he completely masters the buddhadharmas that are superior in all aspects. What is that single dharma? The attitude of adamant unwillingness to abandon sentient beings.*

The totally pure intention referred to in the phrase "totally pure intentions and actions" is motivation that is not non-virtuous, like envy, malice or distorted outlook, but instead is virtuous, like love, compassion and bodhicitta. Further, as the "Twenty Pledges" says:

> *A virtuous mind is without shortcomings.*

By murdering a devious merchant, a compassionate ship's pilot amassed the meritorious accumulations of many eons. Geshe Ben tossed a fistful of ashes on his shrine after he examined his motivation for scrupulously cleaning and dusting his offerings and altar in anticipation of a visit from a patron, and discovered that his wish to make a good impression was vain. When Padampa Sanjay heard about this he praised the Geshe's action. As shown in these cases, with powerfully virtuous motivation, actions that might otherwise be somewhat impure are just like pure ones.

Totally pure actions are those that are properly carried out physically or vocally, and moreover have been generated solely through virtuous motivation.

This totally pure intention and action is depicted as a snow mountain. The collection of virtues that spring from it include both the mutable and immutable principal virtues, such as the ten virtues of body, speech and mind, generosity and the rest of the six pāramitās, and the thirty-seven factors conducive to enlightenment; and these are portrayed as streams. These streams of amassed virtue are also "uncontaminated by the three concerns," that is, free of the contaminants stirred up by focusing on the three concerns, for with such focus the path is never a legitimate path of awakening. Also, as is said in "Embarking [on the Central Course]":

> *Though it may be towards the enlightenment which is perfect buddhahood,*
> *if it retains focus on the three concerns, the dedication is mundane.*
> *In the absence of such concerns it is what the Buddha*
> *spoke of as the "transcendental parāmitā."*

In the "Mother of Victors"[8] and elsewhere, all virtue that is accompanied by such concern is called "action that is the curse[9] of bodhisattvas."

The example of generosity in "Embarking [on the Central Course]" illustrates the three concerns: "In giving, the gift is given by the giver to the recipient." That is, concern with a recipient, an agent and an object.

Genuine prajñā that is devoid of any focus on these three concerns is possessed by Āryas alone; ordinary persons can, however, possess an approximate understanding through reliance on scripture and the guru's formal instructions.

In general, the result of prajñā that is divorced from method is bondage to the extreme of serenity, and method without prajñā produces bondage to saṃsāra; therefore, the two must be practiced jointly. That is why "all sentient beings" is mentioned here to teach method, compassion, and "uncontaminated by the three concerns" to teach prajñā, emptiness. Likewise, the sūtra "Expounded by Lodrö Mizaypa"[10] directs:

> *Prajñā lacking method causes bondage within nirvāṇa, and method devoid of prajñā produces bondage within saṃsāra; therefore they must be conjoined.*

The four kāyas of the Victors to which the collections of virtue are dedicated are the dharmakāya, saṃbhogakāya, nirmāṇakāya and svabhāvikakāya.[11]

The dharmakāya is a cognitive state in which the ulimate nature of the dharmadhātu is directly ascertained, and is the primary operative condition for the Sugatas' preeminent activity for the benefit of beings. Nāgārjuna says:

> *I offer tribute to that which is neither single nor multiple and is the foundation for great and splendid benefit for oneself and others; is neither abstract nor solid, is uniform like space and by nature difficult to comprehend; is stainless, invariant, serene, unparalleled, ubiquitous and extremely simple, and experienced only for oneself, the peerless dharmakāya of the Victors.*

The saṃbhogakāya is described in the "Ornament for Clear Realization":[12]

> *The embodiment of the thirty-two marks*
> *and eighty distinctive features*
> *is totally immersed in the Mahāyāna, hence*
> *it is termed the Mighty One's kāya of perfect experience.*

Because [the saṃbhogakāya] appears on a plane in which none of the attributes of the physical kāya of the Sugatas is lacking, yet is devoid of an inherent nature, it is unlimited and therefore the same as what is spoken of in the Vajrayāna as the kāya or face possessing all features. Also, since the realm and retinue are totally pure, the dharma that is consummately engaged in is solely Mahāyāna.

The nirmāṇakāya appears in any among the pure and impure realms, and is the embodiment of activity spontaneously occuring as soon as a Sugata manifestly attains buddhahood in the sphere of the saṃbhogakāya, like radiance produced from the sun. Although Tibetan scholars assert that there are supreme nirmāṇakāyas who exhibit the twelve deeds in Jambudvipa, born nirmāṇakāyas who assume the form of sentient beings, whether superior or ordinary, and also appear in material guises as supports,[13] rafts, bridges and so on, and craft nirmāṇakāyas such as the guitar player who manifested in order to train Rab Ga, king of the gandharvas, it is clear in authoritative sources by Indian scholars that a supreme nirmāṇakāya, with regard to accepting birth within the royal caste and so forth, is a born nirmāṇakāya; when displaying expertise in the arts, is a craft nirmāṇakāya, and after demonstrating the attainment of enlightenment is a supreme nirmāṇakāya. This explanation is also in accordance with the meaning found in scriptural sources. On this point, the "Ornament for the Sūtras" says:

> *Craft, birth and great enlightenment, the transcendence of misery;*
> *continually demonstrating all these signs,*
> *this nirmāṇakāya of the Buddha*
> *is the greatest of means for total liberation.*

Svabhāvikakāya is the great serenity that is the essential nature of all phenomena, and is obtained through the force of the dharmakāya of realization.[14] Since in the Vajrayāna it is distinguished by supremely unchanging great bliss, it is called mahāsukhakāya. Ācārya Nāgārjuna:

> *I offer tribute to the sukhakāya, the unequalled equanimity of the Victors, beyond the concerns of the three transient worlds, abiding equally with space, the essential nature of all entities, purity and peace, the yoga of total isolation with the nature of supreme tranquility, precisely what yogis must comprehend, yet difficult to comprehend and difficult to analyze, full of benefit for oneself and others, without characteristics and nonconceptual, the unitary dimension.*

And so, "may the" previously mentioned "river of accumulated virtues flow into" these "four kāyas," which are depicted as an ocean, the epitome of vastness and profundity. This verse is therefore a condensed aspiration prayer for the qualities of both the path and fruition of the Sugatas, so you should understand that all of the following words merely elaborate upon what is expressed here. This figurative use of an image to represent an abstract subject is explained in poetical treatises.

[II.B] SPECIFIC COMPONENTS OF THE ASPIRATION PRAYER

[These are treated in five sections:] aspiration for an outstanding support for the path, aspiration for prajñā that understands the path, aspiration for the path that is not mistaken, aspiration to correctly effect that path, and aspiration for the fruition upon completing the path.

[II.B.1] *Aspiration for an Outstanding Support for the Path*

The first of these, aspiration for an outstanding support for the path, also has two parts: common, and uncommon.

[II.B.1.a] *Common Aspiration for an Outstanding Support for the Path*

3. **For however long that may take to accomplish,**
   in all lifetimes through my succession of lives,
   may even the sounds "nonvirtue" and "suffering" be unknown,
   and may I enjoy the wealth of oceanic virtue and happiness.

The first two lines mean "through all of my lifetimes, beginning with this very life, until the attainment of the exalted status of the Victors' four kāyas" (explained earlier), and the latter two mean "in those lifetimes, without the cause, 'nonvirtue,' or the result, 'suffering,' even being mentioned, may I experience only the ocean-like grandeur of the cause, virtue, and its result, happiness."

Also, from the "Precious Garland":[15]

> *From passion, aggression, stupidity and*
> *their offshoots nonvirtue arises,*
> *and from nonvirtue, suffering and*
> *likewise all inferior migrations.*
>
> *From passionlessness, nonaggression and lack of stupidity*
> *and what these imply there arises virtue,*
> *and from virtue, all pleasant migrations*
> *and happiness in all lifetimes.*

Further, from "Embarking on the Course of Bodhisattva Conduct":[16]

Suffering arises from nonvirtue.
"How can I be surely liberated from that?"
It is worthwhile for me to think of this alone,
incessantly, day and night.

[II.B.1.b]
Uncommon Aspiration for an Outstanding Support for the Path

4. Possessing the greatest leisure and endowments,
with faith, industry and prajñā,
serving an excellent spiritual advisor, may I obtain
quintessential instructions,
and with no hindrance to their proper implementation,
may I practice superb dharma in all my lifetimes.

The reference earlier to "for however long it may take" is applicable here as well.[17] Leisure and endowments in the phrase "possessing the greatest leisure and endowments" refer to a human situation replete with the eight leisures and ten endowments.

The eight leisures are called "leisures" because they are respites from the eight resourceless states. These eight resourceless states are listed in "Close Attention through Mindfulness":[18]

The hells, pretas, beasts, barbarians, long-lived gods, inverted view, absence of Buddhas and idiocy are the eight resourceless [states].

The ten endowments are:

To be human, born in a central land, with complete faculties, a non-errant occupation and faith in matters [of dharma]. . . .

[These] are the five personal endowments, and

The arrival of a Buddha, his teaching the dharma, the continuance of the transmission, its followers and their concern for others. . .

are described as the five impersonal endowments.

A life that possesses these eighteen leisures and endowments is said to be supreme because it is a proper support with which to accomplish liberation and omniscience. Among supports, one with the stupendous leisure and endowments of birth in Jambudvipa, because its force of virtue and nonvirtue is greater than that of others, is supremely supreme. To wit, from "Origin of Saṃvara":[19]

> *Superior to the six permutations of birth on three continents is wonderful birth in Jambudvipa, famed as the "land of karma."*

Despite obtaining an excellent support which is well endowed and at leisure, one could not traverse the ocean of suffering of saṃsāra without consolidating faith, industry and prajñā. From the "Common Group":[20]

> *Beings of the world with little faith cannot possibly know buddhahood or enlightenment.*

From the "Ten Dharmas" sūtra:

> *White virtue does not arise for persons without faith, just as a green shoot [does not arise] from a seed seared by fire.*

These address the fault of faithlessness, and the sūtra "Requested by Lodrö Gyatso" describes the fault of lacking industry:

> *The lazy lack everything from generosity to prajñā. The lazy lack activity on behalf of others. For the lazy, enlightenment is very distant, extremely distant.*

The fault of lacking prajñā is described in the "Concise Versified Prajñāpāramitā":

> *How could a trillion million blind people, without a guide, who do not even know the way, arrive at a destination? Without prajñā, enlightenment cannot be reached with the sightless five pāramitās, because they would have no guidance.*

and by Vasubandhu:

> *For those who are ignorant and without fine discernment of phenomena,*
> *there is no way to totally pacify afflicted states of mind,*
> *and so they wander in this ocean of worldly existence.*

I will not delve into this in further detail. For the above reasons, "with faith, industry and prajñā" is mentioned. You may ask, "Well then, what exactly are these three, faith, industry and prajñā?" Faith is, from the "Compendium of Abhidharma":

> *What is faith? Explicit trust in actions and their results, Truth and the Jewels; longing, and clear conception.*

The classification of faith is threefold: faith that trusts in the doctrine of the interdependence of actions and results, faith that longs for the enlightenment of the Buddhas, and faith that forms a clear conception of the Three Jewels.

Industry is a frame of mind that acts as a remedy for laziness, which is apathy towards virtue. The abhidharma teachings say:

> *What is industry? The antidote for laziness, that is, unreserved enthusiasm for virtue.*

There are various ways to classify [industry], such as into persistence and respectfulness.

Prajñā is the faculty of mind that distinguishes among all entities that are objects of knowledge. From "Excerpts from Validity":[21]

> *What is prajñā? That which finely distinguishes among dharmas.*

When you classify prajñā there is both a mundane and a supramundane variety.

Even though these factors of faith, industry and prajñā may be present, without the primary condition of reliance upon a spiritual advisor there is no way one will be able to achieve the state of omniscience. From the "Eight-Thousand [-Verse Prajñāpāramitā]":

> *And so, since a bodhisattva mahāsattva wishes to awaken in a perfect and complete manner into absolute, perfect, unsurpassable enlightenment, he should from the very outset approach a spiritual advisor, should attend him, and should serve him.*

There are countless scriptural references like this, especially in the great secret Vajrayāna. For instance:

> *The lama is the Buddha, the lama is the dharma*
> *and likewise the lama is the saṅgha;*
> *the lama is glorious Vajradhara,*
> *the lama is the one who does all.*

and, from "Guhyasamāja"[22]

> *From me, the form emanation of the ācārya. . .*

and in "Kālacakra":

> *The vajra staff wielded at māras is renowned in this inhabited land as Vajrasattva.*

A vajrācārya from whom one requests ultimate empowerment, although exhibiting the form of an ordinary individual, must be regarded as Vajradhara himself, and in fact is ultimately none other than Vajradhara. Without this lama who is Vajradhara one will not even attain slight siddhis, let alone enlightenment. As is said, "siddhi follows the ācārya," and

Without gripping the oars,
one cannot cross over in a boat.
Though one may have perfected all good qualities,
without a lama one's conditioned existence cannot end.

and in "Hevajra":[23]

That which resists expression, is connate
and not found anywhere at all,
shall be discovered through prolonged service to the lama,
reliance upon his methods, and one's own merit.

Therefore, the spiritual advisor whom one aspires to rely upon ("serving an excellent spiritual advisor") must be someone whose abilities match the needs of the trainees who attend him, who is capable of teaching whatever dharma is appropriate to the occasion, and is a compassionate person. He must in no instance be at a loss for methods to instill positive qualities in his disciples that they previously lacked, and to foster the development of whatever qualities previously existed in them, thus liberating beings in his care from the straits of conditioned existence.

For example, someone who has the good fortune of being worthy of entrance to the holy dharma of the vinaya requires, accordingly, a lama to guide him who is a *kenpo*[24] "possessing the four limbs," i.e., who is venerable, learned, steadfast and beneficent. Similarly, secret preceptor and functionary ācāryas must also meet all the appropriate standards, cause [the disciples] to newly generate bodhicitta, both conventional and ultimate, and continually foster its development where it already exists. In this regard, Śāntideva says:

At all times, a spiritual advisor
should be expert in the meaning of the Mahāyāna and
never abandon the supreme conduct of a bodhisattva,
even at the cost of his life.

When the time arrives for guidance with the exceptional techniques of Secret Mantra, as "Kālacakra" states,

> *First of all, lamas who are perfectly suitable to rely upon are keepers of samaya and advanced in the Vajrayāna, experienced meditators, passionless and purified of stains, and fully detached. They have embarked upon the path whose intrinsic trait is tolerance, which they in turn transmit to their disciples, stealing away the horrors of the hell realms; these disciples themselves are brahmacaryas. [Such a lama] wields the vajra staff at māras and is renowned in this inhabited land as Vajrasattva.*

There are also vajrācāryas who meet the qualifications stipulated in the various different classes of tantra.

In general, since a trainee could attend a lama who, when the trainee resides within a dense shell of obscuration in saṃsāra, takes the form of an ordinary person, and when the same trainee's obscurations have diminished somewhat, appears in the guise of an ārya bodhisattva, and when the trainee passes beyond the greater path of accumulation is perceived as a supreme nirmāṇakāya, and finally, once the trainee has attained the ārya path is perceived in the form of the sambhogakāya, at this stage one should remain non-judgmental toward whomever one aspires to attend.

The lama is also styled "spiritual advisor"[25] since, as presented in terms of the pāramitā dharmas, there is no kindness received from any of one's parents, relatives or friends that is comparable to the kindness of extracting one from the ocean of conditioned existence, and therefore the lama who does so is the finest of all friends. He is also purified of faults and perfected in all good qualities, and thus "excellent." "Serve" him with the five pleasing measures and the ninefold service, and so on. Just as the merchant's son Excellent Jewel and the bodhisattva Perpetually Weeping served spiritual advisors, and just as the revered ones of this practice lineage served their lamas, so too should one fulfill the wishes of a holy friend who is the master of compassion.

The "instructions" [referred to in the phrase] "obtain quintessential instructions" are dharma teachings of the three vehicles, three trainings, etc., presented in either a provisional or definitive, ordinary or extraordinary format to coincide with the trainee's personal aptitude, whose purpose is to progressively fuse the positive qualities of the path with the trainee's spirit; since these are the means for seizing the life-essence of liberation, they are "vital" [quintessential]. Once you receive such instructions, don't be complacent, thinking "I've got it," but practice correctly, that is, solely in the manner prescribed by your lama and as elucidated in the dictates and treatises of the Sugatas.

"With no hindrance" to practicing in this fashion means, in brief, being free of any and all obstructions along the path to attaining liberation and omniscience, including outer obstacles brought on by the four elements, humans, nonhumans, and so on, and inner obstacles such as sicknesses, afflictive mental states, and conceptuality.

The final phrase in the verse summarizes the meaning found in the first three: attainment of a situation with leisures and endowments, possession of faith, industry and prajñā, and through them, a spiritual advisor to attend, from whom the oral instructions can be heard and correctly put into practice without the interference of obstacles. A trainee with all these advantages is one who possesses the utmost good fortune of perfect involvement in the sacred dharma, and that is why one prays that such fortunate circumstances endure from this very time until the attainment of enlightenment, throughout one's succession of lifetimes.

[II.B.2]
Aspiration for Prajñā That Understands the Path

5. Study of scripture and reasoning delivers one from the pall of nescience.
Reflection on the oral instructions vanquishes the darkness of uncertainty.
The light cast by meditation vividly illuminates the enduring condition.
May the radiance of the three prajñās intensify.

The first line of this verse concerns prajñā that arises from study; the second, prajñā that arises from reflection; the third, from meditation; and the fourth is a condensed version of the [three] aspiration prayers.

[II.B.2.a]
Prajñā That Arises from Study

As to the first: in this instance, of the two scriptural sources, dictates and treatises,[26] dictates are, from "Higher Continuum":

> *Whatever is wholly concerned with meaningful dharmas,*
> *is spoken to abolish the rampant afflictive mentalities of the three realms,*
> *and instructs in the advantages of peace*
> *is the speech of the Sage. Anything contrary is otherwise.*

This means all sublime speech that arises based upon the [teachings of the] perfect Buddha, who is the primary condition. If one classifies these there are three: dictates spoken by the Buddha, those spoken with his express approval and those occuring through his blessing. Or else, in terms of their actual content, vinaya, sūtra and abhidharma. In that case, one may wonder whether the basket of Secret Mantra is included within any of these three. In fact, since it is the heart of all three, though one may refer to it as the "basket of the vidyādharas" simply to draw a distinction, it is definitely included. Rangjung Gyalwa says "through the profound sūtra, vinaya and abhidharma," and the "Vajra Heart Commentary"[27] says that "a fourth and a fifth for buddhahood are not the intention of the Sage."

Treatises are, as stated in "Higher Continuum":

> *Whatever is solely influenced by the doctrine of the Victor,*
> *is composed by a totally undistracted intellect*
> *and is in accord with the path for attaining liberation,*
> *that too raise to the crown of your head like the dictates of the Sage.*

These are the entire spectrum of explications of the intent of the Buddhas' dictates which concur with his intended meaning and have been composed by noble bodhisattvas, hearers and ordinary paṇḍitas ever since the Teacher exhibited the manner of passing beyond misery in our world. These can be divided into general treatments and specific explications, and in fact there are many other avenues of classification as well.

Reasoning refers to positions, arguments and examples,[28] such as those derived from the textual systems of the "Validity Sūtra" and "Series of Seven"[29] and so forth, which are employed in order to reach decisive conclusions, which in turn enable one to understand, in an abstract fashion, the meanings of all things to be realized.

By learning about and coming to understand both scripture and reasoning from one's lama, the prajñā that arises from study will be born and one will be delivered from its counterpart, the "pall" of not knowing scripture and reasoning. Moreover, Ācārya Candrakīrti says:

> *Just as an entire company of blind people is easily guided*
> *to its desired destination by a single sighted person,*
> *likewise, here, understanding*[30] *lifts up*
> *the sightless qualities*[31] *and journeys to Victory.*
> *The manner by which this [understanding] realizes the extremely profound dharma is*
> *"through scripture and also through reasoning"; therefore....*[32]

In "Sequence of Lives":[33]

> *Learning is a lamp, for it dispels the darkness of bewilderment;*
> *the greatest of all wealth, for it cannot be carried off by thieves;*
> *like a weapon, for it conquers the enemy, perpetual bafflement;*
> *and the best of companions, for it proffers advice on how to proceed.*

[II.B.2.b]
Prajñā That Arises from Reflection

"Oral instructions": in Sanskrit, *upadeśa*. "Reflection on the oral instructions" means to take to heart and properly reflect upon the meaning of what the Sugatas taught exhaustively, out of loving-kindness, in order to liberate us from bondage to conditioned existence and serenity. In particular, since the Sugatas taught a multiplicity of vehicles to suit individual inclinations, a variety of provisional and definitive teachings emerged, and even more critically, since the tantras of the great secret Vajrayāna are totally circumscribed by the six limits[34] and as a result are extremely intricate, one must reflect upon the instructions of an ācārya who with completely immaculate dharma vision (prajñā), teaching in a manner sensitive to the four maxims,[35] edifies one through properly and fully elucidating the vital issues. Reflecting upon the instructions this way produces the prajñā that arises from reflection, and conquers its antithesis, the darkness of ambivalence, which consists of uncertainty about profound issues.

[II.B.2.c]
Prajñā That Arises from Meditation

By duly reflecting over and over again upon the meaning of what one has studied, one discovers a certitude that is entirely free of ambivalence. Resting equanimously and meditating upon that meaning produces the prajñā that arises from meditation, and the glow of that prajñā illuminates the essential nature of the enduring condition just as it is.[36]

"Enduring condition" refers to the nature, or manner of subsistence, of all dharmas, from forms up until omniscience, and is also referred to as ground-state mahāmudrā, innate suchness, the original Lord,[37] the tathāgata potential or tathāgatagarbha.

There is both the "enduring condition of the entity of the body" and the "enduring condition of the entity of the mind."

Regarding the former, from "Hevajra":

In the great bliss bhaga of the Lady
dwells the Teacher with the thirty- two principal attributes
and eighty physical signs,
in the aspect of vital fluid.
Without that, the bliss is lost.
Since there is no vitality, the rest follows.
The bliss from deity yoga
is not the concrete entity of the Buddha,
nor is it a mere abstraction.
That which is formalized in the aspect of face and arms
is the embodiment of supremely unchanging bliss.
Therefore, all beings are connate.

The term "vital fluid" refers to what is produced and appears from conventional bodhicitta, the rarified essence of the channels, winds and drops that is the support for supremely unchanging bliss, which transcends the state of coarse materiality and is therefore of the essence of primordial wisdom.[38] This is the innate body itself. Glorious Rangjung Gyalwa also said this can be called "the enduring condition of the vajra body" since the channels, winds and drops are interdependent, appearing out of the radiance of the mind, and are composed of and appear from conventional bodhicitta, thereby serving as the basis for connate, primordial wisdom.

The seventh Lord[39] described this self-essence lacking the stains of the eight groups and abiding as the four kāyas as "the evolving potential" having no time of inception, and this description appears to coincide and concur with the explanation of Rangjung Dorje himself, which can be satisfactorily established through a plethora of scriptural citations and arguments, though for the moment I will not elaborate upon these.

Secondly, the enduring condition of the entity of mind is the dharmadhātu, unrestricted, impartial and free of conceptually constructed limitations.[40] From "Drop of Liberation":[41]

> *Because it is devoid of all conceptuality,*
> *it is far beyond the realm of the ponderable or expressible.*
> *Like space, it is stainless and the source of everything.*
> *It defies analysis, is the "truly profound."*
>
> *It purifies the spiritual continua of oneself and others,*
> *giving form to mahāmudrā*
> *that is illusory and like a rainbow,*
> *known as "perfect clarity."*
>
> *The supreme nature that is the nonduality of these,*
> *the identity pervading all entities,*
> *totally unhindered by saṃsāra,*
> *is described as "the dharmadhātu."*

That which is explained as nondual profundity and clarity, the innate mind, and the intrinsic, enduring potential is just the same as this.

The meaning of "enduring condition" has here been just touched upon so as not to neglect it entirely, and can otherwise be understood through the explanations that will follow later.

The fundamental, enduring condition of the mind, and of the body, like water and ice, are indivisible, and are therefore called "the union of the two kāyas of the ground-state," which can only be illuminated by unmediated self-disclosive awareness that is capacitated by meditation, and not by any other method. As is said:

This[42] *has nothing whatsoever to be removed*
and [in] this nothing in the least [need] be installed.[43]
Regard the perfect[44] *perfectly.*[45]
When perfection is glimpsed, liberation is total.[46]

The order of progression of the three prajñās is precisely as presented here, and although this may not be definite for those persons who can learn all at once, it is widely known that in the case of gradual learners the stages are interrelated such that without each prior step, its successors will not occur:

Maintaining discipline, with learning and reflection, apply [yourself] fully to meditation.[47]

[II.B.2.d]
A Condensed Version of These Three Aspiration Prayers

The three prajñās of study, reflection and meditation are represented by the image of the sun; by acquiring them, may the great incandescent radiance that dispels any occlusive or obscuring clouds greatly intensify, directly illuminating the nature of the "that alone"![48]

[II.B.3]
Aspiration for the Path That Is Not Mistaken

6. The meaning of "ground" is the two truths, beyond the polarity of existence and nonexistence.
Through the supreme path of two accumulations, beyond the extremes of embellishment and discredit,
the fruition of the two purposes, beyond the limits of conditioned existence and serenity, is attained.
May I encounter the dharma that neither errs nor misleads.

The first phrase concerns the meaning of the non-mistaken, enduring condition, which is the ground [state]. The second explains the non-mistaken agency, which is the practice of the path. The third explains the objective, the stage of fruition. The fourth advocates the dharma consisting of the previous three elements as the correct, unerring path, and ends with the aspiration for such a path.

[II.B.3.a]
[The Poles of] "Existence and Nonexistence"[49]

There are two kinds of incorrect suppositions that arise due to confusion about the nature of mahāmudrā, the fundamental, enduring condition: the existence view and the nonexistence view. The defining characteristics of these are, respectively, the persistent belief that a given phenomenon "exists" and the persistent belief that a given phenomenon "doesn't exist." As is said,

> *"It exists" is the existence view; "it doesn't exist" is the nonexistence view.*[50]

Where, then, are the advocates of such views found? Principally within heterodox schools, but also among Buddhists.

Among the non-Buddhists, there was the ṛiṣi Purbu, who in order to facilitate the triumph of the gods in their warfare with the anti-gods, composed a treatise asserting the nonexistence of virtue and nonvirtue, or previous and future lifetimes. Subsequently, the ṛiṣi Jugtop[51] and others promulgated this doctrine, which became known as Cārvāka[52] and is a nonexistence view school.

There are also four heterodox schools that are well known as existence view holders:

(1) The followers of the teacher Serkya who assert that there are twenty-five kinds of objects and that liberation is achieved through understanding their nature—the Sāṃkhyas;[53]
(2) The followers of the ṛiṣi Zekzen (or Kangmig) who was specially blessed by the great god Wangchuk (Śiva), who assert that all knowable entities are included within six semantic categories—the Śaivas;[54]
(3) Those who hold Viṣṇu to be god and follow the teachings of Gyalpag and so forth—the Vaiśnavas;[55] and
(4) Those who follow the ṛiṣi Gyalwa Dampa and assert the existence of the six substances—the Nirgranthas.[56]

Furthermore, although those, like the Persians (known as the Barbarians), who uphold the doctrinal system composed by the teacher Mohammed, the follower of the anti-gods, and the Yung

Drung Bon of Tibet who follow Shenrab Miwo, and also the Zinshing tenet-holders of India are not tīrthikas[57] *per se*, the practices of the Persians are even more base than that of tīrthikas, while the latter two don't assert self-identity and the like and are thus perhaps slightly better than tīrthikas; nonetheless, they are all classified as existence-view holders.

Among Buddhists, the Vaibhāṣikas and Sautrāntikas generally don't refute the self-identity of phenomena and assert external objects to be composed of tiny, partless particles.[58] The Cittamātrins assert nondual cognizance to be truly existent and so it follows that they accept the self-identity of an apprehended phenomenon.[59] These are the views within the Buddhist tradition that adhere to a pole of existence or nonexistence. Ācārya Loten, in his commentary on "The One of Thirty"[60] says:

> *To say "like the mind knowing it, the known object exists" is the pole of existence, and to say "like the object it knows, the mind knowing it doesn't exist" is the pole of nonexistence.*

"The meaning of 'ground' is the two truths beyond...": The true meaning of the fundamental, enduring condition is beyond the two polarized views that result from invalid presuppositions, and is clearly certified to be the union of the two truths.

The two truths are ultimate truth and apparent truth.[61] The former is the intrinsic state of all animate and inanimate phenomena, which lies beyond the eight conceptually constructed limits,[62] is totally pure like the depths of space, unrestricted[63] and impartial, and well beyond the scope of thought or expression[64]—styled the original Buddha, the prototypical Lord, Suchness, and so on. The latter is the way all animate and inanimate phenomena appear to be, full of all sorts of elaborate detail, interdependently arising and illusory.[65] As Ācārya Jñānagarbha puts it:

> *How it appears is just the apparent. What's left is the other.*

These two truths are also primordially unified. Whatever animate and inanimate phenomena of conditioned existence and serenity appear, they all, from the very moment of their appearance, lack any real essence as whatever they appear to be, and so, like a reflection appearing in a mirror, do not fall to the extremity of existence. Yet while they never deviate from being emptiness in essence, phenomena arise unimpededly in multiplicity, and so they do not fall to the extremity of nonexistence. On this point, Ācārya Nāgārjuna says:

> *For whatever emptiness is suitable, everything is suitable.*
> *For whatever emptiness is unsuitable, everything is unsuitable.*

If phenomena were truly established in and of themselves, since they would never relinquish their own characteristics, they would impede one another, that is to say, arisal and cessation would become impossible, but if all phenomena were empty [of such a self-nature] such a fault would not pertain, and so emptiness is compatible with interdependent origination. It is very important for one to understand this and the other topics covered in the "Six Collections on Reasoning" of Madhyamaka. From the "Whence Fearlessness" commentary on the Madhyamaka root text:[66]

> *The dharma taught by the Buddha-Bhagavan arose based upon these two truths. The "apparent truth for worldly people" is that essentially empty phenomena are inaccurately conceived of by worldly people, who view all phenomena as [truly] arising. Since, for them, they [phenomena] are what is taken to be real, they are apparently true. Ultimate truth is that which Āryas have correctly internalized, such that observing all phenomena to be nonarising, they take this to be their ultimate nature.*[67]

and [from the same text]:

> *Whoever doesn't rely upon conventional terms will be unable to teach the ultimate, and without reference to the sacred meaning, nirvāṇa can never be attained. Therefore, both truths must be presented.*[68]

[II.B.3.b]
[The Extremes of] "Embellishment and Discredit"

[These] are misapprehensions of the path that is the means for attaining liberation. If without understanding how it is that interdependent origination springs from emptiness, [one thinks] "only perceptible phenomena such as actions and their results are real; all else is false," one is neglecting the factor of prajñā and falling to the extreme of embellishing the nonexistent with existence. If without comprehending the crucial point that the Three Jewels and karma arise in an interdependent manner and as such are fully capable of functioning, [one thinks] "only emptiness is real, all else is false," one is neglecting the factor of method and falling to the extreme of discrediting the existent with nonexistence.

"The supreme path of two accumulations, beyond...": As was just explained, one gathers the accumulations of merit in order to establish the rūpakāya of the Tathāgatas and not be stuck in the extreme of discrediting [conventional existence], and one gathers the accumulations of primordial wisdom in order to establish the dharmakāya of the Tathāgatas and not be stuck in the extreme of embellishing [the empty nature], and the unified, nondifferentiated practice of these two is the most supreme and non-mistaken path for attaining liberation.

Among the six pāramitās, generosity and discipline accumulate merit, prajñā alone accumulates wisdom, and the three others, patience, industry and concentration, contribute to both. From the "Ornament for Sūtras":

> *Generosity and discipline are [for] the accumulation of merit;*
> *prajñā is [for] wisdom;*
> *the remaining three are [for] both.*

As for the necessity of uniting the practices of the two [accumulations], in the "Lamp for the Path of Awakening," it is said:

> *Since it is said that*
> *prajñā without method*
> *and method without prajñā*
> *are "bondage," abandon neither.*

and, from the sūtra "Expounded by the Renowned, Noble Drima Maypa,"

> *Prajñā not embraced by method is bondage. Prajñā embraced by method is liberation. Method not embraced by prajñā is bondage. Method embraced by prajñā is liberation.*

[II.B.3.c]
[The Limits of] "Conditioned Existence and Serenity"

[These] are inferior results to attain. What this means is that the result of method alone, divorced from prajñā, can never transcend conditioned existence, and the result of prajñā alone, divorced from method, can never transcend mere serenity.

"The fruition of the two purposes, beyond the poles...is attained" means that, in contrast with those extremes of existence and serenity, through engaging in the unified practice of the two accumulations mentioned above, one attains the rūpakāya of magnificent benefit to others and doesn't tumble into the extreme of serenity, and one attains the dharmakāya of magnificent benefit to oneself and doesn't tumble into the extreme of conditioned existence. This is the non-mistaken fruition of the unified two kāyas. As is said in "Higher Continuum,"

> *One's benefit, others' benefit, the ultimate kāya and, on the basis of that, the apparent kāya...*

[II.B.3.d]
[Summary Aspiration for the Path that] "Neither Errs Nor Misleads"

[This last line of the verse] means that, were one to fall towards either of the two poles that have been described for each of the ground, path and fruition, one would go astray. Here, to eradicate all such errors, one dispels all polarized existence and nonexistence views with regard to the ground. By dispelling them, training on the path will be free of extremes of embellishment and discredit, and this freedom will lead to a fruition of spontaneous liberation from the poles of conditioned existence and serenity. That is why the presentation of the non-mistaken path that is error-free is arranged in terms of the ground, path and fruition.[69]

[II.B.4]
Aspiration for Putting the Path into Practice Correctly

[This includes a] concise discussion of what must be understood, [and] the meditation that is to be practiced.

[II.B.4.a]
Concise Discussion of What Must be Understood

7. **The ground of purification is mind nature, unified cognizance and emptiness.**
   Through the purifying agency of the great vajra yoga of mahāmudrā,

may delusory incidental stains be purified
and the result of purification, stainless dharmakāya,
become manifest.

Here is what is most important to understand about practicing path-phase mahāmudrā yoga on a path that meets the specifications of "correctness" described earlier.

There are four aspects: the ground where purification takes place, the yoga that effects purification, the stains that are purified, and the result that is attained through purification, each of which is explained by a separate line of verse, with words expressing aspiration appended.

[II.B.4.a.i]
The Ground Where Purification Takes Place

The first line identifies naturally pristine mind as the basis for purifying all stains that are impediments to attaining liberation, and resolves its defining property to be unified cognizance and emptiness.

First of all, the reason why pristine mind is the ground of purification is explained in "Higher Continuum":

Earth rests on water, water on wind,
and wind rests firmly on space.
Space does not rest upon the elements
of wind, water and earth.

Similarly, the aggregates, constituents and faculties
rest upon karma and afflictive mental states,
while karma and afflictive mental states
rest totally upon improper conceptual engagement.

Improper conceptual engagement
rests upon the pristine element of mind.
The [pristine] nature of mind does not rest
upon any phenomenon whatsoever.

This shows that the ground for all of saṃsāra and nirvāṇa is the pristine mind, tathāgatagarbha (or dhātu). This is the ground for purification but not itself the object to be purified, for within its own nature there is not a single established atom that might be purified. Also, from Nāgārjuna's "Praise to the Dharmadhātu":

The constituent [dhātu] that is the potential
is asserted to be the basis for all dharmas;
through gradual purification
the state of enlightenment will be attained.

and in the "Indication of Emptiness Sūtra":[70]

Everything the Victors taught was to overturn afflictive mind states.
This does not impair the constituent.

On this point, the following misgiving might conceivably arise for some reflective people: "Why say 'mind'? That term denotes 'accumulation' [of experience] and is not an appropriate label for non-composite sugatagarbha. Also, in abhidharma and elsewhere, [mind] refers to an ordinary consciousness that is the ground for all [karmic] potentials, which is exactly the opposite [of what you mean by it]."

There is no fault here; mind can be divided into both a pure and an impure aspect, and that explanation is concerned with the impure aspect. Also, since [mind] possesses, in a nondual fashion, the sixty-four enlightened qualities that reside in the ground, it makes the emergence of all positive dharmas possible, and therefore it is compatible with the sense of 'accumulation.' There are a multitude of sūtras, tantras and treatises in which the pristine purity of mind is referred to as "mind," such as in "Mother [of Victors]": "Mind has no mind, for the nature of mind is luminosity"; the "Higher Continuum" scripture cited earlier, and Ācārya Nāgārjuna:

In that manner luminous mind
is obscured by the five obscurations:
desire, remorse, lassitude,
agitation and doubt.

Secondly, concerning mind being unified cognizance and emptiness, in "Guhyasamāja":

Distinct from all material entities,
devoid of the aggregates, constituents and sense fields,
grasping and fixation,
lacking phenomenal identity and being equanimous,
one's mind is originally unborn,
naturally empty.

This demonstrates that mind is essentially empty. In "Higher Continuum":

> *The mind whose nature is luminosity*
> *is unchanging, like space;*
> *incidental stains, like passion, which spring*
> *from fallible conceptuality, in no way afflict it.*

This shows that because mind is naturally luminous, incidental stains are incapable of defiling it. There are countless similar scriptures that establish mind to be empty cognizance.

Furthermore, emptiness and cognizance are a unified whole, as there is absolutely no such thing as the mind's emptiness apart from its cognizance or its cognizance distinct from emptiness. Lord Maitreya taught us: "[Mind's] defining property is indivisibility."

Various polemicists in Tibet who can't comprehend this sort of subtle point discuss mere cognizance and mere emptiness as though their union were more like a synthesis, a concept which is alien to the doctrine of the Sugatas.

[II.B.4.a.ii]
The Yoga That Effects Purification

The second line concerns the vajra yoga of mahāmudrā, which is the **path that purifies** the **stains to be purified** from the **ground of purification**.[71]

According to the instruction manuals of the Dagpo Kagyu, a receptive disciple who attends a qualified lama, depending on his degree of progress, might or might not initially obtain an elaborate empowerment; either way is fine. Some, after practicing the common, uncommon and special preliminaries and then the main practice of calm abiding and penetrative insight, gain exceptional realization through glimpsing the very nature of ordinary cognizance, having previously resolved [what it is] in a direct introduction; and realization that is basically identical to that also arises through reliance on the two-stage yoga.

Furthermore, due to the variability of the calibre of the disciple and the ability of the master, realization occurs for some solely through the "blessing of the transference of primordial wisdom," while others progressively receive the four empowerments and sustain the continuity of the experience of the third empowerment that is indicated during the word empowerment. Primordial wisdom is actualized by all of these rich and diverse methods.

During the phases of accumulation and juncture, primordial wisdom is present primarily in the form of experiences, but once one attains the path of vision it arises fully manifest in one's continuum of being. Thereafter, during meditative sessions it becomes increasingly stabilized, and in post-meditation, as confused appearances become progressively lighter, the objects to be abandoned are gradually relinquished. The process is like the upward and downward swing of the two pans of a weight-scale. Finally, the "vajra-like samādhi at the end of the continuum" completes the process of abandonment without leaving any remainder, and this is perfect enlightenment.

If you were to ask what this primordial wisdom that is realized is like, the "Mahāmudrā Drop" tantra says:

> *Listen, goddess, great mudrā:*
> *mahāmudrā is great secrecy;*
> *inexpressible; unceasing; unborn;*
> *all-encompassing yet without form;*
> *formless yet the supreme, sacred form;*
> *without coarseness, fineness and so on;*
> *inestimable by nature.*

Ācārya Nāgārjuna, in "Commentary on Bodhicitta," says:

> *The bodhicitta of the Buddhas*
> *is unobscured by thoughts*
> *occupied with self and skandhas,*
> *and continually observes the characteristics of emptiness.*

The Honorable Saraha says:

> *How can I describe what is unutterable,*
> *without analogy in color, letter or quality?*
> *Like the joy abiding in the heart of a maiden,*
> *how could this sacred Īśvara be communicated to anyone?*

As these statements, along with many others, imply, even though it is beyond the scope of expression, thought or verbalization, it is vividly experienced by means of one's own internal, self-disclosive awareness, whereby one beholds the true nature of the ground of purification explained earlier.

This explanation of how the primordial wisdom of mahāmudrā can arise even without being preceded by an elaborate empowerment ceremony does not fit into the preconceived notions of certain reputed scholars who have come into prominence in earlier and later times here in Tibet, who find in it many glaring faults, such as how without empowerment and the two stages, [this practice] cannot be established as mantra mahāmudrā, and how although it might be just barely possible to comprehend the Madhyamaka view if one's meditative approach is really outstanding, still, without schooling in the dialectical method of considering and refuting the four alternatives, as explained in the seminal works of Madhyamaka, even that remote possibility is unlikely.

Such criticism would appear to be quite deprecating, like saying "Only what I understand is true; everything else is not," disavowing the fact that the Bhagavan employed illimitable training methods for training diverse sorts of disciples, and that his teachings have been individually and thoroughly interpreted and transmitted by paṇḍitas and siddhas.

The aforementioned "faults" are not present in this superior Kagyu system of instruction. As will be explained later, although it is not suggested that elaborate empowerment, among the different approaches to instruction, is indispensable for exceptionally sharp disciples, they nevertheless must receive the blessing of a vajra-jñāna empowerment bestowed by a vajrācārya as a prerequisite. As a result of that, the two stages [of yoga] are also, *de facto*, indisputably present.

Furthermore, some maintain that the empowerment of blessing-transference does not qualify as true empowerment and practicing guru-yoga does not qualify as two-stage [yoga]. In that case, empowerment through a colored-sand maṇḍala also would not qualify as empowerment, since the word "empowerment" means "that which has the power necessary to generate realization of the meaning of empowerment in one's being," and in that respect elaborate empowerments are inferior in potency to non-elaborate ones.

Also, practicing deity yoga would not qualify as two-stage [yoga], since here in mantrayāna it is necessary to regard the lama and yidam as nondual, and the yidam is confirmed[72] by the lama. A confirmed without a confirmer is a mere designation of a deity, and therefore cannot bestow supreme siddhi.

And so, in our system, since samādhi empowerment, or vajra-jñāna empowerment, is supreme among all forms of empowerment, it goes without saying that it qualifies as empowerment.

In fact, should a realized lama guide an extremely astute disciple, suited for mahāmudrā, with an elaborate empowerment, as opposed to this one, he would be at fault. Indrabhūti, in "Accomplishment of Wisdom":

> *Through the empowerment of vajra-jñāna*
> *that banishes all concepts and*
> *grants supreme and excellent wisdom,*
> *all supreme siddhis will be accomplished.*
>
> *What, you may ask, would be the result,*
> *on the other hand, of empowering with a drawn maṇḍala*
> *when one possesses all perfect wisdoms?*
> *It would impair one's samaya.*
> *The sufferings associated with impaired samaya*
> *are impairment of one's body and mind*
> *and their purposes,*
> *and a swift death.*
> *After one dies, one experiences*
> *hundreds upon millions of eons of hellish suffering,*
> *and even if one gets out of that predicament,*
> *one is born an outcast, or into an inferior caste,*
> *dumb, or deaf,*
> *or else blind, through life after life—*
> *of that there is no doubt.*
> *The primordial wisdom of all Tathāgatas*
> *is called vajra-jñāna. When the astute empower with that,*
> *know that to be true empowerment.*

This is discussed in great detail and is something to be understood well.

Because the dividing line between obtaining or not obtaining empowerment is whether or not the import of the empowerment has dawned in one's being, it has to be understood that when realization of inseparable appearance and emptiness arises in a disciple's being, he has obtained the vase empowerment, and so on.

Similarly, at this level, meditation on the guru alone is also sufficient as generation stage practice, because through the power of proficient guru yoga meditation the entirety of phenomenal existence appears as the vibrant display of the lama; and guru yoga is far more effective than even meditation on the yidam for arresting clinging to ordinariness. Also, in many tantras and commentaries it is said that "the lama is all the Rare and Sublime Ones" gathered into one, and by meditating upon the lama all siddhis will be attained.

Also, in terms of perfection stage, through intense devotion [to the guru], awareness becomes freed of any reference point, and preserving that experiential state is acknowledged to be the very finest path, free of any hazards or impediments.

Recondite subjects like these, the province of exceptionally gifted individuals alone, always prove to be beyond the ken of pedants, and, conversely, the very fact that their talents are so overmatched in such matters tells us just how extraordinarily profound and secret they are.

The second "fault" is also dubious. From the point of view of being devoid of conceptual constructs, the view of mantra mahāmudrā is entirely in accord with Madhyamaka. Therefore, realization of the Madhyamaka view cannot be a defect of mantra. Since these arguments posed by polemicists were made with an eye to disputes with heterodox scholars, it turns out that analytic meditation is not even the highest priority within the Mādhyamikas' own system, as is said, "Without adornment by the lama's speech, Madhyamaka too is merely mediocre."

More on the reasons why, in view of the pacification of all limiting conceptual constructs, mahāmudrā is in accord with the view of Madhyamaka:

> *If there were a view higher than Madhyamaka, that view would be a construct.*

As this explains, in the doctrine of the Buddha it isn't possible for a view to be superior to the Madhyamaka aprapañca.[73] It is with this in mind that Ācārya Jñānakīrti, in order to explain how prajñāpāramitā taught in sūtra and mantra mahāmudrā are synonymous, wrote in "Proceeding to 'Just That Alone'":

> *Mahāmudrā is another name for the mother, prajñāpāramitā, for it is the very essence of nondual primordial wisdom.*

[II.B.4.a.iii]
The Stains to Be Purified

[Next is] the topic of what is to be purified, the [subject of the] third line of verse.

You may wonder, what are the stains that are to be purified from the ground of purification by the agent of purification? They are dharmas grasped or fixated upon that are generated by incidental, temporary confusion, but don't exist in their own right. And what is this confusion? That will be dealt with a little later on in discussion of the verse "self-display with no existence," etc.

[II.B.4.a.iv]
The Result That Is Attained Through Purification

The subject of the fourth line of verse [is this]: What is the result of purifying what must be purified by the process of purification? The completely actualized dharmakāya, the fundamental, enduring condition forever rid of any and all incidental stains, [rid of] phenomena subsumed under grasping and fixation.

Further, from "Praise to the Dharmadhātu":

> *When it is covered by the web of afflictive patterns, it is called "mind."*
> *When it is rid of afflictive patterns, call it "Buddha."*

You may wonder, if the result of purification is just dharmakāya, whether the two rupakāyas might not then be results of purification. From the point of view of their essence, the two rupakāyas are indistinguishable from the dharmakāya; therefore they are established to be results of fruition just by the mention of dharmakāya itself.

The way all three kāyas are assigned to the dharmakāya is as follows: When the dharmadhātu, mahāsukha, naturally free of all stains, is also purified of incidental stains, it becomes the dharmakāya of abandonment possessing twofold purity, also known as svabhāvikakāya; and when (1) the universal ground consciousness, (2) the consciousness bearing afflictive patterns, (3) the sixth (mental) consciousness, and (4) the consciousnesses that engage objects are wholly purified and transformed, they become primordial wisdom knowing all that is just as it is, the dharmakāya of realization, also known as the jñānakāya. These two indivisibly comprise the complete dharmakāya.

Of these two, with regard to the dharmakāya of realization, the purified consciousnesses, in the order that I have just mentioned them, are divided into four wisdoms: (1) mirror, (2) impartial, (3) discerning and (4) effective, of which impartial wisdom would be saṃbhogakāya, effective wisdom would be nirmāṇakāya and discerning wisdom would be included in both.[74]

If you want to learn about these in more extensive detail, look in the "Ornament for Sutras" and the Lord's own "Autocommentary on the Profound Inner Meaning."[75] However, since I fear I am becoming too long-winded, I shall not elaborate on this further here.

[II.B.4.b]
The Meditation That Is to Be Practiced

The aspiration for putting the meditation into practice has two explanations: brief, and extensive.

[II.B.4.b.i]
Brief Explanation of the Meditation That Is to Be Practiced

8. **Cutting off embellishments of the ground, the view is assured.**
   Sustaining that without distraction is the point of meditation.
   Gaining full proficiency in meditation is the finest activity.
   May I have confident view, meditation and activity.

To meditate properly on the path of mahāmudrā, first cut off all claims that embellish mahāmudrā, the fundamental, enduring condition. This makes the view accurate. Undistractedly cultivating and settling evenly into that very view is the exact point of meditation. Training one's proficiency in the vital points of meditation swiftly brings out its full benefits. This is the supreme activity. Since it is with such crucial points of view, meditation and activity as these that one becomes accomplished with the least struggle, one casts the aspiration prayer accordingly.

[II.B.4.b.ii]
Extensive Explanation of the Meditation That Is to Be Practiced

The extensive, detailed explanation of this verse of the aspiration has four parts: aspirations dealing with how to cut off embellishments of the ground through the view, how to achieve certitude by meditating upon that view, how to bring that to its culmination through activity and complete the path, and the result of completing the path.

[II.B.4.b.ii. A']
How to Cut Off Embellishments of the Ground with the View

The first part itself has [both] a brief and an expanded treatment.

[II.B.4.b.ii. A'.1']
Brief Treatment

9. **All phenomena are apparitions of mind.**
Yet mind is not there, for mind is essentially empty,
and while empty, unimpeded, displayed any way at all—
examining well, may I sever the underlying root.

The first line resolves that all perceptible things are projections of mind; the second concludes that mind lacks self-nature; the third teaches that emptiness and interdependence are unified without contradiction; the fourth says that embellished claims about the meaning of the ground must be severed through investigation with the prajñā of fine discernment; and all these instructions are presented in the form of an aspiration.

[II.B.4.b.ii. A'.2']
Expanded Treatment

The expanded explanation has four parts, treating each line [of the verse] separately.

[II.B.4.b.ii.A'.2'.a']
Resolving That Perceptible Objects Are Mind

10. Self-display with no existence is mistaken for an object.
Out of ignorance, self-awareness is mistaken for one's self.
Driven by dualistic clinging, one wanders the vastness of creation.
May I strip away ignorance, the source of confusion.

Since on its surface this verse explicitly deals with ascertaining how the phenomena of saṃsāra are the vibrant display of mind, while on a more refined level it intends to make understood, by implication, that the dharmas of total purification are the prowess of mind [as well], there are two topics here: explicit and implicit.

[II.B.4.b.ii.A'.2'.a'.i']
Explicit Topic

In the form of an aspiration, this section teaches how the mistaken duality of subject and object arises, how that impels circulation within saṃsāra, [and] the need for exposing the hidden recesses of that confusion.

[II.B.4.b.ii.A'.2'.a'.i'.aa']
How the Mistaken Duality of Subject and Object Arises

From "The Profound Inner Meaning" by the Lord himself:

The cause, mind nature with no beginning,
although without restriction or partition,
due to its unimpeded vibrant energy
has an empty essence, a nature of clarity
and an aspect of unimpededness, appearing any way at all.
That [mind nature] does not notice itself.
Out of the stirring of formative cognitive force,[76]
which moves like waves upon water,
things and [their] apprehension both appear.
[Mind] attends to and seizes upon itself.
From the appearance factor, cognitive force moving outward,
[appear] objects taken to be real things, and consciousness arises.
Feelings, whose function is to accept and reject, take birth;

ideas, seizing on the characteristics of these,
regard fabricated appearances of objects as "other."
Due to clinging, the form skandha is produced.

As this passage explains, and as the autocommentary of this work explains more fully still, the fundamental, enduring condition, naturally pure, luminous vajra mind, fails to notice its very own essence with its own prowess, and as a result, formative cognitive force stirs. These, then, appear as the cause and condition, in dependence upon which [mind] comes to bear afflictive patterns; this is [the process of] ignorance.

This cognitive force has two aspects. The instigative mental force plants the potency of the six collections of consciousness on the universal ground at the moment they are made to arise and cease, and the afflictive mental force fixates on the universal ground as "I." So the former makes consciousness be generated and the latter makes it afflicted.

The universal ground, which serves as the basis for these two mental forces, is called "the seed totality," because it stores all impressions of afflictive thought patterns. The mental forces and the universal ground, appearing as cause and condition relative to each other, functioning just like water and waves, are the very root from which all the confusion of saṃsāra is produced.

This is also what Vasubandhu says:

The universal ground consciousness,
the totality of ripened seeds,
always retains the mental activities
of contact, engagement, feeling and ideation.
It is neutral in feeling,
unobscured and morally neutral.
It is like the constant rush of a river.
Arhats reverse its course.

and

Because it rests upon and emerges from [the universal ground]
to regard it, it is called "mental force."
Its nature is to conceive of consciousness as an ego,
and it is always accompanied by the four afflicting patterns.

Look in the "Abridged Vehicle"[77] and other sources with more extensive discussions for more details about this.

By the power of the mental force stirring from the universal ground, the six objects grasped externally and the six internal consciousnesses, while ultimately in no way established as distinct entities, come to *appear* that way. This comes about when the object, faculty and consciousness interdependently come together. When the resultant appearance is *reinforced,* it becomes connected to the thought process. This creates the *finished* idea of a thing. That is how tripartite appearance, reinforcement and attainment are established.[78] It is solely the potency of the seed-potentials of objects, faculties and consciousnesses continuously present in the universal ground, acting in interdependence, that produces appearances.

From "Vajra Pinnacle":[79]

> *The universal ground bearing all seeds*
> *is asserted to be the substance of [what is] outer and inner.*

Furthermore, concerning the progression of appearances, you should know that the mental force, incited by formative mental elements,[80] forms ideas of the six [types of] objects, which gives rise to consciousnesses that regard them as external things. From that, feelings of happiness which wish to accept, feelings of suffering which wish to reject, and neutral feelings which wish neither alternative are born. When these are born, perception, which fixes upon the object's properties, arises. When that has arisen, tendential impressions which consider the object to be "other" follow; and last, the skandha of solid form is created.

In that way, although these phenomena, which are entirely displayed out of mind nature's own innate vibrancy, have never been found to [truly] exist within mind nature's own condition and never could come to exist there, mind nature, by not realizing that, takes itself to be an object and thereby becomes confused.

Under the power of that [confusion] which ignorance has generated, [mind nature] fails to realize self-awareness to be groundless and without foundation and thereby confuses that which apprehends an object with a self. For that reason, every single phenomenon that falls into the categories of subject or object is merely mistaken, and yet the basis for that mistake is the mind. So none are established apart from the mind, not even a particle's worth. It is like using mantra spells to conjure horses and cows out of thin air; still, there is nothing there but emptiness.

You might wonder at what point in time mind became caught up in confusion. The appearance of temporality is also mistaken, therefore it, too, is an embellishment. Since for all eternity it is unestablished [as real], there is no "that time" we can pinpoint. However, it can be said to be mistaken over a span of time without inception, while it remains in the phase of being ignorant of itself, at which point the empty essence of pristine mind is called "universal ground," its nature of cognizance is called "afflictive mental force," and its unhindered expression "consciousness," since on account of ignorance these [three] appear in a distorted fashion.

Scriptures that talk about this include "Departed for Laṅka," "Densely Arrayed Ornaments," and other sūtras of the last [dharma]cakra, and the commentaries on their meaning give even lengthier accounts, but I shall not go on about them here.

Are the accounts of how confusion comes about that are found in tantras and commentaries of mantra[yāna] similar to this one? Although there are, obviously, differences because of their purpose and subject matter, the basic meaning found in them is identical. For example, from "Hevajra":

> *All migratory beings come from me.*
> *The three regions also come from me.*
> *I encompass all of these.*
> *Indeed, no other nature of beings is to be found.*

and from "Stainless Light: The Great Kālacakra Commentary":

> *Supremely unchanging great passion is awareness. Lack of awareness is sentient beings' ingrained predisposition towards passion since time immemorial.*

and

> *"Mara" is the stain of ingrained predispositions in the saṃsāra-oriented minds of sentient beings. "Buddhahood" is mind freed of saṃsāra-oriented ingrained predispositions.*

and from "Commentary on Bodhicitta":

The conventional and afflicted arises from karma.[81]
Karma is what arises from thought activity.
Thought activity collects from tendential imprints.[82]

[II.B.4.b.ii.A'.2'.a'.i'.bb']
How That Impels Circulation Within Saṃsāra

In that way, while subject and object are not truly separate, confusion which holds them to be two continues to manifest without interruption until the universal ground has been overturned, and so until then wandering and circling within this sphere of conditioned existence will go on like the inexorable turning of a water wheel.

Once cognitive force has arisen from the universal ground and the six engaging consciousnesses have arisen from the cognitive force, the cognitive force once again deposits the tendential imprints of the experience of objects back onto the universal ground. These [two] continue to interdependently manifest without interruption, appearing in turn as each other's cause and condition, and so, until the attainment of Buddhahood, the universal ground continues to flow along in its course like a river, unobserved and without cessation. That is why it is said:

It is like the steady flow of a river. That is what Arhats reverse.[83]

and, from "Departed for Laṇka":

Mind is pellucid by nature.
It is the cognitive force that agitates it.
The cognitive force associated with consciousness
continually implants tendential imprints.

and

Consciousness arises from cognitive force;
cognitive force arises from the universal ground.
All phenomena are stirred up
from the universal ground like waves.

From the perpetual flow of seed-potentials arise the twelve interdependent phases of conditioned existence, which also continue without interruption. (1) *Ignorance* (as explained before), (2) *craving* for sensation, and from the spread of craving,

(3) *appropriation* which reaches out for the object of desire, the three kinds of *afflictive patterns,* produce the actions of (4) *configuration* and (5) *impulsion;* and from those, the aggregation of *suffering* arises, which is constituted by the seven aspects of (6) *name and form,* (7) the six *sense fields,* (8) *contact,* (9) *sensation,* (10) *birth,* (11) *aging* and (12) *death.* From those, once more, the three afflictive patterns arise, and so forth, and the cycle continues step by step. Ācārya Nāgārjuna says:

> *From the three come two,*
> *from two come seven,*
> *and again from seven come three—*
> *the whole of conditioned existence.*

and

> *The first, eighth and ninth are afflictive patterns.*
> *The second and tenth are actions,*
> *and the remaining seven are suffering.*

[II.B.4.b.ii.A'.2'.a'.i'.cc']
The Need for Exposing the Hidden Recesses of That Confusion

If one is unaware of the particulars of what confusion is, one won't recognize confusion on sight, and not seeing confusion as confusion, one will be unable to eliminate it. This aspiration has therefore been composed in order to edify us about how essential and necessary it is to understand confusion.

[II.B.4.b.ii.A'.2'.a'.ii']
Implicit Topic

From the coarser demonstration that phenomena within saṃsāra are the display of mind, one can understand that, on a more refined level, phenomena of nirvāṇa are also merely displayed from mind. The coarse appearances of real things, which are created by intense habituation to tendential imprints of reified reality, are starkly opposite to the properties of mind, therefore it is difficult to gain certitude that they are just mind. However, if one can become certain about this, then since phenomena of total purity bear strong resemblance to what is mental, realizing them to be merely mind should not be too formidable a task. Therefore the aspiration shows that phenomena of total purity also do not transcend the nature of pristine mind. Just as mind nature, so long as it has stains, is classified into mind, cognitive force and consciousness, so when it is free of stains is it classified into the three kāyas.

That is why, during the course of the bodhisattva path, as the stains to be purified become more and more slight, the enlightened qualities that reside within prisitine mind become more and more evident, manifesting as the [thirty-seven] qualities conducive to enlightenment. When all of the stains are purified, all of the enlightened qualities of the ground-state fully manifest. You can learn how this works in more detail by studying the account given in "Higher Continuum."

"How can you reconcile that with this explanation by Candrakīrti:

> *By burning the dry tinder of each and every knowable entity,*
> *they are extinguished—that is the Victors' dharmakāya,*
> *which is then unborn, and also unceasing.*
> *That termination of mind is made actual by the kāya.*

[which suggests] that mind is extinguished at the time of attaining enlightenment?"[84]

That explanation concerns relinquishment of the mind which is indicated by "mind, cognitive force and consciousnesses," whereas the term "pristine mind" is being used here to talk about mahāsukha dharmadhātu, which is devoid of arising, dwelling or ceasing. Since even omniscient wisdom is not something separate from the dharmadhātu, it is totally beyond the phenomenal condition of impure mind. For the very reason that phenomena of total purity are not established apart from pristine mind, the displays of nirmāṇakāya and saṃbhogakāya are disclosed to disciples whose minds have become somewhat purified or mostly purified, respectively.

What are the sources for the actual and implied subjects presented here, namely, the manner in which one reaches the conclusion that all phenomena contained within saṃsāra and nirvāṇa are one's own mind? They come from Mahāyāna sūtras and tantras and commentaries upon them. From the "Vajra Canopy" tantra:

Outside of precious mind
there are neither Buddhas nor sentient beings.
The places and things [mind is] conscious of
have not the least external existence.

and from the same source:

Mind nature, pure like space,
is also pure saṃvara's[85] *mind nature.*
The nature of objects and faculties
does not exist outside of mind,
and even what appear distinctly as form and the like
are solely the display of mind nature.

Also, from the "Secret Charnel Ground" tantra:

Buddhahood separate from mind,
and other phenomena separate from mind,
are not even observed by Buddhas;
[Buddhas] have never spoken of them, nor shall they ever speak of them.
That is why this mystery of the mind of all Buddhas
is supreme among all mysteries.

From "Sūtra of the Tenth Level":[86]

Kye! Children of the Victor, these three worlds are just mind!

From "Departed for Laṅka":

The mind provoked by tendential imprints
comes to appear vividly as a thing.

Ācārya Nāgārjuna, in "Praise to the Dharmadhātu," says:

Regard mind nature as having two aspects:
that is, mundane and supramundane.
From apprehension of a self, there is saṃsāra.
When awareness is self-disclosed, it is "just that way,"[87]
which exhausts passion—that is nirvāṇa.
Because it exhausts aggression and bewilderment
and terminates them, Buddhahood itself
is the actual refuge of all embodied creatures.

From "Commentary on Bodhicitta":

There are no external things at all
that exist apart from consciousness, whose
essence is to grasp and apprehend.

Venerable Saraha says:

I offer homage to mind, which is like a wish-fulfilling jewel,
giving whatever fruit is desired,
whence conditioned existence and serenity radiate,
the seed of all, singular mind nature.

Such statements are endless in number.

[II.B.4.b.ii.A'.2'.b']
Gaining Conviction That Mind Has No Self-Nature

From "Commentary on Bodhicitta":

Having dwelt upon mere mind,
the fortunate relinquish that too.
For the vijñānavādins
this multifaceted [display] is established to be mind.
What, then, is the nature of vijñāna?
It is that described as tathatā.
The teachings by the Muni that
"all these [things] are just mind"
were meant to allay the fears
of the immature; but this is not so.[88]
Designated, heteronomous and
the fully established itself, these
are attributions to mind of the essence
of the one unique, master emptiness.[89]

and from "Ornament for the Sūtras":

Once you intellectually understand there to be nothing but mind,
then realize mind, too, not to be.
Use the intellect to understand that both do not exist,
then rest in dharmadhātu without recourse to [intellect].

As this says, though one may know the phenomena of conditioned existence and serenity to be mind, if one doesn't realize mind nature to be emptiness, groundless and without basis, one will not be able to once and for all be rid of fixation upon the self-identity of phenomena. Therefore it is extremely essential that one understand the intrinsic nature of mind. This topic has two parts: abandoning the limitations of existing or not existing, and abandoning the limitations of being or not being something.

[II.B.4.b.ii.A'.2'.b'.i']
Abandoning the Limitations of Existing or Not Existing

11. It is not existent, for even Buddhas have never seen it.
It is not nonexistent, for it is the basis of all saṃsāra and nirvāṇa.
This is the unified central course, not a paradox.
May I realize the unlimited dharmatā of mind.

The meaning of the first line is this: One may wonder, might this pristine mind that was explained earlier be truly established as real? Never mind whether it is truly established to be real, it doesn't exist in either a true or false respect, since even the wisdom of Victors which sees all has not seen it. From the "Densely Arrayed Ornaments" sūtra:[90]

> *There is not even mere nonexistence of mind,*
> *for it has neither extent nor measure.*

and in the sūtra "Requested by Ösung":

> *Ösung, mind does not exist inside, it also does not exist outside. It also isn't observed [to be] between the two. Ösung, there is no mind to discover, none to show, none to support, none to perceive, none to form an idea of, none that abides. Ösung, none of the Buddhas has ever seen, sees or ever will see mind.*

From "Mother [of Victors]":

> *There is no mind in mind, for the nature of mind is luminosity.*[91]

From the "Manifest Awakening of Vairocana" tantra:

> *Mind, the master secret one, has never been, is not, and never will be seen by the Tathāgatas.*

and

> *How should one properly understand one's own mind [to be]? Like this: even if you search thoroughly for it as having an aspect, color, shape or location; as a form, sensation, perception, thought configuration or consciousness; as a self, or possessed by a self, as something to grasp or apprehend, as pure or impure, as a constituent or sense field, or in any other way at all, you won't observe it. This lord secret one is "the portal to the totally pure bodhicitta of a bodhisattva," the gateway for the appearance of dharmas, the original way in which dharmas appear...*

and so on in great detail.

Therefore, when the Victor says that he sees dharmadhātu just as it is and that mind is self-disclosive awareness and is self-cognizant, he is expressing how wisdom's great vision views the dharmadhātu which is free of any limiting constructs and has not even a particle's worth of properties to look upon, and expressing what is beyond cognizer or cognized, discloser or disclosed with the words "awareness" and "cognizance." This profound point should be understood well so that no ready comparisons be made to the kind of sight, etc., that worldly beings possess. In other contexts "self knowing itself" and the like are [considered] contradictions. "Departed for Laṅka":

Like the blade its own edge
and the finger its own tip
does not cut, does not touch,
likewise mind sees not mind.

and from "Embarking on the [Course of Bodhisattva] Conduct":

Is it akin to the manner in which
a butter lamp perfectly illuminates itself?
A butter lamp is not thus illuminated
since it is not obscured by darkness.[92]

These and other faults [of reasoning ordinarily] ensue.

The meaning of the second line: "Well then, can we settle upon the nature of mind being radical nonexistence and inconceivability?" We can't hold to that either. Were the naturally pure constituent of mind utterly nonexistent, the appearances of conditioned existence and serenity could not possibly occur even on the conventional level, since the distinction between conditioned existence and serenity hinges precisely upon whether or not the fundamental ground has been realized. Likewise, in the "Praise to the Dharmadhātu":

Because the constituent is there,
by working upon it you will find its pure extract.
With no constituent, though you work,
surely only afflictive patterns will arise.

and

Like that, from all seeds
arise fruit kindred to their causes.

What knowledgeable person could establish
the existence of a fruit without a seed?

This constituent which is the seed
is asserted to be the basis for all phenomena.
Through gradually cleansing it,
the state of enlightenment will be attained.[93]

This last statement, which provides an example, is very clear.

At this juncture, one point must be understood well: the phenomena of conditioned existence and serenity displaying characteristics do not abide as their own entity and do not enjoy true existence, yet they all still have the capacity to appear, without contradiction. Although we speak of "mind vajra" and the "naturally pure constituent," it is absolutely not the case that these exist in the extreme sense of being real and true, forever and ever.

How can this be reconciled with the sūtras of the final dharmacakra[94] that talk about the pāramitās of purity, permanence, bliss and selfhood, and with the innate, indestructible and invulnerable primordial wisdom talked about in mantrayāna?

What is nonexistent is
said to be the most sacred existent.
What is not observed in any way
is the most sacred observed.

As this quote from "Densely Arrayed Ornaments" shows, the intrinsically pure "just that itself" is not broken down into components and properties, is beyond the range of the intellect, and is provisionally described in these ways to point out that it is not changeable into something else,[95] and so on. The purpose of speaking in this way is also to eliminate the great evil of grasping onto emptiness, which is even more vile than the existence view. From sūtra:

Mt. Meru's worth of grasping at a self is simple [to correct], but grasping at the absence of self is not.

and venerable Nāgārjuna:

A defective view of emptiness is the ruin of those with little prajñā.

The reason for teaching this is to undermine fixation on solidity, since in teaching emptiness, if emptiness is taken to be a solid thing, this holding onto solidity would become even greater than [the fixation] of worldly people, and extremely vile, like, for example, taking an emetic to cure an illness and having the emetic itself turn poisonous. Therefore, the "Absorptions of Four Youths" sūtra says:

Someone who thinks what is empty is empty
has no notion of what is empty.
Those who do not see emptiness
are the ones who understand [it].

From "Principal Exposition [of the Central Course]":

If there were even slight non-emptiness
there would also be slight emptiness.
If there is not the slightest non-emptiness,
how could there be emptiness?
The Victors have said that emptiness
disrupts all views.
Whatever "views" of emptiness there are,
they are all of no use.[96]

The meaning of the third and fourth lines: If the enduring condition of mind were explained to be both existent and nonexistent, wouldn't it succumb to the fault of forcing opposites together, since it isn't possible for one subject to be both existent and nonexistent? No, that wouldn't happen, since what preceded was a refutation of both existence and nonexistence rather than a proof that [the enduring condition of mind] is both [existent and nonexistent].

In short, in order to facilitate the realization of that which is not located anywhere and lies outside the bounds of the intellect, that which any terms, such as existent, nonexistent, empty, not empty, and so on are unable to actually express, we simply [seek to] demonstrate, in our unrealized way, how to disprove the extreme positions of existence, nonexistence, embellishment and discredit.[97] And yet, once those extremes have been abandoned, there is not a particle's worth of anything that we attempt to prove. Venerable Nāgārjuna:

To reject all designations
we teach the nectar of emptiness.
Should there arise attachment to that,
then that, too, should be abandoned.

From the "Sky Treasury" sūtra:

The wise do not subscribe to views of real and not real.
"Emptiness" is a verbal expression.
The sound does not contain emptiness,
which is not a sound, not an expression.
Therefore, what is called "emptiness,"
although it is taught by all Buddhas,
is not something to be expressed,
and when something is said to be empty,
what that means is inexpressible.

Therefore, the essence of mind is not found at either polarized extreme and does not even abide in the center; that is what is meant by the term "unified, utterly non-abiding central course" (Madhyamaka), which, again, is just a label we stick on. So this aspiration has been composed as an instruction on the necessity of realizing the meaning of mahāmadhyamaka, the defining property of mind, freedom from every polarized position.

[II.B.4.b.ii. A'.2'.b'.ii']
Abandoning the Limitations of Being or Not Being Something

12. There is nothing to indicate that "it is this."
There is no refutation to show "it is not this."
Unfabricated dharmatā that defies the intellect
is the perfect, ultimate limit—may I be certain of it.

The meaning of this verse can be understood from the previous section refuting existence and nonexistence, but just to say a little more, the nature of mind that is free of extremes can be referred to by a multitude of sonorous names, like emptiness, the unborn, unification, the ultimate, the connate, great bliss, and so on, yet even though we say it is these things, mind nature cannot actually be represented in any way whatsoever, because at no time is there ever a truly established quality within mind to be represented. Likewise, though [qualities such as] singularity and plurality, existence and nonexistence, coming and going and the like are all refuted, since it is not possible for mind's nature itself to diminish or change, it is not refutable.

For instance, though you can [try to] refute it by saying "That which is devoid of any nature is not like such and such," since the very subject that is to be refuted is not established, there isn't anything to refute. Further, from "Ornament for the Central Course":

In reality, it is free of
all collections of constructs.
Since there is no such thing as birth,
being unborn and so forth is just not possible.

From "Distinguishing the Two Truths":[98]

Refutations of birth and so forth,
since they approximate the truth, are accepted.
Because what is refuted does not exist,
it is evident that in reality there is no refutation.

and

What is in reality nondual
is not mentally constructed.
In response to Mañjuśrī's inquiry into reality
the Victor's son remained silent.

For such reasons it "defies the intellect." Śāntideva:[99]

The ultimate is not in the domain of the intellect.
The intellect is on the level of conventions.

That is to say, it is not possible for the conventional to take the ultimate as its object. Because that which is beyond the reach of the intellect primordially dwells as the dharmatā of all phenomena, it is "unfabricated," as it is not changed by any extrinsic, constructed, conditioning factors. It is referred to as the "perfect, ultimate limit" since it follows that where all phenomena finally end up[100] is their true, ultimate end. From "Distinguishing the Center from the Extremes":

In brief, tathatā,
the perfect limit, the uncharacterized,
the ultimate, and dharmadhātu
are all synonymous with emptiness.

"May I be certain of it": If one is burdened with doubts about the meaning of the enduring condition, then during meditation one's mind won't reach a state of focused equipoise. That is why this verse counsels us that it is necessary to gain conviction about this explanation [of mind], and so be rid of all uncertainty.

Is this also the kind of view that is taught in Mantrayāna? As I have already discussed, since there is no difference at all in sūtra and tantra Mahāyāna with regard to the view that is devoid of constructed ideas, this is in fact precisely what is taught [in Mantra]. From the "Kālacakra" principal tantra:

> *Fully released from being or not being,*
> *not dual, past being something or nothing,*
> *indivisible emptiness and compassion,*
> *vajra yoga, great bliss,*
> *beyond the condition of matter, coarse or subtle,*
> *entirely without empty dharmas,*
> *fully released from existence or nonexistence,*
> *unrestricted vajra yoga. . .*

There are countless statements from the profound classes of tantra that are like this one.

[II.B.4.b.ii.A'.2'.c']
How the Unity of Emptiness and Interdependence Is Not Paradoxical

13. Simply not realizing this stirs the ocean of conditioned existence;
just realizing this, there is no enlightenment elsewhere.
Being all, it is never "this but not that."[101]
May I discover the hidden dimensions of the universal ground, dharmatā.

As was explained in an extensive fashion earlier, from lack of realization of this recondite, enduring condition of mind comes the forward system of interdependence, which is circulation within conditioned existence; whereas when realization takes place, the reverse system of interdependence produces enlightenment—in fact, this enlightenment is not something distinct from what is meant by the enduring condition. Therefore, this enduring condition of emptiness, which abides primordially as the enlightened nature, encompasses all phenomena, and so no matter where you search for some phenomenon that it is, as opposed to others that it is not, you won't succeed in locating anything.

The fact that phenomena occur interdependently can also be used as an argument that establishes their emptiness, since if they were not empty, there would be no way for them to occur in dependence upon one another. From sūtra:

> *Whatever arises conditionally does not arise,*
> *for it has no nature of arising.*
> *What is dependent upon conditions is described as empty.*
> *Whoever know emptiness is circumspect.*[102]

Venerable Nāgārjuna says:

> *There is not a single phenomenon*
> *that is not interdependently arisen.*
> *That is why there is not*
> *a single phenomenon that is not empty.*

Therefore, interdependence is not established apart from emptiness, and emptiness is not established apart from interdependence, and that is why their unification is permissible. Since that [unity] is the dharmatā of all dharmas, [the aspiration] says "May I discover the hidden dimensions," that is, the determinant features, of "just that" (tathatā), here referred to as "the universal ground." In this instance "universal ground" just means the naturally prisitine mind. As is said in "Densely Arrayed Ornaments":

> *The innate condition of the universal ground, virtue,*
> *is seen and heard by the children of the Victors. . .*

and

> *By the merit of the stainless universal ground, one becomes a Tathāgata.*

Therefore, don't confuse this with the universal ground consciousness that is the cause of conditioned existence.

[II.B.4.b.ii.A'.2'.d']
The Need for Investigation with Discerning Prajñā to Sever Embellished Claims About the Ground

14. Since appearance is mind, and emptiness also is mind,
realization is mind, and confusion also is my own mind,
arising is mind and cessation, too, is just mind,
may I sever all embellished claims within my mind.

Here we have instructions, in the form of an aspiration, on the need to cut through "apparent" or "empty," "realized" or "confused," "arising" or "ceasing," and all other contrivances concerning the enduring condition, through the conviction that [mind] has no self-nature. One acquires this conviction by assimilating all the reasons forwarded thus far.

How is it that, according to Vijñānavādins, realizing all phenomena to be mind is the realization of the ultimate? In this case, as mentioned before, the fundamental enduring condition is being called "mind," so there is no contradiction.

[II.B.4.b.ii.B']
How to Achieve Certitude, Through Meditation, About the Meaning of Severing All Embellished Claims About the Ground

[There is both a] concise explanation and an expanded explanation.

[II.B.4.b.ii.B'.1']
Concise Explanation

15. Without being corrupted by deliberate, fabricated meditation,
and without being disturbed by the commotion of common affairs,
knowing how to settle into what is natural and uncontrived,
may I expertly sustain practice of the vital point of mind.

This verse will be easier to explain if the second line is put first, so that first is the way to enter into meditation, next is the way to remain steadily in equipoise, and last is the way to sustain that state.

[II.B.4.b.ii.B'.1'.a']
How to Begin Meditation

A qualified person who has been blessed by an outstanding lama, whose mind is able to accomodate the profound dharma, and who possesses the four qualities of faith, industry, prajnā and tolerance, in order to put the yoga of mahāmudrā into practice, should first remove himself or herself from physical, verbal or mental contact with ordinary social affairs. This is very important.

[To have] contact with common affairs means to busy one's three gates in the pursuit of fame, fortune, and the eight worldly dharmas, out of passionate interest in conditioned existence. Without abandoning that, one can't even attain higher states, let alone liberation. From "Embarking on the [Course of Bodhisattva] Conduct":

In the forest the deer, the birds
and the trees listen not, and do not speak.
Those so pleasant companions —
when shall I dwell amongst them?

In a cave, an empty temple, or
before an enchanted tree,
without so much as a look back
and freed of passion, oh when shall I be?

In wilderness regions
and natural, open vantages,
on my own and carefree,
when shall I dwell?

As the guidance manuals suggest, dwell in an isolated place, like the ones spoken of here in "Embarking on the Conduct," with a mind well trained in the preliminaries. By relying upon external isolation and through familiarity with the common path, the whole lot of common affairs will automatically lose their lustre. Take to heart these words from the lips of Ācārya Maitrīpa [Avadhūtipa]:

The fair lady, the water fowl, the snake,
the hunter for game in the woods,
the arrowsmith and the maiden,
these are my masters.
Surrender of hope, material wealth, and home,
meditation in remote forests,
steady focus and solitude—
these I discovered from my gurus.

Here is the meaning: Avadhūtipa himself, on one occasion, saw a woman named Serkyamo (Fair Lady) who had arranged a tryst with a man and was anxiously awaiting his arrival, but then later, when she became convinced that he was not going to come after all, went to sleep feeling very relieved. From this he knew that he must abandon expectations. Next, he saw a water fowl riding around on a large fish with the rest of the birds chasing behind until the rider gave up his spot, whereupon another took its place, and this sequence was repeated over and over. From this he gathered that material wealth must be abandoned because no matter who holds it, it is always the basis for dispute.

Similarly, he saw a snake lying in its lair with its many children, who were busy playing and being a nuisance, so it went to another hole where it could lie comfortably. From this he realized one must abandon one's home. Observing a hunter who regularly went into the forest in search of prey meet a sannyāsin yogi there and begin to meditate, and eventually become a yogi, he understood the importance of meditation in isolation. When he saw an arrowsmith so engrossed in fashioning an arrow that he failed to notice the king and his entourage passing by, he learned the importance of totally focused attention.

When a young lady was grinding incense, her many bracelets were clattering noisily so she finally tore them off and was more comfortable. Seeing her do this, Avadhūtipa knew that he must give up companionship and stay by himself. Practicing just what he had learned from these episodes, [Avadhūtipa found] exquisite samādhi within.

After abandoning the bustle of social affairs, the next step is [to practice] the four uncommon preliminaries that set into motion the interdependent process that effortlessly produces the wisdom of mahāmudrā. These are absolutely indispensable.

[II.B.4.b.ii.B'.1'.b']
How to Rest Steadily

This has two parts: first, the pertinent points of body, and second, the pertinent points of mind.

[II.B.4.b.ii.B'.1'.b'.i']
The Pertinent Points of Body

Although not discussed explicitly here, the pertinent points of body are tacitly included. They are, from the "Vajra Rosary" tantra:

> *A practitioner should rest on a comfortable seat,*
> *direct the gaze to the tip of the nose*

and look no further than the nose.
Keep the shoulders level and touch the tongue to the palate.
Allow the lips and teeth to relax.
Without forcing the inhalation and exhalation of the breath,
without the least exertion or effort,
maintain proper vajra posture.

and from "Vajra Pinnacle":

In a tidy place free of social interaction,
assume the posture.
Just like a bodhisattva
seated at bodhigarbha,[103]
close the eyes and let teeth rest on teeth.
Performing the mudrā of straightening the body,
[sustain] one-pointed mindfulness, mahāmudrā.

As these texts state, properly observing the pertinent points of physical posture, such as the "seven dharmas of Vairocana" and the "five dharmas of dhyāna," as they are presented in oral instructions, is very important.

[II.B.4.b.ii.B'.2'.b'.ii']
The Pertinent Points of Mind

Don't corrupt practice with your own fabrications of resting in clarity, resting in emptiness, or resting in unification, with deliberate attempts to stop thinking or hold your attention on the subject, or with, in short, any deliberate, contrived meditation. From "Guhyasamāja":

No meditation on no subject.
To do meditation is not meditation.
In that way, with the subject of no subject,
meditation is nonreferential.

and from "Hevajra":

Since it isn't imagined by the mind,
all beings should meditate in this manner.

From "Connate Accomplishment":

What is thought of as empty,
like the hollow within the vase
or what the intellect may claim to be empty,
these are not called "connate."

Honorable Saraha says:

Knowing that what is displayed as self and other is of a single nature,
and completely fixating upon just that, undistractedly,
is painful to the mind, so abandon this [approach], and then,
without grasping at anything, elicit bliss.
Being rid of all actions that harm the mind,
and with all attempts to acquire or obtain become superfluous,
freed of effort, and while spurious conditions are absent,
this mudrā of multifaceted display is truly spectacular.

Even in the sūtras, from the "Seven-Hundred-Verse Prajñāpāramitā":

Not seizing, grasping or rejecting any dharma is the meditation of prajñāpāramitā. What does not dwell on anything at all is the meditation of prajñāpāramitā. Not considering or identifying anything is the meditation of prajñāpāramitā.

and from "The Eight-Thousand [-Verse Prajñāpāramitā]":

This meditation of prajñāpāramitā is not meditation on any dharma.

From the "King of Absorptions":

When the thought "I must get rid of this thought" arises,
that is immersion in thought constructs,
which will not liberate one from thought constructs.

From the sūtra "Requested by Lodrö Gyatso":

Don't preoccupy the mind with dharmas.
Totally abandon superior interests.
Comprehend all dharmas in equanimity,
with perfect composure.[104]

Countless such statements are found in Mahāyāna sūtras, tantras, and their commentaries. So just let yourself settle into a state of natural ease without contrivance. From the sayings of the masters of oral instruction in our Kagyu school:

Don't linger in the past. Don't anticipate the future. Come to rest in present wakefulness without altering or modifying it.

Lord Gampopa:

The saying "don't linger in the past" means we shouldn't pursue the thought that has just passed through our minds. "Don't anticipate the future" means we shouldn't await the thought about to enter our minds. Saying "rest vividly in present, natural wakefulness" means don't keep

> *track of anything in the present moment. If mind is not tampered with, it will become clear. If water is not disturbed, it becomes pellucid. So rest freely and alertly in a state without contrivances.*

Since the gist of the scriptural statements cited above is that there is no idea fabricated by the mind that can qualify as meditation, this superlative, profound point of oral instruction on not pursuing thought constructs of the three times is well-corroborated.

Further, mahāsiddha Wangpo'i Lo says:

> *So long, so long as there is thought,*
> *then all is total artifice.*
> *When that itself*[105] *is not examined,*
> *then that is what is proper, and that is truth.*

and Saraha:

> *So not preoccupying the mind with the three times*
> *in any way whatsoever is non-separation, the intrinsic state;*
> *and sustaining "just that" is what we refer to as "meditation."*

In this context, "intrinsic state" should be understood to mean the natural condition of the fundamental ground that is not corrupted by thought activity. "The Authoritative Commentary on 'Embarking on the Conduct'" by Sherjung Baypa[106] says:

> *Having no nature is the intrinsic condition of all things, and so it is the natural and enduring condition of ultimate [truth]. That is why it is called the supreme purpose of all creatures, and is highly exalted.*[107] *But don't have a lot of attachment to this.*

Some people say, "Your system of mahāmudrā, by blocking thought activity concerning the three times, amounts to the meditation of the Chinese teacher Hua Shang." Although there are certainly people with this opinion, they say it without careful forethought, since this Kagyu system does not advocate deliberately blocking thought activity and then resting upon that idea of blocking thoughts, but rather, as I have already explained, recommends that one preserve present wakefulness in an unfabricated way. These critics might think that, nevertheless, the fault still applies, because sustaining present wakefulness without fabrication will inevitably result in thoughts engaged with the three times coming to a halt.

Well then, those of you who feel this way are apparently rather fond of thoughts and reluctant to discard them, and since it does seem that the kind of people who prefer this sort of perfect view are in the vast majority, you are entirely welcome to join them in reveling in thoughts, and need not trouble yourselves further with us.

At no time have we ever ventured onto any course that diverges from the one taught by the Sugatas and travelled by the master siddhas. From "Kālacakra":

Since "A" and "Ka," candra, and the single surya are not the seat
of the vajra-one,
and the "Hung" syllable itself does not admit of sign
and transformation [into] another, with color and form,
then, to the "changeless" diminishes generation and transformation,
which bears the power of supremacy,
the ubiquitous bindu possessing all aspects, the Lord of Victors
that embraces manifold illusion, to that I offer praise![108]

This tells us that thoughts and contrived meditation cannot bring about the supreme, immutable state, and as both the "Guhyasamāja" and "Hevajra" scriptures quoted earlier, and the lines:

The holy Victor has taught that
that which retains signs
[produces] siddhi with signs.
Remaining in what is signless
can also produce that [siddhi] which has signs.

from the "Manifest Awakening of Vairocana" explain, the yoga free of concepts and signs is suitable not just for producing signless, supreme siddhis, which goes without saying, but also common siddhis with signs. Ācārya Nāgārjuna:

Wholly abandoning thought and investigation
of dharmas that are principally mental,
meditate within the dharmadhātu,
the very nature of all dharmas.

From the "Four Mudrā Stages"[109] of Pa'o Dorje:

Prolonging the continuity of moment-to-moment nonconceptuality is conveniently labelled "meditation."

and from "The Oral Instructions of the Succession of Lineage Gurus" of Ācārya Vajrapāṇi, translated by Drogmi,

"Then there is no meditator, and no meditation,
there is no deity and there is also no mantra.
Within the nature which is without limiting constructs
deity and mantra perfectly abide."

Therefore, for nonconceptual mahāmudrā itself, deliberate, purposive meditation is not acceptable.

and

"There is no meditator whatever.
There is no meditation whatever.
There is not even something to meditate upon.
Meditate upon the tathatā of that."

Therefore, rest undistractedly upon what is without meditator, object of meditation or intention to meditate. Meditate undistractedly upon "just that," and since all thoughts are generated in dependence upon extraneous, moment-to-moment conditions, whereas the natural essence is unborn, when the conditions for thinking of something have not assembled, cognizance not corrupted by passing conditions is the unfabricated natural state, free of embellishment or discredit—this is mahāmudrā.

This source is quite thorough, offering many supportive scriptural statements.

Statements from the profound classes of sūtra are also in agreement with this [meaning]. From the "Excellent Qualities" sūtra:

Don't follow the past. Don't have hope for the future. What is in the past is over and the future has not yet come. Looking well at dharmas arising in the present without being captivated by thoughts, comprehend them all.

and from the sūtra "Requested by Lodrö Gyatso":

Past ideas are finished. Future ideas have not arrived. Ideas arising in the present do not remain. One who does not focus upon ideas in the three times understands ideas well.

So there are many sources which validate this [meaning].

Does one just start right out sustaining the unfabricated natural state? Since people's capacities vary, if one is able to start there, that's terrific, but if not, then as those wise in the oral tradition say, "Tether the elephant of mind to the pillar of a reference point with the cord of attentive mindfulness."

There is outward mental retention and inward mental retention, and each has both a subtle and a coarse variety. In connection with these, there are a variety of figures of deities, bindus, syllables, prāṇa, and so forth, which act as supports for retention of mind. When the time comes, if you put into practice the instructions given to you by your lama, you won't go wrong. Nāgārjuna:

> *Supported by points of reference*
> *the referenceless will fully emerge.*

[II.B.4.b.ii.B'.1'.c']
How to Sustain That State

Being expert in this kind of practice of the crucial point of mind through possessing the critical oral instructions, and having expertise as well in the ways to get rid of faults like torpor and agitation, the way to circumvent deviations, and the way to extract maximal benefit, then until you actualize genuine fruition mahāmudrā, as is said,

> *"Like the steady flow of a river*
> *and the tip of a glowing butter lamp,*
> *follow the tathatā of mantra,*[110]
> *and you will attain uninterrupted dhyana."*
>
> *That is how [the practice] must be sustained.*

The aspiration is therefore composed as a lesson to us.

[II.B.4.b.ii.B'.2']
Expanded Explanation

[This section discusses the] yogas of serene abiding and higher insight; how they give rise to experiences and realization; and the practice of unified emptiness and compassion.

[II.B.4.b.ii.B'.2'.a']
Yogas of Serene Abiding and Higher Insight

[This is divided into the yoga of] serene abiding, [the yoga of] higher insight, [and] the yoga of unified serene abiding and higher insight with a listing of synonymous terms.

[II.B.4.b.ii.B'.2'.a'.i']
Serene Abiding

16. May the waves of coarse and subtle thoughts subside on their own
and the placid river of mind gently come to rest.
May the ocean of serene abiding, without the silt and mire
of torpor and dullness, remain steady and unperturbed.

As I have already explained, because there are different calibres of people, one might practice steady placement first with and then without a support, or else one might from the outset start to practice without a support. In any case, in meditation one must first establish the samādhi of serene abiding. This term "serene abiding" means to settle down the thought process that afflicts the mind and to abide one-pointedly in the essence of virtue. As Dīpaṃkara[111] puts it:

Looking out upon the activities of the world
[one sees that] all deeds are futile and create suffering.
Since there is no benefit in anything you can think of,
meditate looking at your own mind.

and from "Manifest Awakening of Vairocana":

Thoughts are enormous ignorance;
[they] send you plummeting into saṃsāra's ocean.
If you remain in the samādhi of non-thought
you will become as pure as the sky.

This is the samādhi of nonconceptuality, which demands that one first abandon worldly affairs.

Thoughts can be divided into coarse and subtle. A coarse thought is just the mind thinking of an object, and a subtle thought is reflection that analyzes that thought. From "Abhidharma Treasury": "Thought and analysis, rough and fine," which is quite clear. Here, in the context of the oral instructions, it is taught that thought or analysis of an object that is explicitly noticed is coarse, whereas when the engagement of an object is not felt, it is subtle.

That is why, without forcibly blocking the thought waves that emerge from the mind, you should allow them to naturally come to a halt, for they will subside on their own. Then the flow of the river of mind, the universal ground consciousness, will also become stilled and naturally come to rest.

This is the aspiration for a still and steady ocean of serene abiding with none of the turbid filth of torpor and dullness. This verse also makes use of decorative imagery.

At this point the impediments to serene abiding, represented in the verse by "torpor and dullness," are presented, and the prayer teaches the necessity of eliminating them. From "Letter of Friendly Advice":[112]

> *Agitation, remorse and regret, lassitude and*
> *sleepiness, longing for the desirable, doubt—*
> *these five are thieves who steal the riches*
> *of virtuous dhyāna—so the Muni has said.*

The impediments are agitation, regret and remorse, sleepiness and lassitude, longing for the desirable, and doubt — five in all. The agitation caused by thoughts scattering towards various objects and regret for inappropriate actions one has done prevent the mind from abiding serenely. Remorse prevents it from abiding happily. Torpor that occludes the mind, dullness (which is a more overwhelming form of torpor), and compulsion to sleep prevent the mind from resting lucidly. Longing, which is desire for material goods or sentient beings, prevents the mind from resting in an effective way. Doubt about whether or not this is leading to samādhi prevents the mind from resting with sharp focus.

These five can also be condensed into two. Torpor, lassitude and sleep are included in torpor, while the rest are included within agitation, so there are just the two, torpor and agitation. The method for eliminating them is reliance on the individual remedies given in the guidance manuals, or else,

> *This has nothing whatsoever to be removed;*
> *there isn't the slightest thing to be added on.*
> *Look at perfection perfectly.*
> *When you see the perfect you are totally liberated.*[113]

So the main thing is to look at the very essence of torpor and agitation and just rest in that essence without contrivance. That is the most profound [remedy]. This is also absolutely necessary as a basis for higher insight. As Śāntideva says:

Once you know that serene abiding
with full measure of higher insight
completely destroys afflictive patterns,
then first strive for serene abiding that,
with no attachment to the world,
is accomplished with evident joy.

According to the sūtra system of classification of serene abiding, there are what are known as the "nine means of bringing mind to rest," which are ancillary to the commencement of serene abiding. Then there are the seven engagements of mind, which are known as "the prerequisites" because they are endeavors aimed at reaching the actual main practice of dhyāna. Then there are the four dhyānas (the first and the others), the four formless samādhis, and cessation absorption. Of all these, the dhyānas and formless samādhis, along with cessation absorption, are known as the nine absorptions.

The nine means for bringing mind to rest are, from "Mother [of Victors]":

Bring the mind to a steady state of rest. Bring it properly to rest. Bring it totally to rest. Train it. Fully train it. Pacify it. Utterly pacify it. Unify it. Bring it into samādhi.

The seven engagements of mind are, from "Ornament [for the Sūtras]":

Then, the first step for one who maintains precepts
is to differentiate the unambivalent meaning
of dharmas, such as those of the sūtra class.[114]
Fix the mind upon the name of the sūtra
then, in order,
isolate its individual words, analyze them,
and further, properly analyze
the internal meaning of each of them.
Having identified these meanings,
bring them into coherence as dharma
then make aspirations, in order that

one may attain their meaning.
With utterance of mind, continuously
examine each topic of investigation.
Discover, too, that being of one taste,
engagements of mind are inexpressible.
Also connect the name of the dharma.[115]
Know this to be the path of serene abiding.

Of individual consideration, interest, isolation, joy, withdrawal, discernment, completion of preparation, and result of completion, the seven engagements of mind,[116] the last one is called the "noncompulsory prerequisite."[117]

The four dhyānas [are], from "Abhidharma Treasury":

The first has five: conception, analysis,
joy, bliss, and samādhi.
The second has four branches:
extreme lucidity, joy and so forth.
The third has five: balance,
recall, attention, bliss and rest.
The last is the four samādhis of recall,
balance, no happiness and no sadness.

At this point, as a result of the fourth dhyāna, the six paranormal cognitive powers also occur. As is said:

Once the fourth samādhi has been attained with extreme purity
then, by embracing [it] with nonconceptual wisdom,
through engaging the mind upon the topic of how it is[118]
paranormal cognitive powers readily emerge.[119]

The four formless absorptions are limitless space, limitless consciousness, total vacuity, and neither existence nor nonexistence. Once perception of form ends, the meditations continue to get more and more subtle.

Cessation absorption proceeds to end suffering and all other sensation. No persons besides ārya bodhisattvas and hearer and solitary realizer arhats have access to this level.

You should understand that bringing the mind to rest through the nine methods of resting is solely serene abiding practice, and all stages beyond that are serene abiding in concert with higher insight.

You might wonder whether there is a contradiction in this statement, since higher insight is supramundane prajñā, and I have just explained that, other than the state of cessation-absorption, all these absorptions are also common to mundane paths. There is no problem on this point, for although there are certainly instances of referring to mundane prajñā as higher insight, here I am describing that which is uncommon [prajñā], in view of its being linked to the transcendent path from the very beginning.

I have given just the kernel here of an explanation of the absorptions and the rest simply because I felt it would make the topic more comprehensible, even though it isn't of paramount importance for practical purposes. Look elsewhere for more detailed presentations.

The stages laid out in the "Extraordinary Definitive Secret of the Kagyu Masters,"[120]

> *First, resting is like water rushing down a steep decline.*
> *Second, like a gently flowing river.*
> *Third, like a still ocean.*

concern serene abiding practice alone.

[II.B.4.b.ii.B'.2'.a'.ii']
Higher Insight

[There is both a] main explanation, [and advice on] severing the root.

[II.B.4.b.ii.B'.2'.a'.ii'.aa']
Main Explanation

17. When invisible mind is looked at again and again,
the unglimpsed meaning is beheld distinctly, just as it is.
With the severing of all doubts about what is and is not,
may the non-mistaken inner essence reveal itself.

Resting steadily upon the enduring condition of the entity of mind, which is not something to be looked at since it transcends the realm of the visible,[121] yet looking again and again with the eye of prajñā born out of meditation and the lama's oral instructions, one will very distinctly[122] see that which is not a sight, exactly as it is, and thereby cut through, right on the spot, all doubts and theoretical claims about the meaning of the enduring condition, such as what it is or is not, and whether it is or is not.

In that way, the non-mistaken innate essence is vividly experienced in a self-disclosive manner. "Giving rise to higher insight wisdom of this kind, may I fully realize connate mahāmudrā!"

Furthermore, the realization of the enduring condition, which is itself devoid of all the characteristics of thought, meditation, view, cognition, sight, experience, and so on, is merely designated using those words. You should understand, for instance, that being free of the obfuscations that come out of ignorance, such as grasping onto void emptiness or a non-affirming negation as ultimately real, or describing [the enduring condition of mind] as akin to the emptiness of lifeless matter, it is asserted to be "self-disclosive awareness"; and as a result of cutting through all doubts and superimposed claims, it is the "discovery of certainty"; and due to the elimination of the ebb and flow of dissatisfactory thoughts, it is asserted to be "great bliss."

Also, from "Origin of Saṃvara":

Wholly free of grasping and fixation,
totally devoid of philosophical speculation,
the foundation of mind and mental factors,
the natural tathatā of migrant beings,
like pure crystal, precious stones and
open space, mind's indwelling perfection,
by nature without beginning or end,
not of the senses, not a construct,
not apparent and free from variation,
empty in toto, unafflicted,
not phraseable in words, breaker
of the chains of existence, a lamp for beings,
not material for the intellect,
unafflicted and free from duality,
the sacred ultimate, bestower of liberation—
to the constant tathatā, I offer homage.

When you come into contact with that[123]
all ideas become unthinkable.[124]
When mind beholds the unthinkable,
at that moment it becomes inconceivable.[125]
As sentient beings are without concepts,[126]

so what is free of concepts emancipates[127]
because Buddha who is free from concepts
explained this concept very well.

That mind that is free of concepts[128]
is not accompanied by any thoughts,[129]
not dressed up with myriad embellishments,
passionless, great bliss,
the supreme among all aspects
[yet] beyond all the senses, with no aspect,
the essence of what is tangible and intangible
[yet] without tangibility or intangibility,
self-cognizant, since it is not material,
[yet] not cognizance, and not something visible,
not located anywhere, since it has no form,
permanent, because it never changes.

From "Mahāmudrā Drop":

Ultimately, not something visible
or invisible, nor even both.
That which is disclosed to itself, supreme serenity
this supreme mahā-tathatā
is the essence of the tangible and intangible, serenity.

and from "Hevajra":

The essence of self-disclosive awareness, purity,
is not liberated by some other purity.

and from "Kālacakra":

Not what is increased by increase,
not what is balanced by equanimity,
not what setting sets,
not what rising raises,
not what vivid clarity makes vividly clear,
and not what covering covers over.
Not what is born at birth,
and not what dies at death, either.
Not what is liberated by liberation,
not what does not abide in nonabiding,
not the entity of what is no entity,
but also not the entity of what is an entity.
Not what is changed by change
and not what is unchanged by no change.[130]

We could go on and on.

Even in the profound sūtra classes, we find in "Concise Prajñāpāramitā":

> *Sentient beings speak easily enough of "seeing space"—*
> *how does one see space? Look carefully at what this means.*
> *The one who sees that way sees all dharmas;*
> *no other example has the power to convey what is seen.*

and even in treatises, from "Entry to the Two Truths":[131]

> *By examining in a nonconceptual manner*
> *emptiness is "glimpsed," conventionally speaking.*
> *As the extremely profound sūtras say,*
> *the invisible is glimpsed.*

and so on.

[II.B.4.b.ii.B'.2'.a'.ii'.bb']
Severing the Root

18. Looking at an object, there is none; I see it is mind.
Looking for mind, mind is not there; it lacks any essence.
Looking at both, dualistic clinging is freed on its own.
May I realize luminosity, the enduring condition of mind.

Objects are visual, auditory, olfactory, gustatory and tactile phenomena, that is to say, all perceptible appearances. Holding one's attention upon those and then resting steadily, with prajnā born of meditation one will observe that places and objects are not established in their own right but are just mind. Then, similarly, through the force of looking at the innate essence of mind nature and then resting steadily, one will realize that mind, too, is groundless and without any basis. By resting steadily upon the sameness of taste of both appearances and mind, apprehension of the duality of subject and object will become undermined and released right where it stands.

Therefore, relying on such methods, "May I give rise to the wisdom of higher insight which realizes the enduring condition of mind just as it is—luminosity, naturally free from obscurations."

On this topic, the presentation of the guidance manuals is arranged to first introduce appearance as mind, then mind as emptiness, then emptiness as spontaneous presence, and finally spontaneous presence as self-liberated. The reason for this is that although initially, through the oral instructions on the eleven engagements of mind and so on, one might recognize the enduring condition, afterwards one needs introduction via the oral instructions of severing the underlying root, or else one won't reach the stage of absolute certainty.

The main set of formal instructions for arriving at such final, definitive understanding, such as the cycle on "searching for the mind," are apparently, for certain Tibetans, a source of great amusement. However, I can put up with all the sly comments I hear. From "Manifest Awakening of Vairocana":

> *Thoroughly search for enlightenment and omniscience within your own mind. How so? Because that mind is by nature utterly pure, not observable within or without, or somewhere in between.*

and

> *Son or daughter of the lineage, since you wish to completely understand enlightenment, thoroughly search out your own mind nature.*

and so on, going on at great length about the reasons why mind must be sought out, the way to go about it, etc. It ends:

> *This lord of mystery, called "the gateway to the completely pure bodhicitta of bodhisattvas," is the portal through which dharmas appear, the original manner in which dharmas appear. Wherever bodhisattvas may be, with little difficulty they attain samādhi that dispels all obscurations, and with that attainment bodhisattvas are able to travel in the company of all the Buddhas. They also obtain all five paranormal cognitive powers. They acquire the language, sound and melody of limitless dhāranis. They know the thoughts of sentient beings, and because they are blessed by all Tathāgatas, they are not subject to sinking back into saṃsāra. They become indefatigable in the service of sentient beings. They rest exquisitely within unfabricated discipline, totally renounce distorted views and gain consummate realization of the perfect view.*

A capsule account of what this means can be found in "Commentary on Bodhicitta" and other texts which, it seems, those critics have not looked at. Furthermore, since Kamalaśila himself, in his "Stages of Meditation,"[132] offers a lengthy explanation of how to seek out mind, and supports this with [verses from] the "Arrangement of Precious Ones" scripture, this oral instruction does seem to be something of importance within the Madhyamaka meditation [tradition] as well.

Looking at objects, mind and both at once is done with the eyes of prajñā, that is, with the three prajñās that were explained earlier. Of the three, it is nonconceptual prajñā arising from meditation that brings about the direct encounter with authentic dharmatā, and that is why, for this lineage, not carrying out analysis while resting the mind steadily is a most crucial and profound point. Those who assert that even āryas need to analyze while in equipoise have gone outside the pale of the Buddhist tradition, since not one of the genuine doctrinal systems within Buddhism claims that conceptuality is a requisite feature of remaining in equipoise. Rather, they all unanimously state that higher insight consisting of analysis with prajñā of the appropriate level[133] occurs during postmeditation. In particular, according to the Mahāyāna, from "Segments of Oral Instruction":[134]

> *These branches are only to be abandoned;*
> *while abiding in equipoise on the path,*
> *perfect thought, speech, livelihood, endeavor*
> *and recollection are impossible.*[135]

This teaches us that it is not even possible for āryas to practice their perfect mode of conceptual analysis while remaining in steady equipoise. Likewise, all sūtras and tantras uniformly teach the way to settle the mind into a balanced state using nonconceptual wisdom, so those critics should think long and hard about what purpose is ultimately served by deliberately obscuring this fact.

[II.B.4.b.ii.B'.2'.a'.iii']
The Yoga of Unified Serene Abiding and Higher Insight, [Along] with a List of Synonymous Terms[136]

[First is] the main explanation, [and then there is] additional discussion of how the two are unified.

[II.B.4.b.ii.B'.2'.a'.iii'.aa']
Main Explanation

19. Free from being mind-made, this is mahāmudrā;
free of extremes, it is mahāmadhyamaka;
this contains all, and so is "mahāsaṃdhi" too.

Through knowing one, may I gain firm realization of the meaning of all.

Realization of just how the connate nature is has nothing to do with forming ideas about it. That is why it is called mahāmudrā. This goes by other names as well. It is "mahāmadhyamaka" since it avoids all polarized extremes. It is "mahāsaṃdhi" (great perfection) too, because all dharmas are contained within this realization.[137]

The pupose of this verse of the aspiration prayer is to teach us that we must achieve that confidence [of view] which, through understanding the singular dharmatā alone, realizes the inner meaning of all dharmas without exception.

The word "too" is used to show that both the names and meanings of all profound and vast dharmas are contained in this, and for that very reason knowing any one will liberate all. With this in mind, Pagmo Drupa said:

Pacifying all thoughts and afflictive patterns, this is vinaya.
This is where certainty that thoughts are dharmakāya is generated.
Because it cuts off all embellishments from within,
this is the formal instruction of the guru.
Shunning the extremes of existence, nonexistence,
embellishment, discredit and the rest, this is Madhyamaka.
Inexpressible, inconceivable and incommunicable,
this is the formal instructions of [prajñā]pāramitā.
Because the phenomena of conditioned existence and serenity
are complete within mind, this is the great completeness.[138]
Because the mind entertains neither good thoughts
nor bad ones, this is mahāmudrā.
Quelling all suffering, this is pacification;[139]
bringing all afflictive patterns and thoughts
onto the path, this is Secret Mantra.
Mind, thought and dharmakāya are connate from the start.
Conjoining these three through special instructions—
this is described as "connate conjunction."
This is said to be praised even by spirits,
māras, and the other obstructors.

How is it that the names and meanings of all vast and profound dharmas are contained within mahāmudrā? Each of the many distinctive names does not rest upon its own unique basis or referent; therefore, they are fully interchangeable and each avenue of elucidation is acceptable and informative. They can all be [said to be] "contained" within [mahāmudrā], insofar as all representations [of the enduring condition of mind] are only slightly [successful], and it is by means of the demonstration that has just been given of how [the meaning of mind nature] is captured in several names that we are able to [approach an] understanding of what it is like.[140]

Among meanings, the profound meaning is the one flavor to the reality of emptiness, and the manifold vast meaning is just whatever enables one explicitly or implicitly to approach mahāmudrā, and is therefore contained within the branch of "that which facilitates realization."[141] As is said in "Higher Continuum":

> *How can one show what the subtle and profound is like?*
> *It is like the unique flavor of honey.*
> *What would show what the vast and multifaceted is like?*
> *Know that it is like a colorful flower bud.*

Therefore, this is the final intent of all the various sublime utterances of the Sūgatas, and by realizing just this alone one will arrive at what underlies all dharmas, perfect all positive qualities and remove all obscurations. That is why this is honored with the title "the single sufficient white one," which can also refer to the meditation which brings about its realization. This is no contradiction, as Dignāga makes plain:

> *Prajñāpāramitā is not dual.*
> *That wisdom is what is achieved*
> *by Tathāgatas, and because they possess that meaning,*
> *the great paths too are described by that term.*[142]

"Free from being mind-made, this is mahāmudrā." On this point, some highly esteemed scholars might well be concerned that explaining mahamudra to be free from any mental engagement might be going too far; however, there is no fault here. In Sanskrit, the "a" of *amansikāra* expresses the meaning of emptiness beyond all thought constructs, such as "lack of self-identity," or "the unborn," while the remaining syllables express engaging the mind in a total lack of engagement without any attachment at all to that emptiness. This expresses [exactly] what unified mahāmudrā free of extremes is. From "Perfect Declaration of the Names of Mañjuśrī":[143]

> *"A" is the paramount letter,*
> *the sacred, most significant syllable—*
> *self-emergent, not born,*
> *the abandonment of verbal expression...*

and from "Hevajra":

> *The primary vowel is innate.*
> *"Intellect" is examination with prajñā.*[144]
> *Tathatā is [what is known by] the prajñā of bhagavans,*
> *the actual application*[145] *of perfection stage.*

From the "Dhāranī for Entering into Nonconceptuality":

> *Son of noble family, for what reason is the nonconceptual expanse called "engagement of mind"? When all of the characteristics of thought are totally left behind, [that is] abandonment.*

and

> *Thought activity bearing the characteristics of method is thought bound up with appearances; this is what the bodhisattva mahāsattva's disengagement of mind thoroughly relinquishes.*

There are many scriptural statements like these. Ācārya Maitrīpa:

> *The engagement of mind that is principally the syllable "A" is not mental engagement. Like the king of leaves, it is the pith that verbally guides [one] to the central course.*

and he further informs us:

> *Or else, "A" is the word for luminosity, while "engagement of mind" is the word for self-empowerment. This too is "A," and it is also the absence of mental engagement; therefore do not engage the mind. In this manner you will generate an understanding of the inconceivable matter of disengagement of mind, namely, the essence which bestows empowerment of luminosity upon itself, the origin of indivisible, unified, nondual emptiness and compassion.*

Here, the term "mahāmudrā" means this: *mudrā* is the Sanskrit equivalent of [the Tibetan word] *rgya* [pronounced "ja"], [which means] sealing in or containing, and in order to eliminate other potential grounds for confusion, the translators volunteered the additional term *phyag* [pronounced "chak"], so that [mahāmudrā] was translated as *phyag rgya.* It means that none of the phenomena of conditioned existence or serenity go beyond this, and *chen po* [Skt. *mahā;* great] means there is no dharma that is higher than this one, or else that it is distinguished above the mudrās of dharma, karma and samaya.[146] Therefore, it is *phyag rgya* on the one hand, and *chen po* on the other, and so the two terms are combined since their bases are in agreement.

Likewise, Ācārya Vajrapāṇi explains:

> *Since the intrinsic essence of mahāmudrā is not breached, it is* phyag rgya. *For instance, just as the seal of command of a great universal emperor cannot be violated by any outlying vassal provinces or by the ministers of the land, so none among the diverse inner and outer dharmas passes beyond the essence of unified, spontaneously manifest wisdom, mahāmudrā. Therefore it is* phyag rgya. *As for* chen po, *since it is the very essence of dharmamudrā, karmamudrā and samayamudrā, it is the great mudrā.*

and Ācārya Gakyong says:

> *Since it seals the three mudrās in confirmation, this is both* chen po *and* phyag rgya.

and from the explanation in the "Lotus-Laden Authoritative Commentary":[147]

> *What we call "great mudrā" is the prajñāpāramitā that produces all of the Tathāgatas, past, present and future. Since it seals supremely nonabiding nirvāṇa or even nonvolatile bliss in confirmation, it is* phyag rgya. *It is distinguished above karmamudrā and jñānamudrā, and because it is devoid of the tendential imprints of conditioned existence, it is called* chen mo.

[Someone might wonder,] "If your [Kagyupa] mahāmudrā is the highest one of the four mudrās, since the other three mudrās would obviously have to be practiced first, why is it that you don't explain it that way?" There is no fault on this point. According to the tantras, the very sharpest among the highest calibre of disciples, who aren't interested in pursuing the siddhis of the desire and form [realms], are able to enter mahāmudrā practice from the very beginning. For instance, from "Kālacakra":

Completely dispensing with karmamudrā and
abandoning imputed jñānamudrā,
through the supremely invariant application
meditate on the aspect of mahāmudrā.

and

Accomplish the siddhis experienced in kāmadhātu
with the [aid of] a karmamudrā.
In highest Akaniṣṭha realm
know the embrace of jñānamudrā.
An omniscient mahā-yogi
does the blissful singular enlightenment
attain through meditating
on the branch of mahāmudrā.

and from the "Great [Kālacakra] Commentary":

Completely dispense with karmamudrā
and totally abandon jñānamudrā.
Perfection is born from mahāmudrā.
The connate does not consort with others.

and Kālacakrapāda, in his "Oral Instructions on the Six Branches of Application," says:

The best attain realization with the first;
the average, with "life-essence" and others;
and the worst practice the six in order.

As he explains, those of the very highest capabilities realize mahāmudrā just through "concentration" and "collection," the branches of "approach" among the six branches of application.

It is not a contradiction to say that those who lack the highest capabilities can still start out practicing the yoga of mahāmudrā, as is said:

As soon as you obtain abhiṣeka
abandon worldly activities
and meditate upon nondual primordial wisdom.
Not wavering from nonconceptuality
one never strays outside of emptiness.
Therefore, at first a yogi
meditates continually on emptiness;
then, once he sees various forms,
in order to achieve supremely invariant bliss
he relies upon a karmamudrā.

and

> *Without an understanding of mahāmudrā,*
> *practicing just karmamudrā alone,*
> *he will fall from the lineage;*
> *that yogin will cry and wail.*

Also, it is far too restrictive to say that if it is mahāmudrā then the other three mudrās must necessarily precede it, for there are numerous well-known and authentic accounts from both Tibet and India of siddha ācāryas effortlessly eliciting wisdom in their more qualified disciples merely through blessing or through showing them a symbol, without any need at all for elaborate empowerment ceremonies, scriptural transmissions, or formalized instructions, and there are also cases of the wisdom of mahāmudrā arising during the "descent of primordial wisdom," so the format is not rigid. The "Oral Instructions on Glorious Kālacakra,"[148] the quotation from Kālacakrapāda's person-to-person lineage presented above, and other [sources] explain that since disciples have different capacities, there are any number of ways mahāmudrā can be accomplished through one of the other three mudrās.

Therefore, our very own system derived from the divine physician from Dagpo,[149] the instruction tradition of connate conjunction, because of the different levels of ācāryas' abilities and students' faculties, possesses many different styles of presentation, just as I explained earlier.

One of these concerns disciples who are not extraordinarily qualified recipients of mantra [teachings], but who are just of the Mahāyāna lineage of either the definite or indefinite variety.[150] In the context of this instruction tradition, it is said that even though there may be no presentation of the other mudrās, when through their [Mahāyāna] path they give rise to the unified wisdom of the pāramitā-yāna, they advance and become deserving, astute mantra disciples, and then through special blessing and direct introduction they accomplish the supreme siddhi of mahāmudrā.

There are evidently some Indian paṇḍitas who suggest that the unified wisdom of the pāramitā vehicle is itself mahāmudrā. [However,] in his "Lengthy Commentary on 'The Tenth Tattva,'"[151] Lhen Kye Dorje says,

Some call this "the wisdom of just that itself, mahāmudrā." As is said,

> *"Meditation combining method and prajña*
> *is the supreme yoga.*
> *The Victor taught that meditation*
> *of their blending to be mahāmudrā."*

Mantrikas contend that meditation which combines method and prajñā is not itself the meditation of mahāmudrā, for then the system of the pāramitās and the system of mantra would become indistinguishable.

There are therefore these two different ways of looking at the question.

Although our own system does not speak out definitively on this matter, it is clear that with regard to the view, it explains these two as not divergent. Look carefully in the principal commentary[152] on "The Tenth Tattva" and you will see that this is the case.

Although I could go on at great length providing more scriptural and logical reasons in support of these points, this should suffice.

[II.B.4.b.ii.B'.2'.a'.iii'.b']
Additional Discussion of How the Two Are Unified

Well then, about this "unified serene abiding and higher insight" mentioned earlier: exactly how are they unified?

When, above and beyond the practice of serene abiding, there arises the wisdom of higher insight, and that wisdom blends together with samādhi, that is called "unification," since the person who realizes it does not differentiate between his practice of serene abiding and his practice of higher insight during a meditative session.

Genuine wisdom of higher insight only begins to occur at the stage of superb dharma on the path of connection and then improves further and further, becoming sharper and more stable, and from then on there is actual unified serene abiding and higher insight. However, according to the pāramitā-yāna, until one reaches the point where meditative sessions and postmeditation have blended together, one analyzes with prajñā during postmeditation and remains in equipoise, without thinking about the object of analysis, during the meditation session.

Once session and post-session have coalesced into one state and theoretical constructs of analyzer and analyzed have been pacified, then spontaneously present prajñā will effortlessly comprehend the tathatā of dharmas. Therefore, prajñā which engages in conceptually bound analysis belongs to the category of "that which enables one to attain higher insight," and so even though we might *call* it higher insight, you should understand that it is not *actual* higher insight. For this reason you should understand that what is described as concerted serene abiding and higher insight and is practiced before one finally reaches the actual practice of unified yoga involves this latter kind of higher insight.

Some people are totally baffled by talk about unified [serene abiding and higher insight], since they believe that higher insight is prajñā that distinguishes among refined dharmas and therefore does not go beyond conceptually based analysis, whereas serene abiding admits of no conceptual analysis. Still others apparently assert that what "unified" means is that there is something which, while remaining coated with serene abiding, at the same time undertakes conceptual analysis, like a tiny fish darting around inside a limpid pool of water that is not agitated by wind. The source of their respective bafflement and confusion is their attachment to [the belief that] the wisdom of higher insight is essentially conceptual. I have to respond that this [idea] is highly improper.

The meaning of higher insight is, according to the sūtra "Certain Liberation of Mind":[153]

> *Lodrö Yangpay, since a bodhisattva sees neither his own internal apprehension nor an apprehending consciousness, sees not the universal ground, the universal ground consciousness or accumulation, the mind, the eye, or the form, sees nothing from the visual consciousness up until the body consciousness, nor even his own internal cognitive power, that is perfect and precisely as it should be. That is "the bodhisattva's expertise with the ultimate."*

and from the "King of Absorptions":

> *Like the sky above the horizon—*
> *that is how the defining property of dharmas is.*
> *All that has passed, all that shall be*

and all that is now, too, will be seen.
The sky is described as ungraspable:
there is nothing there to hold on to.
That is the nature of dharmas exactly—
like ungraspable space.
Showing dharmas whose nature is this way,
there is nothing at all to be seen;
no one sees such dharmas.
Dharmas like this are inconceivable.

and from the sūtra "Absorption Gathering All Merit":

At the point when one sees that
all dharmas are naturally fully pacified
and naturally absorbed
and eternally unborn and nonarising
and perpetually fully gone beyond misery,
and when one does not see even what one sees
and sees how it is that one sees not and fully sees not,
then one is "seeing properly."

As these along with countless other sūtras of the profound class show, when an analytic frame of mind that closely resembles true prajñā investigates dharmas, the cognitive mind that does not discover anything there also dissolves into that nature, and then non-mediated, apperceptive awareness in which subject and object have become nondual is experienced. That is also prajñāpāramitā, for it has the power to remove the dense shroud of ignorance, and its power even extends to finely distinguishing among dharmas, as [ordinary] prajñā does.

If the wisdom of higher insight were not like this, but were instead a serial string of thoughts, we would not even bother asking how it would be able to alleviate the pall of ignorance, for thoughts themselves are ignorance in their very nature, as "King of Absorptions" shows:

Thoughts are great ignorance:
they send you plummeting into the ocean of saṃsāra.
If you remain in nonconceptual samādhi
the clarity of nonthought will be like the open sky.

Some will say that [if this is so] then the secret mantra teachings which rely heavily upon likenesses to practice "reversal meditations" are faulty,[154] and you [Kagyupas] are also repudiating your own system's classification of thoughts as dharmakāya.

There are no such faults here. What is taught in reversal meditation is, for instance, to use passion under the control of the exceptional methods of mantra to eliminate ordinary passion. When one does that, the passion that contains skillful means no longer has the usual characteristics of passion, but is instead the very antidote to passion.

"In that case, it is not reversal meditation." It is reversal meditation. To take passion as an example, when practicing karmamudrā there is a similarity in kind to the workings of desire, such as embracing, kissing, grinding of hips, etc., and the same is true for the other forms as well: they are similar in kind. You must try to remember that when we speak of a "likeness," since it is "like" some thing then it is not actually that thing. On the other hand, if you wonder whether or not full-blown afflictive mental states can be used to dispel themselves, go ahead and try to remedy the passion of sexual intercourse by engaging in it over and over again, and then you will find out.

"Well then, when we settle into equipoise in unified serene abiding and higher insight, the conceptual analysis that we perform is also conceptual analysis under the control of skillful means, so it is not wrong."

That too is not right. The graded meditations of Madhyamaka teach that analytic meditation is used to bring about the attainment of the wisdom of higher insight when one has not yet attained it, whereas once one has attained it, not only is analysis out of place in the session of equipoise, it also serves no purpose. And even at the very beginning of mantra mahāmudrā practice, there is no instruction that says one has to practice analytic meditation.

Also, in general, the exceptional methods of the mantra system that are known as reversal meditations are explained to be methods for accomplishing mahāmudrā, so once one has actually become established in the unified yoga of mahāmudrā, one no longer needs them.

The meaning of the well-known dharma expression of ours that "thoughts are dharmakāya" is that all of these phenomena that are on display, which are merely concepts, do not exist outside of the mahāsukha dharmadhātu and are therefore, from the very moment they appear, established as dharmakāya. For example, the reflection of the moon in water is not composed of anything other than water, and so from the very instant it appears it is established as just water. It seems that idiomatic, evocative phrases like these evolve out of the personal inspiration [of yogis], but that it must just not be your lot to understand them. Do understand, however, that in no way are we saying that thoughts themselves are the dharmakāya and that therefore if you just continue conceptually analyzing for long enough you will eventually be liberated.

Then there are those who have never heard of using such terms as "serene abiding" and "higher insight" when talking about Secret Mantra. Those people have heard very little indeed.

The majority of tantras and commentaries of mantrayāna offer presentations of serene abiding and higher insight, and in particular, in his commentary on the meaning of what is taught in the tantra "Ubiquitous Conduct of Yoginīs," Pa'o Dorje says:[155]

> *First the dharmakāya is taught—this is expressed by 'mahāmudrā' and other [terms]. Mahāmudra is the dharmadhātu. 'All yogas' are what create understanding—[namely,] serene abiding and higher insight.*

and

> *It is explained that [the verse] 'the grand champion of all yogas' means that the aforementioned serene abiding and higher insight practices are the foremost producers of [the attainment of] dharmakāya.*

Here serene abiding and higher insight are not just mentioned by name but are in fact hailed as the foremost yogas for accomplishing mahāmudrā.

[II.B.4.b.ii.B'.2'.b']
How They Give Rise to Experiences and Realization

[There are two topics:] experiences and realization.

[II.B.4.b.ii.B'.2'.b'.i']
How Experiences Occur

20. Great bliss with no attachment is continuous.
Luminosity without grasping at characteristics is unobscured.
Nonconceptuality that goes beyond intellect is spontaneous.
May unsought experiences occur without interruption.

When one remains in equipoise in the yoga of serene abiding and higher insight, three faultless experiences will occur: the experience of continous great bliss that is free from any attachment, the experience of unobscured self-disclosive luminosity that is free from any grasping onto the characteristics of objects, and the experience of spontaneously present emptiness, nonconceptuality that transcends the sphere of the intellect.

The nature of all three of these experiences of bliss, clarity and nonconceptuality is that they happen automatically and uninterruptedly, without being deliberately produced, when you rest at ease in the intrinsic state without corrupting it with any hopes that experiences will occur or worries that they will not occur.

Then there are the faulty experiences of bliss accompanied by attachment, luminosity coupled to grasping at characteristics, and intellectually held nonconceptuality.[156] Of these, the first misdirects one into the desire realm, the second into the form realm and the third into the formless realm. That is why one has to abandon these faults of attachment and so forth at all times, and in particular, trying to deliberately create [these experiences] and trying to retain them when they have occurred are both equally faulty tactics. The first error prevents experiences from arising and the second disrupts experiences when they arise. That is why it is absolutely crucial to give up thought activity like hope, worry, grasping at properties and deliberate effort, in all ways and at all times. This verse was written to advise us to do just that.

What is meant here by the experience of bliss is blissful sensation in both the body and the mind. The experience of clarity ranges from the experience of self-illuminating, self-disclosive awareness when cognizance is unobscured by torpor or agitation, to effortless understanding of the tathatā of dharmas, and also the shining forth of the ten signs.[157] The experience of nonconceptuality ranges from a state that is predominantly nonconceptual to the vision of "total emptiness."

When one can remain in meditative equilibrium in the natural state, without deliberately holding onto or being attached to any one of these experiences, one will become masterfully proficient in the yogas of unified bliss and emptiness and indivisible bliss, clarity and emptiness, and out of those all positive qualities will manifest spontaneously.

The reason why such experiences arise is explained by honorable Saraha:

> *Cessation of mind and cessation of prāṇa*
> *are the oral instructions of the glorious guru.*

By taking hold of mind you control prāṇa.[158] That generates warmth. Warmth generates bliss, and in dependence upon that, clarity and nonconceptuality also arise. Because of this, even though in this system one doesn't deliberately meditate on the path of skillful means, still the signs of progress on the path of Secret Mantra, such as the ten signs, occur in exactly the right way.

In general, when one's three experiences of bliss, clarity and nonconceptuality achieve sameness through realization that is not just of an abstract image, but is direct and actual, one has crossed over the dividing line from experience to realization proper. At that point, because one's obscurations have become so slight, that which abides in the fundamental ground is made apparent, and so, for example, the bliss that occurs at that stage is "supremely unchanging bliss," since one has abandoned the ordinary mutable bliss of body and mind. Therefore [this bliss] is not located within the paradigm of pleasure and pain.

It is with this meaning in mind that the "Hevajra" tantra says:

> *This has no beginning, middle or end*
> *in either conditioned existence or serenity.*
> *This is supreme, great bliss itself,*
> *with no self and no other.*

It is misguided to set off some phenomena as being clear or empty, as opposed to being great bliss, since the natural condition of mind, unified clarity and emptiness, is itself great bliss. Āryadeva, in the "One Hundred Essences Creating Understanding" treatise, says:

> *By relinquishing thoughts*
> *interest in the superior does not arise.*
> *This radiant clarity is*
> *self-disclosive great bliss.*

[II.B.4.b.ii.B'.2'.b'.ii']
How Realization Occurs

21. Preferential grasping at experiences is liberated on the spot.
The confusion of negative thoughts is purified in the natural expanse.
Natural cognizance adopts and discards nothing, has nothing added or removed.
May I realize what is beyond limiting constructs, the truth of dharmatā.

As was just explained, the subjective mind that feels conceit about the excellence of experiences that have arisen is naturally liberated. Thoughts are determined to be negative since they stand in the way of glimpsing the meaning of the enduring condition through their pursuit of delusory phenomena. But even though one doesn't set out deliberately to abandon them, the power of remaining in equipoise naturally purifies them into the expanse of just what is so.

When that happens, "ordinary cognizance," the intrinsic condition of mind, becomes fully manifest. Then one achieves a state of intuitive realization wherein not a single one of the obscurations, which are things to be discarded, need be abandoned, and likewise remedies, which are things to be adopted [need not be adopted]. Removal, which is the abandonment of things to be discarded, and addition, which is the attainment of fruition through adopting and discarding, do not apply to that nature itself and do not reside therein. When one intuits exactly how this is so, that is what we refer to as realization of the truth of dharmatā that is devoid of all limiting mental constructs, such as arisal and cessation, existence and nonexistence, coming and going, and singularity and plurality.

This verse has been composed in order to teach us this.

There is a reason why we assert that through the effortless pacification of all the characteristics of adoption, abandonment, addition and removal in ordinary cognizance one will glimpse the enduring condition. From the "Great Acclaim" sūtra:

Mind and awakening are not seen
to have two aspects.
Whatever properties define awakening
are also the defining properties of mind.

and from "King of Absorptions":

It is not taught that the nature of form
is one thing and emptiness another.
Whoever knows form well
also knows emptiness well indeed.
Whoever knows emptiness well
knows nirvāṇa as well,
and trounces upon those with points of reference
who see things not this way.

This point is applied to all five of the skandhas. Further, from "Jewelry Case":

There is not even the slightest distinction to be made between afflictive mind states and buddhadharmas.

and from "Kālacakra":

Nirvāṇa and the mind apart[159]
do not pass beyond saṃsāra.
Sure liberation from existence and nonexistence
is the alternate, nondual application.

As countless scriptures attest, the nondual, nonreferential mode in which "conditioned existence" and "serenity," or else the "two truths," do not even exist at all is the truth of dharmatā, the enduring condition of ordinary mind. When one recognizes [dharmatā] to be that way, the characteristics of adoption, abandonment and so forth fade away of themselves. It is just as Ācārya Nāgārjuna says:

For what nirvāṇa is not to be generated
and saṃsāra not to be dispelled,
examine what, for that,
saṃsāra could be, nirvāṇa could be.

For that reason, until one glimpses the enduring condition, there is no way that the characteristics of adoption and dismissal could ever just disappear on their own.

When one has correctly realized what is meant by there not being anything to add on to or take away from the enduring condition, then, the way those who are familiar with the oral teachings of the Dagpo Kagyu would put it, one has "seen the intrinsic mind-essence." Ācārya Ḍombīpa stated it very succintly this way:

Give up doctrines that create unusual complexity and pursue the wondrous awe-inspiring mind that is intrinsic in nature and enlightened in essence. When you have become totally absorbed within that, then all will coalesce like space blending with space. The particulars that arose previously through the distracting influence of taking pleasure and delight in objects will be gone. In a state of expansiveness, like open space, without any concepts, one will be blessed by all of the mudrās, and then will arise what goes beyond the sense faculties, is qualified by being unborn, is the subject of the sphere of experience of self-disclosive awareness, transcends definition, is the nature of method and prajñā never before manifest and is the principal embodiment of bliss.

The profound sūtras also speak of trusting in this, which is said to be the gauge of fortunate non-returners. For example, in the sūtra "Teaching the Conduct of Bodhisattvas," Kyeu Rinchen Gyin responds to Mañjuśrī's question about how to teach dharma to beginning bodhisattvas in this way:

"Don't relinquish passion. Don't defuse hostility. Don't alleviate stupidity. Don't escape from the transitory composite."

and so on, and continues,

"Don't keep the buddhas in mind. Don't think of the dharma. Don't worship the saṅgha. Don't take on the trainings. Don't seek to pacify conditioned existence. Don't ford the river." This is the kind of advice you should offer when instructing beginning bodhisattvas, this is what you ought to teach them. Why so? Because the dharmatā of all dharmas

> *is just "remaining." Those neophytes have been taught to regard dharmas as arising and ceasing. Tell them, "This dharmadhātu is distinguished by nonconceptuality, and the one who comes to realize this about the nature of phenomena is a bodhisattva," and if this information does not frighten or alarm them, and they remain unalarmed, then how wondrous! You should know that those bodhisattvas are non-returners with the fine fortune of [having attained] the non-returner level, and this instruction will instill joy within them over and over again.*

This kind of glimpse of the truth is nothing other than the arising of the wisdom of mahāmudrā, as "Hevajra" says:

> *Self-cognizant primordial wisdom*
> *transcends the realm of discourse.*
> *Since it is the outgrowth of blessing,*
> *earth and water, wind and fire*
> *and space as well, along with*
> *sensations that isolate self and other,*
> *all cannot overwhelm omniscient*
> *wisdom like this for an instant.*
> *Higher, human and subterranean realms*
> *become uniform in an instant, and*
> *the force of thoughts that factor in*
> *self and other cannot be brought to bear.*

At the very moment when path-phase mahāmudrā arises, one immediately realizes all dharmas contained within the duality of what is grasped and what fixates to be one with [wisdom's] nature, and as a result the complexities of characteristics can no longer weigh one down at all. That is what the cited verses mean.

Although some contend that the measure of whether or not mind-essence has been glimpsed is the ability to identify thoughts, that doesn't really suffice as recognition of mind-essence, since it conflates nature and essence, and thoughts are not, after all, the nature or essence of mind, since they are only incidental and mistaken.

[II.B.4.b.ii.B'.2'.c']
The Practice of Unified Compassion and Emptiness

[The next verse] identifies compassion [and the following one describes] how it is united with emptiness.

[II.B.4.b.ii.B'.2'.c'.i']
Identifying Compassion

22. The nature of beings is ever enlightened,
yet not realizing this, they wander endlessly in saṃsāra.
May intense compassion arise within me
for sentient beings, whose suffering knows no bounds.

In general, there are said to be three kinds of compassion. There is compassion with reference to sentient beings and compassion with reference to dharmas. Finally, there is compassion without any object of reference. The first two of these, within this system of instruction, are to be practiced during the preliminary phase, and once one has glimpsed the meaning of the enduring condition, nonreferential compassion will be born. This is the emergence of what we call "emptiness with a core of compassion." The compassion presented in this verse is this last kind.

What is it like? As was explained earlier in the section teaching the meaning of the view, the nature of each and every sentient being ever and always resides within the essence of the enlightened dharmakāya, and yet, merely through not realizing that this is so, they stray into conditioned existence with no end and there drown within an infinite ocean of suffering. For these sentient beings there arises within [us] effortless, continual, intense and virtually unbearable compassion. This compassion comes into being through the force of glimpsing the meaning of the fundamental, enduring condition, as is said:

When a bodhisattva remaining in equipoise
finalizes the power of that meditation,
exceptional compassion will arise for those
in the grasp of the demon of reification.

and Ācārya Nāgārjuna:

In that manner, when a yogi
has meditated upon this emptiness,
a mind concerned with the aims of others
will undoubtedly arise.

Supported by that kind of compassion, bodhisattvas occupy themselves solely with the welfare of others, and so in accordance with the ways of beings in general and [the needs of] particular beings, they embrace existence within the world. Yet even though they do not relinquish conditioned existence, it does not taint them with any faults, as is said:

Someone whose meditation has brought stability,
who comes into contact with the suffering of others
and relinquishes the bliss of dhyāna,
becomes involved, but still is not tormented.
This is wondrous and this deserves praise;
this is the greatest form of holiness.
Following their own customs and
offering wealth is not that impressive,
but knowing that phenomena are empty
and then teaching action and result
is a wonder of wonders,
and remarkably remarkable;
even though those who wish to
protect sentient beings are born
in the mire of worldly existence,
this event does not corrupt them.
They are like the petals of water lilies.

"May" is added to the verse to make it aspirational.

[II.B.4.b.ii.B'.2'.c'.ii']
How It Is United with Emptiness

23. In the moment of love, when the vibrant power of intense compassion
is uncontained, the empty essence shines forth nakedly.
May I never step off this supreme path of unity that never goes awry,
and practice it at all times, day and night.

At the very moment when the vibrant energy of compassion without any object of reference shines forth unimpededly and love is present, emptiness, the essence of the enduring condition which is free of limiting conceptual constructs, also appears nakedly in a very direct way, not just as a vague generality. In that way, emptiness and compassion blend into a single experience. This path of their unification, which has no danger points, is the very best path of all. As is said in the tantra "Binding the Network of Ḍākinīs":

The mind that realizes
indivisible emptiness and compassion
is taught to be the buddha,
the dharma and also the saṅgha.

and even in "Vajra Pinnacle":

Emptiness and compassion are distinct,
like a butter lamp and its glow.
Emptiness and compassion are also identical,
like a butter lamp and its glow.

This is also the meaning of bodhicitta and prajñāpāramitā. As "Segments of Instruction" explains:

Here the fully nonabiding mind of inseparable emptiness and compassion is bodhicitta and prajñāpāramitā.

When prajñā—emptiness, and method—great compassion, are not coupled together, but instead are only practiced separately, one will be unable to attain the highest state of realization. Because one will be unable to do so, this also cannot be vajra yoga. From "Guhyasamāja":

It is neither the manner of yogic method
nor prajñā in isolation, but the yoga
of the confluence of method and prajñā
that the Tathāgatas taught.

and:

What is method comes into being;
prajñā terminates the existence of the fallible.[160]

From the sūtra "Requested by Gyatso, King of Nāgas":

Māras have two activities:
method devoid of prajñā and
prajñā devoid of method.
Knowing these to be māras' work, abandon them!

In Jowo Je's "Lamp for the Path":

Since it is said that
prajñā without method
and method without prajñā
are "bondage," abandon neither.

and from the "Ornament for Clear Realization":

> *Through prajñā, not remaining in worldly existence, and through compassion, not remaining in serenity....*

These passages tell us that in order to attain nirvāṇa which does not abide within either worldly existence or serenity, one needs unified method and prajñā. There are countless more statements [like these].

On top of that, even though one might pretend to be working towards the welfare of others using just compassion that doesn't realize emptiness, what one ostensibly does for others, instead of accomplishing their aims, at times actually creates impediments for them, since one's own virtuous application is chancy and contaminated. And by only meditating on emptiness, one strays onto the paths of hearer and solitary realizer Buddhas, which becomes a long-term obstacle to fulfilling the aims of others. As is said,

> *Going to hell does not interfere*
> *with awakening forever;*
> *but hearers and solitary realizers*
> *ever stand in the way of awakening.*[161]

Since there is no doubt about this, this is clearly a dangerous deviation from the Mahāyāna path.

And so, this verse, couched as an aspiration prayer, teaches us that it is necessary to meditate unbrokenly and at all times, indicated here by "day and night," on this unified path that never steers us off course, until we finally attain the great unified state of Vajradhara. As is said in "Commentary on Bodhicitta":

> *The bodhicitta of the buddhas*
> *is not obscured by thoughts*
> *absorbed in the skandhas and dhātus.*
> *It is what is meditated upon assiduously*
> *by a mind knowing authentic emptiness*
> *at all times, and doused with compassion.*[162]

Another point to be understood here is that the earlier, single verse showing how experiences arise teaches about the paths of accumulation and junction, and the single verse on how realization occurs, along with the two verses that follow it, teach about the paths of vision and meditation.

"If that is so, then has activity[163] not been taught anywhere up to this point?"

Just teaching about meditation was enough to teach activity as well. Generally speaking, activity in [Secret] Mantra is said to be of two types: elaborate and simple. The first of these is termed external activity and the second, internal. Of the two, the latter is superior, and not found anywhere other than in this practice of the yoga of mahāmudrā. It is also referred to as "Samantabhadra activity" because remaining within [the realization of mahāmudrā] will produce all that one requires. "Guhyasamāja" says:

> *This is the finest yoga of all, and thus*
> *is worthy of the Tathāgatas' veneration.*
> *Because of this are the countless practices*
> *of renunciation so very well known.*
> *Due to this do the countless samādhis*
> *of gods arise so perfectly.*
> *From that yoga, the utterly perfect*
> *mudrā, maṇḍala and guhyamantras [arise].*
> *Activities of both pacification and expansion,*
> *and all else that arises from mantra,*
> *in numbers like the sands of the Ganges River,*
> *all of the subtle siddhis that there are,*
> *all of the other mudrā siddhis*
> *that are renowned on the bhūmis—*
> *the Mind-Vajra has said*
> *arise from this very yoga.*

This is something you should know. The meditation of primordial wisdom in which method and prajñā are nondual is itself the activity of mantra. As the "Subsequent Guhyasamāja"[164] says:

> *The mental power that creates associations*
> *from the linkage of faculties and objects*
> *is what is described as* "man."
> *The syllable* "tra" *has the meaning of* "*protection.*"
> *The samayas and vows that are taught to*
> *fully emancipate one from worldly conduct*

> *were called "mantra conduct" by*
> *all the Protection Vajras.*[165]

Jigme Shab[166] explains the meaning of this in his commentary:

> *That which associates the faculties and so forth is mental power, and this is itself described as* "man."[167] *In a deeper sense,* "man" *is cognizance as such, and we can extrapolate from this that* "man" *is "Śūnyatājñāna." The addition of "protection from" tells us that the two obscurations are absent from this cognizance. This is the attainment of Samantabhadra [purity]. Therefore, here* "tra" *means fully non-relinquished. What this term* "mantra" *means, then, is just the activity of the wisdom of inseparable emptiness and compassion.*

This activity is also the supreme form of activity, as "Segments of Instruction" explains:

> *Since purity of body and speech are solely the result of total purity of mind, mental activity takes priority over all other forms of activity.*

[II.B.5]
Aspiration for the Fruition upon Completing the Path

24. With eyes and paranormal powers that arise from potent meditation,
sentient beings are matured and buddha fields well cleansed.
Aspirations to accomplish buddha dharmas are fulfilled.
May I complete fulfillment, maturation and cleansing, and attain enlightenment.

The explanation of this verse has both a main part, and a short, tangential explanation of the stages of the path.

[II.B.5.a]
Main Part

The first of these also has two parts: explanations of [the] eyes and paranormal[168] cognitions, and [of] fulfillment, maturation and cleansing.

[II.B.5.a.i]
Explanation of Eyes and Paranormal Cognitions

The final fruition that one will attain with the power of one's meditation through putting the correct formal instructions into practice is the unsurpassed state of enlightenment, complete awakening that brings all dharmas to actual fulfillment. This state is endowed with absolutely pure enlightened qualities, such as eyes and paranormal cognitive powers, and is the completion of fulfillment, maturation and cleansing. While on the path, one must first generate paranormal cognitive powers and then gradually complete the processes of fulfillment, maturation and cleansing. Therefore, the eyes and paranormal cognitive powers are asserted to be the first fruit.

There are five types of eyes and six types of paranormal cognitions. The five eyes are: fleshly eyes, divine eyes, prajñā eyes, dharma eyes and buddha eyes.

The first of these is described in sūtras as "the fleshly eyes of bodhisattvas which can see over a distance starting at one hundred yojanas anywhere up until the entire billion-world system."

The second: "The divine eyes of gods from the domains of the four mahārājas up until Akaniṣṭha are known well by bodhisattvas. The divine eyes of bodhisattvas are [however] not known at all well by them" and are also said to be exceptional, relative to the eyes of gods, in that they can see the circumstances of the transitions from death to rebirth of all sentient beings throughout the ten directions.

Third are the eyes of prajñā which behold lack of self-identity.

The fourth type, according to Ācārya Vasubandhu's account, is the nine powers that are left of the ten powers when you subtract the power to know places and non-places.[169]

The fifth is the fully manifest, complete and perfect realization of all dharmas in every way possible.

The six paranormal cognitive powers are [the power to perform] miracles, divine hearing, telepathic knowledge of others' minds, recollection of prior location, divine sight and unblemished cognition.

The first of these is the supernatural ability to display miracles, the second is the power to hear sounds from countless realms, and the third is knowledge of what is specifically going on in the mind of each and every sentient being. The fourth is knowledge of the previous and future birthplaces of every sentient being, in sequence. The fifth is knowledge of the births and deaths, along with the actions and their results, of sentient beings. The sixth is cognition from which all obscurations and impediments are gone because they do not inhere in the very essence of mind.

The divine sight that belongs to this group of six is not equivalent to the one within the five types of eyes. That one comes from complete maturation whereas this one arises from meditation.

"How can you claim that the eyes and paranormal cognitions are positive qualities unique to Buddhas, while at the same time explaining that they also arise along the path?"

As Abhayākaragupta explains in his "Ornament for the Thought of the Muni,"

> *No matter which path [we speak of], at the stages of accumulation, and further along the higher and higher phases of mental development, they are generated gradually, and as a result one obtains, stage by stage, "supreme," "highly supreme," etc. versions of each of the five eyes, and likewise the six paranormal cognitive powers...*

and

> *How can it be asserted that the eyes and six paranormal cognitions of the Buddhas are found on the bodhisattva bhūmis? On the eighth bhūmi, bodhisattvas obtain both of those, one by one, which later, on the bhūmi of enlightenment, are totally perfected and utterly purified, assuming their final form.*

Thus on the bhūmi of enlightenment the eyes and paranormal cognitions become extremely pure and reach the ultimate level, and as a result can, for example, penetrate every single object in a totally unmediated way. That is what is unique to Buddhas.

[II.B.5.a.ii]
Explanation of Fulfillment, Maturation and Cleansing

With their superior intentions, aspiration prayers, and immersion in vast activities, utilizing the great might of their eyes and paranormal cognitions and using the plethora of skillful means at their disposal, bodhisattvas bring all manner of sentient beings to maturity, thoroughly cleanse Buddha fields,[170] and reach true fulfillment through completing their aspirations to fully perfect all of the enlightened qualities of the Tathāgatas.

After discussing the fact that a bodhisattva must first ready himself in conformity with the ninefold manner of authentic maturation, "Ornament for the Sūtras" talks at length about maturing sentient beings:

Just as a wound and food are accepted as mature
when they [respectively] suppurate and are ready to consume,
so it is taught that this support must be
both pacified and operational.
The explanation is given that
the subject is to be ripened separately, and likewise
fully ripened, highly ripened, appropriately ripened
and also well ripened, ripened to realization,
permanently ripened and ripened in toto.

For example, once a suppurating wound has matured, it is ready to be drained, and when food has ripened it is ready to be eaten. Likewise, when disciples are prepared to abandon what must be relinquished, the remedy is ready to be put into effect. If you break this process down into its component parts, there are eight, including "separate ripening" and the rest. These need not be elaborated upon here.

Cleansing the fields is mentioned often in the "Aspiration Prayer for Excellent Conduct":

In that manner, may I enter the array
of all the Victors' fields throughout all directions...

and

Atop one particle, fields as numerous as all the particles there are...

and [also]

May I fully purify the ocean of fields....

One enters an ocean of fields by integrating into oneself the wisdom that comprehends the defining properties of an immeasurable number of boundless realms within the external universe, and knowing them directly. One accomplishes the complete purification of those fields through the seven aspects of complete purification. These seven are common purification, rule, fine utilization, sentient beings, causes, results and complete purification itself. I won't go into more detail about these here, so if you want to know more about them, look in "Sūtra of the Tenth Level" and elsewhere.

Concerning the fulfillment of aspiration prayers to accomplish buddha dharmas, the sūtras contain countless aspiration prayers pertaining to each of the ten bhūmis, each accompanied by hundreds, thousands or millions of subsidiary aspirations, and when all of these have been fully accomplished, then buddha dharmas have been completely fulfilled.

"Buddha dharmas" refers to what is within the realm of experience of a Buddha and, to a slight extent, that of an ārya bodhisattva.[171] But because one could never exhaustively delineate [these buddha dharmas], the imaginations of childish beings are clearly not competent to grasp their true extent. And yet, sūtras and śāstras do group them into kāyas, wisdoms, positive qualities and enlightened activities. Within the [category of] kāyas, there is the single dharmakāya, and also the rūpakāya, which makes two. By dividing the rūpakāya into two there become three, and if you add to those the svabhāvikakāya, there are four. Then there are the five kāyas which embody the five wisdoms, and you can continue to subdivide in this manner until there are simply too many to mention.

As for wisdoms, there are the two wisdoms, one that knows everything there is and another that knows things just as they are, and then there are the five wisdoms, mirror wisdom and the others. If these are further divided for each kāya and every disciple there is, their number becomes unfathomable.

Then there are the sixty-four positive qualities of separation and maturation, and subdivisions of those like we calculated for the [kāyas and wisdoms] that make them limitless in number.

Finally, you can begin to assess enlightened activity by dividing it into two aspects, spontaneous activity and unceasing activity, and from there you can continue to divide it until it, too, becomes incalculable.

You should learn the precise details of what these are all like by referring to sūtras, tantras and śāstras.

The meaning of the term *sangs rgyas* is derived from [the Sanskrit word] *buddha*, which denotes both "purify" and "expand," as is said,

> *Because it purifies the sleep of ignorance*
> *and expands the discovery of what there is to know*
> *buddhahood is pure and expansive, like a lotus.*

In that manner, bodhisattvas attain enlightenment once they have finished the processes of cleansing and maturation and then fulfilled all of their original aspiration prayers. It must be understood that in mantrayāna, it is due to one's swift completion of the processes of fulfillment, cleansing and maturation through the inconceivable power of [mantrayāna's] exceptional samādhi and skillful methods that one actualizes the state of enlightenment within the span of a single lifetime. We find this excerpt in Ācarya Jñānākara's "Commentary on 'Entrance to Mantra'":[172]

> *In "Requested by Noble Shiwa Lodro"*[173] *it is said that:*
>
> > *"For example, a swift-footed siddha,*[174] *the sun or the moon will swiftly arrive at a place that would be reached only very slowly by an individual with little strength, or a carriage drawn by oxen. Similarly, the bhūmis that would be attained over the course of a number of eons by a pure child of the lineage who is engaged in the practice of the pāramitās, are attained in this very life through the superb discipline of a vidyā-mantradhārin because the powers of these [practices] are not on a par with each other."*

[II.B.5.b]
Short, Tangential Discussion of the Stages of the Path

When one explains [this topic] using the scheme of the four yoga levels, a dharma lexicon exclusive to this lineage, as it is presented by the mahāsiddha Nāropa in his "Summary of Words on Mahāmudrā," first there is what is called "the yoga of undivided attention." This occurs when single-pointed mindfulness is attained through the practice of serene abiding, and then, as one remains in that state, higher insight appears, and the experiences of bliss, clarity and nonconceptuality arise and continue without interruption.

Next, one sees that all phenomena included within the categories of appearance and mind never depart from the nature of the mahāsukha dharmadhātu. As a result, all grasping at the constructs of dualistic phenomena becomes spontaneously released. One obtains fully qualified higher insight, the wisdom of unified compassion and emptiness, and because of that, serene abiding and higher insight become aligned in a unified yoga. This is "freedom from constructs."

Third, through ever-increasing familiarity with that [yoga], one realizes all dharmas to be of a single flavor, and the wisdom of effortlessness never wavers. This is "one flavor."

Last is the "yoga of nonmeditation." By the blending together of meditation luminosity and fundamental luminosity, all obscurations and veils concealing the enduring condition are drawn away for good. The division between sessions of meditation and postmeditation is destroyed and all positive qualities, in their ultimate form, arise spontaneously.

Each of these four has its own lesser, intermediate and higher levels, making a total of twelve. You can learn in some detail about the precise divisions of each of these and how they generate positive qualities by researching what the great masters of the past have said.

If those [yogas] are matched up with the grounds and paths of the pāramitāyāna, then the three levels of undivided attention are the path of accumulation; lesser and intermediate freedom from constructs are the path of junction; higher freedom from constructs is the path of vision; all the levels of one flavor and the first two levels of nonmeditation are the path of meditation, and finally the higher level of nonmeditation is the stage of enlightenment, where one abides in the ultimate. From "Ornament for the Sūtras":

After the bodhisattva has splendidly gathered
the unlimited pāramitā accumulations of merit and wisdom,
that bodhisattva is most certain about dharmas, and so
realizes the aspect ever expressive of the ultimate

and merely through such expression grasps the meaning.
[S]he dwells perfectly on what is displayed, mere mind,
and then comes to directly realize the dharmadhātu,
which is free of the characteristics of duality.

and

When the power of nonconceptual wisdom tied to the intellect
is permanently dispatched into total equality,
the coarse collections of faults that depend on it
are eliminated like poison counteracted by a supreme antidote.

The well-arranged sacred dharmas taught by the Muni
ease intelligence into the basic dharmadhātu.

The teachings that expose all thoughts as mere imputations
swiftly transport one across the ocean of positive qualities.

The first stanza is describing the path of accumulation; the next half-stanza, the path of junction; the second half of the same stanza, the path of vision; the stanza about "ties to the intellect," the path of meditation; and the last stanza, the path without learning. All of the defining properties of these paths, as they are subsequently described in detail in the section presenting the formal instructions of the "Ornament," are contained in these [verses].

"Well then, must one acquire, on each of those paths, the particular qualities that are associated with them?[175] For instance, when one has reached the higher level of the path of accumulation, does one receive teachings from nirmāṇakāya Buddhas in person, miraculously journey to numerous world-realms, and so forth?"

Because the signs of development of outstanding qualities on the pāramitā path are [ineluctable] like heat [arising from] fire, there is no way they could simply be left behind as irrelevant when one travels along the path of realization of the meaning of the enduring condition.[176] And yet, [a yogi] may or may not display his achievements in a manner that accords with the perceptions of other beings. There are a range of possibilities. However, confining ourselves to the case of attainment of full fruition within a single lifetime, it is true that until one transforms one's body of maturation[177] into a wisdom body, that body of maturation will always retain a small degree of obscuration.

Progress along the paths and grounds in perfection stage practices of anuttara tantra, such as the six branches of application, is also fundamentally the same. In Rangjung Gyalwa's own "Profound Inner Meaning,"

First, empowerment is obtained and development and perfection
are understood well;
considered practice[178] [is the] path of accumulation.
Knowing the vital points of nāḍi, prāṇa and bindu and
abiding in Samantabhadra conduct, when warmth is attained,
one resides on the path of junction.
Then, through the activities of yogic disciplines,
one traverses the path of junction and arrives at vision.

This is the path that has individual collection and the four concentrations,[179]
also described as "training the nāḍis."
When the branch of concentration is perfected
one is said to attain the five paranormal powers of mind
and one enters into the kāya maṇḍala

The four yogas are also connected to the format of the four empowerments. Saraha:

Undivided attention [with the] vase empowerment;
bliss devoid of constructs, the secret empowerment.
The third is connected with equality;
nothing to meditate on, the fourth.

and Nāropa:

The first [step] in realization of mahāmudrā
is to look at [the nature of] incidental,
passing thoughts and overturn ignorance;
realization of clear awareness without grasping
is called "awareness empowerment."
When the five poisons abide as the five wisdoms,
that is the vase empowerment.
When the unimpeded vibrant power of that
appears not partially, and not partly, then
in the state of emptiness bliss arises;
clarity is thus the second empowerment.
Connate, primordial wisdom,
inseparable bliss and emptiness, open space,
the great unified, one flavor,
appearance and mind experienced as mahāsukha
is held to be jñāna prajñā empowerment.
These three empowerments are indivisible, contained within mind;
when mind itself is as pure as space
there is no meditative session, and no postmeditation—
unity of the two truths is the fourth [empowerment].

"Well then, if I practice the instructions of mahāmudrā this way, how long will it take me to accomplish fruition mahāmudrā?" There is no one, definite answer to that question.

An extremely astute [disciple] of absolutely the highest calibre taught by an ācārya who has attained supreme siddhi will accomplish [mahāmudrā] in a single human lifetime, and moreover will do so effortlessly. Others, depending on the level of their abilities, will become accomplished in the bardo,[180] within seven lifetimes, or at most within sixteen lifetimes. Even within the context of the unified path of sūtra and mantra, [mahāmudrā] is far swifter than the pāramitāyāna path alone. It is important to understand this. In the "Lengthy Commentary on 'The Tenth Tattva,'" Lhenchik Kyepa'i Dorje explains:

> *There is this important difference with yogis who practice in the manner of that other, pāramitā[yāna]: because [mantra practitioners] definitely realize the tathatā of unified emptiness that is explained in the oral instructions of holy gurus, [this yāna] is exceptional, highly distinguished and superior.*

[III]
A CONCLUDING SUMMARY OF THE PRAYER

25. Through the compassion of Victors and their offspring everywhere
and the power of all the immaculate virtue there is,
may my own and all countless sentient beings'
totally pure aspirations be accomplished exactly as we intend.

This verse is, for the most part, easy to understand. The phrase "all the virtue there is" includes both fabricated and unfabricated virtue. There are, of course, those who deny that the unfabricated dharmadhātu is virtuous. However, in our own system, as is often said very clearly in sūtras of the final dharmacakra, like "virtue, the intrinsic condition of the fundamental ground...," we accept that it is virtue, not in the sense of fabricated virtue that is the opposite of evil action, but rather with regard to its possessing the potential for the development of all the virtuous dharmas of total purity.

"Totally pure aspirations" are principally those aspirations that have been offered here, yet also include all of the endless number of totally pure aspirations that have been made by ordinary individuals and āryas alike.

Now that I have finished explaining the stages of the aspiration prayer of mahāmudrā of definitive meaning in just this superficial fashion, in keeping with my limited abilities, I would like to say a little bit more about both the variety of techniques found within this mahāmudrā system of instruction, and also the lineage of gurus.

As I mentioned only very briefly earlier, there is both an uncommon mantra system and a [common] system which combines the thought of sūtra and mantra. With regard to the former, there is one procedure which applies in the case of powerful ācāryas and extremely adept disciples, where a vajra-jñāna empowerment can be given without any need for an elaborate empowerment ceremony beforehand. Then there is the other case, where a disciple of any lesser ability requires an elaborate empowerment as a preliminary. So there are two variations.

In the first, people who "get it at once" become liberated just through the blessing of empowerment, the presentation of a symbol, or a modicum of formal instruction. Examples of this are abundant in stories about siddha ācāryas from the land of āryas,[181] and in particular, there are so many examples of gurus within this lineage from the land of Tibet becoming liberated in this way that I doubt there would be much purpose in discussing them here at the very end of the commentary. Of the two systems passed down from Kamalaśīla, known as "the elaborate path of means" and "the nonelaborate [path of] connate conjunction," this corresponds to the latter.

With regard to gradual learners, Rangjung Shab says in his "Guidance Manual on Connate Conjunction":

> *For the preliminaries, a guru who possesses the qualifications should teach a disciple who seeks to practice in a correct manner, abandon the works of this life and attain complete enlightenment. First he obtains the pledges of discipline and engenders the attitude of supreme awakening. Then his continuum is thorougly matured through empowerment. He must practice in a place that is isolated and inspiring.*

This approach is exactly what the lineage prescribes. Although it is certainly acceptable for the maturing [empowerment] that comes first to be done using any one of the deities of the anuttara yoga tantra class, it seems that it is customary for the empowerment to be performed using the maṇḍala of Cakrasaṃvara, father and mother. This is also what the mahāsiddha Lodrö Rinchen explains, using the scriptural vajra verses of the person-to-person lineage, and finally, this is what we can see is done in practice.

One custom within this system of instruction is to begin development stage practice as soon as one has received empowerment, and after one has become familiar with it, enter the [practice of] yoga without signs. Another approach is to first become a little bit familiar with the signless yoga of serene abiding and higher insight, and then begin to practice development stage, so that one will attain vivid perception more easily and siddhi more swiftly. In both of these approaches, after one practices development stage, perfection stage practices both with and without signs are employed so that each will enhance the other. That is how they are practiced in unison.

This second approach, which shares elements of sūtra and tantra, was originally formulated by the master Maitrīpa according to the system passed down by Saraha and his successors. He promulgated it and also authored the reference work *"The Tenth Tattva,"* which presents how it works and which therefore belongs mainly to this lineage.

Dagpo Rinpoche[182] enriched this approach with the formal instructions of Jowo Je[183] from the graded path for the three types of individuals,[184] the system of instruction that he learned while attending Kadampa lamas, Geshe Chagriwa, Nyugrumpa, Gyayon Dak, Chayulwa and many others. He made famous "the mixture of the two streams of Kadampa and Kagyupa." Because this technique enables one to arrive at the siddhi of mahāmudrā in a relatively short period of time, its appellation, "the instruction on conjoined, connate non-meditation," is well deserved.

Dagpo Rinpoche said, "Just as I saw in my dreams and as Milarepa predicted, there is much I can do to benefit beings with the teachings of the Kadampas," and "The small amount of help I am now able to offer beings is just the result of the kindness of the Kadampa lamas." He also dreamt of many wild creatures listening to him beat a drum, from which milk then poured out for them. These references are all connected with the second type of instructional system, which has a very specific purpose.

Gampopa recognized that in times when the degeneracies have become not only widespread but predominant, there are extremely few disciples who have the exceptional qualifications needed for Vajrayāna practice, but by guiding those of dull faculties and inferior fortune with the graded path for the three types of individuals, they will eventually become well qualified and worthy receptacles for the exclusive teachings of mantra who can attain liberation in a single lifetime, or who will at least glimpse the true meaning of mahāmudrā through those methods and thereby become established on the path of nonreturners.

Therefore, beginning in the days of Milarepa and continuing until our own times, the techniques of this system of instruction have continued to guide all disciples of both superior and inferior fortunes, without discrimination. However, the teachings of the profound mantra path of method that are given to the most fortunate disciples are the original formal instructions on which this system was founded and based.

It is clear why there is no need to selectively examine the minds of students in the case of those who become involved through their own sincere interest in the profound meaning of these teachings, but even those who feel reservations about them are still bound to derive significant benefit. That is why [discrimination] is unnecessary. From "Precious Garland":

Not even those with little merit
have doubts about this dharma;
and even if they should doubt it,
it will still tear worldly existence to pieces.

And in the "Teaching the Conduct of Bodhisattvas" sūtra that I quoted from earlier, when Kyeu Rinchen Gyin is talking to Mañjuśrī about the meaning of there being nothing to accept or reject, the eight bhikṣus who retain a reference point are indifferent, and because of that they vomit up warm blood and die, and are reborn in hell. However, the Bhagavan explains, in the style of a prophecy, that because of the power of those bhikṣus having heard the profound dharma, albeit reluctantly, they will be freed from this current sojourn in hell and be reborn in the Tuṣita god realm, where they will spend sixty-eight eons serving a trillion billion Buddhas before attaining enlightenment themselves. And in the "Abode of Mañjuśrī" sūtra, it is prophesied that for the eight bhikṣus who are not interested in the profound dharma and are cast down into hell, the effect of hearing that dharma will be subsequent rebirth as Tuṣita gods, and the eventual attainment of arhatship in the retinue of Maitreya. There are many cases in sūtras of this happening, and it is most definitely so.

Secondly, as for the succession of lineage gurus, the lineage of the exceptional mantra system began with Vajradhara, from whom it was passed on to Tillipa,[185] then to Nāropa, and Marpa Lotsā. That is one way it was transmitted. Another was from Vajradhara down to Saraha, Shawaripa, Maitrīpa, and Marpa Chokyi Lodrö.[186] The two lineages were brought together by him and passed on to Wangchuk Milarepa, Je Daö Shonnu[187] and so on down [through] the Kamtsang ultimate-lineage. The style of instruction that blends the thought of sūtra and mantra was passed down only along this latter stream coming from Saraha.

Because of its enrichment with the graded path for the three types of individuals, the lineage also includes the lineage of vast activity, the lineage of profound view and the blessing lineage of practice.

The first of these came from Tupa'i Wangpo,[188] the regent Mapampa, Togme,[189] Yignyen,[190] Pagdrol, Tsundrol, Choggi De, Dulwa'i De, Nangdzay Zangpo, Senge Zangpo, Kusalipa the greater and the lesser, Serlingpa, and finally Jowo Je Dīpaṃkara.[191]

The second went from the perfect Buddha to Mañjuśrī, Nāgārjuna, Āryadeva, Candrakīrti, the two Rigpa'i Kuchugs and Jowo Je.

The third was passed from Vajradhara to Tilli, Nāro, Ḍombīpa and Jowo Je.

Jowo Je brought all three together into one lineage, and from him it went to Geshe Tonpa, then Chen Ngawa, Chayulwa and Gampopa; or else from Chayulwa to all three of the Geshe brothers, and also down to Dromton, whom Nezurwa, Nyugrumpa, Gyachakriwa and Shawalingpa all attended, and all of whom Gampopa studied with. From that point on it is like the ultimate-lineage.

Author's Colophon

The child who counteracted the sixty thousand forms of contrived meditation, the renunciate who well pleased the brahma[carya] siddhas and scholars of India and Tibet, the true charioteer of the fortunate,[1] after accepting birth, made this supreme purifying practice of connate mah›mudr› well-known on the three paths. However, I have wondered to myself what could be done to prevent narrow-minded, troublemaking pedants in these later times from becoming vessels like pretas with slender throats. I felt it was up to me to speak out a little in order to develop their trust, using scriptures and the oral teachings of the gurus.

Therefore, I have presented this very brief commentary on the aspiration prayer of mah›mudr› of definitive meaning as per the wishes expressed from afar by my own *chungpo*,[2] Satsa Kukye Karma Ngelek Tendzin.

I, the Eighth Situpa, Tenpa'i Nyinchay, completed this writing in the water-ox year at Thubten Chokorling. May it bring virtue and goodness.

MAṄGALA ŚRĪ JAYA PUSTIM BHAVATU

Notes

Introduction

1. The biographical information about the life of Situ Rinpoche is supplemented from *The Autobiography and Diaries of Situ Paṇchen*, volume 77 of the Śata-Pitaka Series, edited by Lokesh Chandra and published in 1968 by the International Academy of Indian Culture in a folio edition.

Teachings of the Supreme Siddhas

1. This is a reference to Karmapa as an emanation of Avalokiteśvara (Chenresig).

2. A title for Rangjung Dorje, third Karmapa, the author of the aspiration prayer.

3. This refers to followers of the great vehicle, Mahāyāna.

4. "Support" means the support of, or for, one's faith.

5. Lamas (plural) include those who confer instructions in sūtra, mantra and mahāmudrā.

6. This is a madhyamaka text by Candrakīrti.

7. As opposed to bodhisattvas, who are called heart-scions of the Buddhas because they attain the realization that resides in the Buddhas' hearts, hearers and solitary realizers are children of the Buddhas' speech, because through hearing and relying upon the teachings spoken by the Buddhas on the four truths and the interdependent origination of phenomena they achieve the realization of arhats, foe conquerors.

8. Tib. *rGyal ba'i yum*. The popular name for a single sūtra or the entire corpus of the Prajñāpāramitā sūtras. Although one source identifies this as the (Sanskrit) *Ekākṣarīmātā nāma sarvatathāgata prajñāpāramitā*, this title corresponds, in the index to the Beijing scriptures, to the Tibetan *rGyal ba'i yum yig gchig ma*, which means "Single Syllable Mother of Victors," and is only one syllable long.

9. Tib., *bdud*; Skt. *māra*.

10. The text refers to this as the sūtra "Requested by Lodrö Mizaypa" (Tib. *zhus pa*), though its proper name is the sūtra "Expounded by Lodrö Mizaypa" (Tib. *bstan pa*).

11. Or kāya of truth, kāya of perfected experience, kāya of emanation and the essential kāya. Since clearly the kāyas do not all function as "bodies" (in

any of the usual usages of that term), in this text the term is not translated; its range of meanings will be seen in context.

12. One of the five treasures of Maitreya received by Asaṅga.

13. Tib. *mchod sdong*: any object to which one may present offerings, such as the bodhi-tree or a stupa.

14. Fruition can be described in terms of the complementary aspects of abandonment of all shortcomings and realization of all positive qualities. Here these are associated with two kāyas: the svabhāvikakāya of abandonment and the dharmakāya of realization. This is a distinction of perspective and not of substance.

15. By Nāgārjuna.

16. By Śāntideva.

17. As is the consideration "for myself and all others."

18. A sūtra on *satipaṭṭhāna*, the technique of mindfulness in meditation.

19. A Cakrasaṃvara tantra. A very large literature on this family of tantras is extant in the Karma Kagyu school, including commentaries by Nagpo Chodpa (the Indian master Kṛṣṇācārya), Belu Tsewang Kunchab (the main disciple of and successor to Situ Paṇchen at Palpung Monastery), and Karma Chagmay (compiling meditation instructions from the person-to-person lineages). The liturgical customs were formalized by the eighth Karmapa, Mikyo Dorje, based on the yidam compilations of the fifth Karmapa. The liturgies have continued to be modified and commented upon by the most recent Karmapas.

20. This is the very literal title for a set of sutras on related topics that are grouped together.

21. The text refers to this work by Dignāga as *Kun btus*, as it does the "Compendium of Abhidharma" cited above on page 37.

22. It does not seem advisable to attempt to translate into English titles of tantras that are also the proper names of the yidam deities presented in those tantras (like Cakrasaṃvara, Guhyasamāja, Kālacakra, Hevajra, etc.). Often the name of a deity itself incorporates the meaning of all that is taught in the particular tantra or family of tantras.

23. The Tibetan title means "Two Examinations" and refers to the organization of the tantra, which is nonetheless referred to as "Hevajra," after the deity.

24. Tib. *mkhan po*. In this context, the one who conducts the offices of ordination into the vows of personal liberation (*pratimokṣa*).

25. The term translated as "spiritual advisor," *dge ba'i bshes gnyen*, pronounced "gewa'i shenyen," could also be rendered as "virtuous friend," or "companion."

26. Scripture includes the three baskets, which expound the three trainings—vinaya for proper conduct, sūtra for samādhi, and abhidharma for prajñā—as well as the four classes of tantra. Treatises (*bstan bcos*) are expositions conveying the intended meaning of dictates (*bka'*) spoken by the Buddha.

27. This text could also be *rDo rje snying po'i rgyan gyi rgyud chen po'i bkha 'grel* [*Vajrahṛdaya laṅkara pañjika*] by Rabtu Shiwa'i Shaynyen; see bibliography.

28. A position would be, for example, "all phenomena are empty"; an argument, "because they are neither single nor multiple"; and an example, "like the reflection of the moon in water."

29. "Validity Sutra" (*Tshad ma'i mdo; pramāṇasūtra*) is the work by Dignāga known as "Excerpts from Validity" (*Tshad ma kun las btus pa; Pramāṇa-samuccaya*). The "Series of Seven" (*sDe bdun; saptadeśa*), the seven texts on *pramāṇa* (validity), are commentaries on Dignāga's work by Dharmakirti. Chief among them is the "Complete Commentary on Validity" (*Tshad ma rnam 'grel; Pramāṇavārttika*).

30. In this context, prajñā that directly realizes emptiness.

31. The remainder of the pāramitās.

32. This passage from "Embarking on the Middle Course" is part of Candrakīrti's account of his purpose in commenting on the writings of Nāgārjuna.

33. This sūtra, the source of the Jātaka tales of Śākyamuni Buddha's previous incarnations, is annotated in the *Jātaka-mālā-śāstra*.

34. The six limits (or perhaps parameters) are: provisional vs. definitive meaning, literal vs. nonliteral meaning, and meaning disclosive of intention vs. nondisclosive, i.e., where the true intention is ulterior.

35. The four maxims are: don't concentrate on the person, but rather on the dharma itself; the meaning is more important than the words; the definitive meaning should be emphasized over the provisional; and interpret primarily with reference to primordial wisdom, secondarily with regard to consciousness.

36. That is to say, prajñā manifestly exposes the essential nature of the ultimate, enduring condition or state.

37. Here it is important to understand "original" as meaning "without cause," and "Lord" to personify what is not actually an independent, external, truly existent thing or person.

38. An alternative interpretation would be "goes beyond the mere emptiness of physical particles, being of the essence of primordial wisdom."

39. The seventh Lord Karmapa, Chodrak Gyatso.

40. Here "restriction" refers to eternalistic and nihilistic tropes and "partiality" refers to leaning towards saṃsāra or nirvāṇa.

41. It has been stated that this refers to a work by Treng po Terton, Sherab Ozer, a near contemporary of Situ Paṇchen, who published an edition of his well-known grammatical work. However, it is in fact a quotation from a text by Sanjay Yeshe (Buddhajñāna), an Indian commentator. See the bibliography for the exact reference to the Beijing edition of the Tangyur, or see folio 55b of volume *ti* of the Narthang edition.

42. Sugatagarbha.

43. Because its qualities are spontaneously present.

44. The indivisibility of openness and awareness that is the enduring condition of the mind.

45. Through unmediated, apperceptive awareness.

46. This is a quotation from the "Precious Sky" [*Nam mkha' rin po che*] sūtra, and is also cited in the "Ornament for Clear Realization" and "Higher Continuum," both of Maitreya, as well as in Gampopa's "Ornament for Liberation" [*Dwag po thar rgyan*]. Although a number of Western scholars have cited this passage in translations of these and other works, no one appears to have found a reference to a sūtra with this title in the scriptural canon. It is undoubtedly a teaching of the third dharmacakra.

47. This is a quotation from Vasubandhu.

48. A synonym for dharmatā, which conveys its singularity, in that it could be no other way and nothing else is quite it.

49. Although these words most commonly mean "permanent" and "disruption" (or interruption), respectively, here they are used in a very formal sense that will be explained below.

50. This is a citation from a stanza in Nāgārjuna's "Principal Exposition of the Central Course" [*dBus ma rtsa shes; Mūlamadhyamakakārikā*], which continues, "therefore the learned rest neither in "exists" nor "doesn't exist.""

51. Who is thought to have been a contemporary of Acarya Dharmakirti. (Footnote in original.)

52. Tib. *tshu rol mdzes pa* or *rgyang 'phen pa.*

53. Tib. *grangs can pa.*

54. Tib. *dbang phyug pa.* The six semantic categories are: substance, opposite, general, specific, collection and action.

55. Tib. *khyab 'jug pa.*

56. Tib. *gcer bu pa.*

57. Tib. *mu stegs pa,* "forders"; holders of non-Buddhist tenets.

58. Even more specifically, the Sautrāntikas assert the general characteristics of phenomena to be mentally imputed upon them and therefore only conventionally real, but their own proper characteristics to be not conceptually generated, but ultimately real.

59. What must be understood here is that although the Cittamātrins themselves don't say that they endorse the self-identity of phenomena, their position, when subjected to Madhyamaka analysis, would appear to lead to just such a conclusion, the phenomenon in question being the non-dual cognizance itself.

60. A work by Vasubandhu. The commentary by Loten is entitled simply "Explanation of the One of Thirty" [*gSum chu pa'i bshad pa; Triṃśikā-bhāṣya*].

61. That is, the truth or reality of what is ultimate and the truth or reality of what is apparent or observable.

62. Birth, cessation, existence, nonexistence, coming, going, single and multiple.

63. In this instance, unrestricted means not able to be designated as solely clear or solely empty.

64. Since it is not something imputed, it is beyond thought. Since it is beyond thought, it is beyond the realm of discourse—inconceivable and inexpressible.

65. Although phenomena are by nature inseparably empty and apparent, they appear as if they truly exist. In this presentation, ultimate reality is aligned with how things truly are and apparent reality with how they appear to be, whereas in some interpretations of Madhyamaka ultimate truth is the indivisibility of how things are and how they appear to be.

66. The commentary is by Nāgārjuna. The root text is Nāgārjuna's "Principal Exposition" (*dBus ma rtsa shes; Mūlamadhyamakakārikā*).

67. The root verse from Nāgārjuna is:

> *The dharma taught by the Buddhas is completely based upon the two truths:*
> *Apparent, worldly truth and sacred, ultimate truth.*

68. The root text from Nāgārjuna is:

> *Without relying upon conventional terms, the sacred meaning cannot be taught.*
> *Without relying upon the sacred meaning, nirvāṇa cannot be attained.*

69. In other words, for the dharma to be error-free, the dual hazards of the ground, path and fruition must be bypassed in turn, and that is why the discussion of the non-mistaken path is organized accordingly.

70. In the text, *sTong pa nyid ni ston pa'i mdo*. I am unable to definitively identify its Sanskrit name.

71. The text highlighted here is bold in the original.

72. This confirmation occurs at the stage of "sealing" the empowerment with the presence of the root guru in the form of the lord of the family on the crown of the head of the visualized yidam deity.

73. The Sanskrit name for the branch of Madhyamaka that claims ultimate truth is that which is free of any limiting mental constructs.

74. Mirror wisdom corresponds to the cognitive factor of the universal ground, while dharmadhātu wisdom corresponds to the emptiness factor. In this way, four of the five wisdoms are related to dharmakāya of realization, while the fifth relates to dharmakāya of abandonment.

75. The third Karmapa Rangjung Dorje's own commentary on his seminal work, "The Profound Inner Meaning" (Tib. *Zab mo'i nang don*).

76. This force is analogous but not identical to the skandha of perception. This is a more fundamental force which creates pattern and relationship, before the skandhas have been formed. It operates upon the universal ground.

77. By Asaṅga.

78. Both the appearance of the phenomenal world and conversely the dissolution of appearances before the experience of luminosity can be described in terms of the three-step process of appearance (*snang*), increase (*mched*) and attainment (*thob*).

79. A tantra probably of the yogatantra class.

80. Here the author is specifically referring to the elements of the fourth skandha, the saṃskāras of formation.

81. A useful illustration here would be the example of a spring. The spring imparts force to the individual coils, and yet because they are all linked together, the coils impart force back to the spring as a whole.

82. All three of these citations employ the same Tibetan word *bag chags*, which I am translating alternately as tendential imprint or impression and ingrained predisposition to satisfy both the sense in which this is the impulse initiating a process and the end result of a process.

83. This is referring to the end of the verse on page 63 above from Vasubandhu.

84. The question and supporting quotation are inserted in quotations to show that they are put forward by a hypothetical speaker. The author frequently uses this device to address an issue or objection not otherwise raised in the discussion.

85. This is a tantra from the Cakrasaṃvara cycle, therefore I translate *bde mchog*, part of one of the names of the deity, as *saṃvara*, to make the reference explicit, though the Sanskrit and Tibetan terms are not strictly equivalent.

86. Part of the "Common Group" section.

87. Tib. *de bzhin nyid;* Skt. *tathatā.*

88. What is meant by saying the teachings are "not so" is that they are not how things actually are, their *de bzhin nyid, tathatā,* earlier translated as "just like that" and "just that way." The implication is that the teachings of Vijñānavāda in the Cittamātrin school are just provisional, for the sake of those who can't yet face the profound emptiness, and are not definitive.

89. Designated, heteronomous and fully established are the three natures attributed to mind in the Vijñānavādin school. The meaning of this quotation is that the presence of these three natures, if interpreted to mean that there is a sense in which mind or a facet of mind truly exists, is only a provisional teaching relative to the definitive truth of emptiness.

90. A sūtra from the turning of the wheel of the dharma of definitive meaning.

91. See page 53 above for another version of this line of verse.

92. Śāntideva is arguing against the Cittamātrin claim of a self-aware consciousness. They offer the example of a butter lamp as something self-illuminating and he is demonstrating that even that mundane example is self-contradictory since something that isn't dark in the first place can't be said to be illuminated.

93. The second verse was also cited above on page 53.

94. The "turning of the wheel" of dharma, referring to the third and final cycle of teachings given by Śākyamuni Buddha.

95. The pāramitā of permanence corresponds to being unchanging, because of not being something composite. The other three pāramitās likewise have meanings which differ from the conventional meanings of the terms used.

96. Because views that make any kind of claim about what emptiness "is" are limiting conceptual constructs, they are unable to establish emptiness, whereas genuine emptiness has the power to dispel all such views.

97. See the explanation of verse six above, pages 46 to 49.

98. This is the root text by Ācārya Jñānagarbha composed in verse. There are also the "Authoritative Commentary on Distinguishing the Two Truths" (*bDen pa gnyis rnam par 'byed pa'i dka' 'grel; Satyadvaya-vibhaṅga-pañjikā*) (P5283) by Śāntirakṣita and "Entry to the Two Truths" (*bDen pa gnyis la 'jug pa; Satvadvayāvatāra*) (P5298, 5380) by Atiśa, which elaborate upon the meaning of those verses.

99. From "Embarking on the Course of Bodhisattva Conduct."

100. Ontologically speaking.

101. There is nothing of which we can say "this in particular is the vibrant display of mind's intrinsic state" and nothing which we can say is not. Another translation of this line would be "All there is is this; nothing whatsoever is not [this]." The meaning is the same in both cases.

102. The thoughts and emotions of someone who understands emptiness are naturally pacified and they are therefore naturally circumspect and mindful in everything they say and do.

103. Tib. *byang chub snying po*. This term usually refers to the attainment of enlightenment, but here it refers to the vajra seat at Bodh Gaya where nirmāṇakāya Buddhas become enlightened.

104. One can interpret this verse to mean either that one should abandon all engagements of mind, including concentration on virtuous subjects, or that one should not engage the mind in any meditation subject and, in particular, one should let go of any subject that is already occupying one's mind. The translation follows the first interpretation.

105. The unfabricated, enduring condition.

106. Prajñākaramatigupta.

107. "Supreme purpose" means that it is what beings must finally realize, and "highly exalted" means that it is the higher of the two truths, and therefore distinctive, superior.

108. There is a plethora of tantric terminology and symbolic references in this quote that make it very difficult to understand. *A* and *Ka* are syllables that are the root of mantra, and *ri bong can*, a metonym which I have rendered here as "candra", and *nyin byed*, rendered as "sūrya", represent the configuration of elements within certain cakras in the practice of the inner yogas. Therefore, the first phrase implies that none of the complexities of development stage yoga with recitation, or perfection stage retaining dependence on signs, is the true basis for ultimate reality, its "seat." The ultimate is not captured by the seed-syllable *hum* and the subsequent stages of development and transformation, and appearance of the complete form of the deity with its colors, aspects, etc. It is ever unchanging, and therefore reduces (by comparison) the significance of generation and transformation, which are still contrived phases of meditation. Meditation that is endowed with the power of this supreme unchangingness is not in any way partial or limited; it cannot be qualified in any way. This universality is described as a bindu endowed with all aspects, that is, emptiness replete with all supreme aspects (the vajra-one), within which all of the diversity of false appearances of conditioned existence and serenity is contained.

109. The Sanskrit title given in the bibliography, *Catur-mudrā-krama,* is reconstructed from the Tibetan, as I have been unable to find an authoritative reference to this work by Viravajra.

110. Here the "tathatā of mantra" refers to fostering the meditative state, and not to a recitation practice *per se.*

111. Tib. Mar me mdzad, the proper name of Atiśa.

112. By Nāgārjuna. "Friendly Advice" is also the title of this section of the Tangyur containing commentaries on the sūtras.

113. This is a slightly different translation of the verse that also appears in the section on the prajnā of meditation, page 46.

114. Each among the twelve branches of scripture.

115. One must associate and unify the words expressing the profound meaning with the inexpressible meaning that they convey.

116. The descriptions in the quotation and this list do not correspond on a one-to-one basis. Some of the ingredients contained in the quotation are numbered (from one to six), whereas the subsequent commentary lists names for each of the seven engagements. "Individual consideration" is looking at the parts separately, "isolation" means nondistraction, "joy" is in samādhi, "withdrawal" means collecting the mind inwardly, "discernment" is of the meaning, and so forth.

117. The final phase is actual samādhi, and not just serene abiding. It is not compulsory because at this point the direction of Buddhist meditation diverges from the common path shared with heterodox traditions; instead of pursuing ever higher states of absorption, we use the preparatory work of the engagements of mind to enter into higher insight practice, which is unique to the Buddhist path.

118.The intrinsic, enduring condition of all dharmas.

119. It is important to understand here that this is the meditation of an arhat, which still involves employment of subtle conceptual processes. Engagement of mind upon how things actually are is still subtly purposeful, and the cognitive powers that occur, too, are still engagements of mind. For example, the arhat would have to deliberately look in order to discover what occurred in someone's previous lifetime.

120. It is unclear whether the author has a specific text in mind or whether he is simply paraphrasing certain codified traditional instructions.

121. Whether material or immaterial.

122. With no barrier or obscuring covering.

123. That is to say, when you are given direct introduction to the enduring condition of mind in the practice of mahāmudrā.

124. All conceptual activity, whether it is immersion in afflictive states of mind or concern with virtue, becomes impossible, and is thus pacified.

125. When all thought activity has been arrested in the mind, the direct experience itself is inconceivable.

126. Both by nature, since the essence of mind is not amenable to constructs, and on the path, when meditating nonconceptually.

127. This state of awareness in which concepts are absent is the remedy which overcomes the object of abandonment, ordinary conceptuality. So here "emancipates" also means "victorious over" (thoughts).

128. By nature.

129. It is not an object for conceptual activity and not a home for conceptual activity.

130. This passage descriptively distinguishes dharmas, phenomena, from dharmatā, their true nature. Any quality one can think of, or any event that can occur within or influence the mind, leaves no mark at all upon the innate, enduring condition of mind, its dharmatā.

131. The author refers to this commentary by Atiśa (P5298) by its popular name, *dBu ma bden chung*, a homonym for a contraction of the proper title, *bDen 'jug* (from *bDen pa gnyis la 'jug pa*).

132. A well-known instruction manual on the graded course of meditation.

133. According to the abhidharma teachings, each of the levels of concentration and samādhi has its own degree of prajñā. At the second level of concentration and beyond, prajñā is no longer conceptually based.

134. By Abhayākaragupta.

135. The various activities of the bodhisattva path cannot be undertaken during the meditative session.

136. These are synonymous names because they all have the same referent (so to speak).

137. In this case "dharmas" refers to buddhadharmas, and in particular all teachings on what ultimately must be known.

138. Another translation for great perfection, mahāsaṃdhi, mahā ati; in Tibetan, *rdzogs pa chen po*.

139. This refers to *zhi byed*, one of the practice lineages, promulgated by Padampa Sanjay.

140. The brackets in this sentence contain comments made by Khenpo Sonam Rinpoche that elucidate the meaning of Situ Tenpa'i Nyinchay's terse explanation.

141. The author is assigning "profound meaning" to what is realized and "vast meaning" to what facilitates realization of that.

142. It is an acceptable convention to assign the name of what is realized to the path or teachings that bring about that realization. So we speak of the perfection of wisdom which the Tathāgatas attain and also the perfection of wisdom scriptures, etc.

143. This text is a true bridge between the sūtra and mantra vehicles, as it is so highly revered in the Tibetan tradition that it is often recited, like mantra, for the power of its blessing.

144. Prajñā which investigates is still bound to intellect, which is the faculty that employs ideas and examines.

145. That is, the ultimate meditation.

146. In the context of the four types of mudrās, mahamudrā is most superior.

147. There are (at least) two important commentaries by this name. This one, *Padmani-nāma-pañjikā* (*Padma can zhes bya ba'i dka' 'grel*; P2067, Vol. 47), is

concerned with the Kālacakra Tantra. The other is a commentary on the "Origin of Saṃvara" tantra and was written by Ratnarakṣita (*Śrī-saṃvarodaya-mahātantrarājasya padminī-nāma-pañjikā, dPal sdom pa 'byung ba'i rgyud po chen po'i dka' 'grel padma can zhes;* P2137, Vol. 51). The title may alternately be translated as "Commentary on the Dictates [entitled] 'The Lotus Laden.'"

148. Also by Dus 'khor zhabs (Kālacakrapāda).

149. An epithet for Gampopa.

150. This refers to the Mahāyāna doctrine of three *gotras* (Skt.) or potentials for attaining enlightenment: those who certainly will, those who might, and those whose development has become arrested.

151. This excerpt from Sahajavajra's work incorporates the root verse from "The Tenth Tattva" by Maitrīpa. See the bibliography.

152. *gZhung 'grel* means principal commentary, or commentary on the primary text. The author is probably referring again to the work by Sahajavajra.

153. The word *dgongs pa* is the honorific term for the mind of a superior being. The title of this section of sūtra is sometimes written *nges 'grel* ("Definite Explication of the Intention") instead of *nges 'grol*, but the latter, in any case, is the name of the first and main part of the section.

154. Such as using passion to overcome passion, etc., with a form of an affliction serving as its own remedy, hence "reversing" itself.

155. This commentary is the "Clarifying the Meaning of the Words of 'Ubiquitous Conduct of Yoginis'" by Vīravajra (Pa'o Dorje). See bibliography. The words enclosed in single quotations are from the tantra.

156. Nonconceptuality that retains a point of reference.

157. Such as of perfection stage illusory body practice.

158. Even though the words used are very similar, you shouldn't confuse taking hold of mind with grasping or fixation.

159. Mind from which obscurations have been removed, so that it is "apart" from them.

160. Here, "method" refers to compassion that prevents one from remaining in serenity. "Comes into being" refers to the unceasing enlightened activity of that compassion. "The fallible" refers to the false self-identity of persons or phenomena, and more specifically may refer to the view upholding the transitory composite of skandhas as real. Prajñā prevents one from being caught in the extreme of reification.

161. The doctrines and attainments of those practicing the minor vehicle impede progress on the major (Mahāyāna) path leading to complete awakening.

162. This is a companion verse to the one found above on page 55, "The bodhicitta of the Buddhas is unobscured...."

163. Activity from among the four: view, meditation, activity and fruition. The question is based on the supposition that no verses remain that explicitly discuss activity if all the preceding verses deal with view and meditation and the remaining verses cover the subject of fruition.

164. This is a third category of tantric scripture, besides principal tantras and explanatory tantras.

165. The mental consciousness responds to the contact between a sense faculty and its object either positively or negatively. This is ordinary worldly mental activity. The mantra samayas and vows that come from Vajrayāna protect against ordinary thought processes and are thus called mantra activity by the Protection Vajras, i.e., Buddhas.

166. Abhayākaragupta, an important commentator on the Guhyasamāja tradition who lived in India in the twelfth century. His commentary is called the "Commentary on the Intention of the Five Stages," and the quotation he is commenting on is drawn from the supplementary Guhyasamāja tantra.

167. The placement of the syllable indicators here suggests *mana*, or *manas*, the Sanskrit term that the Tibetan *yid* most commonly corresponds to, which I am here translating as "mental power."

168. Supersensible.

169. Perhaps one could say "know what is in place and what is out of place," since an example of the former would be knowing happiness to arise from virtue, and an example of the latter would be knowing suffering to not arise from virtue, or happiness from nonvirtue.

170. The word "field" suggests that sentient beings are the field of activity of the compassionate conduct of bodhisattvas training on the path and the enlightened activity of Buddhas. They are the field upon which compassion grows and merit is cultivated. The realms in which beings dwell are "Buddha fields" in the sense that they are innately pure. When the obscurations supporting delusory perceptions are cleansed, the kāyas and wisdoms abiding in the fundamental enlightened potential are activated, and the "ordinary" world cedes its place to all-encompassing purity.

171. A noble bodhisattva who has attained one of the higher grounds (eighth or above) by having directly glimpsed emptiness.

172. "Entrance to Mantra" is also by Ācārya Jnānākara.

173. This would appear to be a quotation from sūtra, but I am unable to ascertain the source.

174. This refers to the skill of rapid walking, one of the ordinary siddhis.

175. The premise of the question is that the long and slow Mahāyāna path presents an outline of qualities that one achieves at each stage of one's progress through the bhūmis and along the paths. The hypothetical interrogator wonders whether the swift mahāmudrā path must produce these same effects.

176. This refers to the mantra mahāmudrā path.

177. That is, of karma.

178. Tib: *mos sgrub*. This is a technical term which means that one considers oneself to already be the fully perfected yidam deity on the one hand, and on the other implies that there is still an element of simulation in one's practice.

179. See the earlier discussion of the six branches of application.

180. Here, specifically, the interval between death and rebirth.

181. India.

182. Gampopa.

183. Atiśa.

184. *sKyes bu gsum gyi lam rim.* This is the common name for the system of instruction from Atiśa. The title of Atiśa's best known work in this area is "Lamp for the Path of Awakening."

185. This is Situ Paṇchen's spelling of the name Tilopa, according to its Sanskrit origin.

186. Marpa's proper name; in the previous sentence he is referred to as Marpa Lotsā (the translator).

187. Candraprabhākumarā ("Moonlit Youth"); another epithet for Gampopa.

188. The mighty muni, i.e., Śākyamuni Buddha.

189. Asaṅga.

190. Vasubandhu.

191. Atiśa.

Author's Colophon

1. Here a note in the original text says "Dagpo Nyigom," yet another name for Gampopa.

2. Younger brother; a term of affection.

Appendix 1: Glossary of Technical Terms

This glossary presents the English and Sanskrit translation equivalents for Tibetan technical terms and expressions found in the text. No claim is made that the translations given can or should apply in all other texts or contexts. The list should prove helpful for a close reading of the commentary; in many cases it shows where different translations have been given for a single Tibetan term. The Tibetan words are also phoneticized for those who may be familiar with them in the spoken language only.

English	Tibetan Phonetics	Transliterated Orthography
abstract image; generality	dön chi	don spyi
ācārya; teacher; master	lop pön	slob dpon
activities of pacification, expansion, domination and intimidation	shi gyay wang drak ki lay	zhi rgyas dbang drag gi las
afflicted states of mind; afflictive thought patterns; mental disturbances	nyön mong	snyon mongs
afflictive mental force	nyön yid	snyon yid
agency of purification	jong chay	sbyong byed
apparent truth	kun dzob denpa	kun rdzob bden pa
appearance, reinforcement and attainment	nang ched top	snang mched thob

English	Tibetan Phonetics	Transliterated Orthography
arguments	ten tsik	bstan tshig
aspiration prayer	mön lam	smon lam
balanced wisdom; impartial wisdom	nyam nyi yeshay	mnyam nyid ye shes
become manifest; make manifest	ngön gyur	mngon 'gyur
blessing lineage of practice	nyam len gyin lap ki gyu	nyams len byin rlabs kyi brgyud
body of complete maturation	nam min gi lu	rnam smin gyi lus
born nirmāṇakāya	kyewa'i trulku	skye ba'i sprul sku
carelessness; carefree	bak maypa	bag med pa
certitude; conviction	ngay shay	nges shes
cessation absorption	gok nyom	'gogs snyoms
cleansing, maturation and fulfillment	jang min dzok	sbyangs smin rdzogs
common path; standard path	tun mong gi lam	mthun mong gi lam
conduct	chö pa	spyod pa
confirmation; seal in confirmation	gyay dep	rgyas 'debs
connate; coemergent	lhen kyay	lhan skyes
connate conjunction	lhen chik kyay jor	lhan cig skyes 'byor
considered practice	mö drup	mos sgrub
controversial issue	ka nay	dka' gnad
craft nirmāṇakāya	zo wa'i trulku	bzo ba'i sprul sku
defies the intellect; beyond the sphere of the intellect	lo lay daypa	blo las 'das pa
definitive meaning	nges dön	nges don
deliberate meditation	chay du gom	ched du sgom
delusory appearances; illusory display	trulpa'i nangwa ba	'khrul pa'i snang ba

English	Tibetan Phonetics	Transliterated Orthography
designated nature; imaginary nature	kun tak ki rang shin	kun brtag gi rang bzhin
dharmakāya; kāya of truth	chö ku	chos sku
dharmakāya of realization	togpa'i chö ku	rtogs pa'i chos sku
dharmas of total purity	nam jang gi chö	rnam byang gi chos
dharmatā; reality	chö nyi	chos nyid
dhyāna; concentration	samten	bsam gtan
dictates	ka	bka'
discerning wisdom	sor tok yeshay	sor rtog ye shes
discipline	tsul trim	tshul khrims
distillate; extract	dang ma	gdangs ma
distorted view; inverted view	lok ta	rlog lta; slog lta
effective wisdom	cha drup yeshay	bya sgrub ye shes
eight limiting conceptual constructs; conceptually constructed limitations	trî pa'i ta gyay	spros pa'i mtha' brgyad
eight resourceless states	mi kom pa gyay	mi khom pa brgyad
embellished claims; doubts	dro dok	sgro 'dogs
emptiness with a core of compassion	tong nyi nying jay chen	stong nyid snying rje can
enduring condition of the entity of the mind	sem ngö ki nay luk	sems dngos kyi gnas lugs
enduring potential; indwelling potential	nay pa'i rik	gnas pa'i rigs
enlightened activities	trin lay	'phrin las
entity	ngî po	dngos po
evolving potential	gyay gyur ki rik	rgyas 'gyur kyi rigs
example	pay	dpe
experience and realization	nyam tok	nyams rtogs
extract maximal benefit	bok dön	bogs 'don
extreme of serenity	shiwa'i ta	zhi ba'i mtha'

English	Tibetan Phonetics	Transliterated Orthography
extreme of transitory or worldly existence	sid pa'i ta	rsid pa'i mtha'
extremes of embellishment and discredit	drokur gyi ta	sgro bkur gyi mtha'
factors conducive to enlightenment	chang chub chok chö	byang chub phyogs chos
five aggregates	pungpo nga	phung po lnga
five eyes	chen nga	spyan lnga
fixating and grasped phenomena; object and subject; dualistic phenomena	zung dzin gyi chö	bzung 'dzin gyi chos
formal instructions	dam ngak; shal dam	gdams ngag; zhal gdams
formative cognitive force	du chay kyi yid	'du byed kyi yid
four maxims	tön pa shi	ston pa bzhi
four thoughts that reorient the mind	lo dos nam shi	blo sdos rnam bzhi
four yoga levels	snal jor rimpa shi	rnal 'byor rim pa bzhi
free of hazards	nyay may	nyes med
fully established nature	yong drup kyi rang shin	yongs bsgrubs kyi rang bzhin
fully nonabiding; not dwelling on anything at all	rab tu mi nay pa	rab tu mi gnas pa
functionary	lay chay	las byed
fundamental, enduring condition	shi yi nay luk	gzhi yi gnas lugs
fundamental luminosity	shi yi ö sel	gzhi yi 'od gsal
gradual learners	rim gyipa	rim gyis pa
ground of purification	jong shi	sbyong gzhi
groundless and without foundation	shi may tsa drel	gzhi med rtsa bral

English	Tibetan Phonetics	Transliterated Orthography
guidance manuals; texts of instruction	tri rim	'khrid rim
heterodox traditions	chirolpa'i luk	phyi rol pai lugs
heteronomous nature	shen wang gi rang shin	bzhan dbang gi rang bzhin
hidden recesses; hidden dimensions	tsang	mtshang
higher insight; penetrative insight	lhag tong	lhag mthong
impersonal endowments	shen jor	gzhan 'byor
incidental and passing stains; adventitious impurities	lobur gyi drima	glo bur gyi dri ma
inconceivable and inexpressible	ma sam jö may	ma bsam brjod med
indivisible	yer maypa	dbyer med pa
innate; intrinsic	nyuk ma	gnyug ma
instigative mental force	de ma tak yid	de ma thag yid
just as it is	ji tawa shin du	ji lta ba bzhin du
just like that; just so; just that way	de shin nyi	de bzhin nyid
knowledge; cognition	shay pa	shes pa
lack of otherness; empty of other	shen tong	bzhan stong
lack of self-identity; empty of self	rang tong	rang stong
lacking any referent or point of reference; without focus	mikpa maypa	dmigs pa med pa
leisures and endowments	dal jor	dal 'byor
liberated on the spot, automatically; where it stands	rang sar drol	rang sar 'grol
limits of conditioned existence and serenity	sid shi kyi ta	srid zhi kyi mtha'

English	Tibetan Phonetics	Transliterated Orthography
limits; extremes; poles	ta	mtha'
lineage of profound view	zabmo ta gyu	zab mo lta brgyud
lineage of vast activity	gya chay chö gyu	rgya che spyod brgyud
mahā ati; mahāsaṃdhi; great perfection; completeness	dzok chen	rdzogs chen
mahāmudrā; great seal	chak chen	phyag chen
making direct perception the path	ngön sum lam du chay	mngon sum lam du byas
making inference the path	jay pak lam du chay	rjes dpag lam du byas
manner of subsistence	ngang luk	ngang lugs
master of the world	jik ten wang chuk	'jig rten dbang phyug
mental retention	sem dzin	sems 'dzin
migrants; migratory beings	drowa	'gro ba
mind instructions or guidelines	sem tri	sems 'khrid
mind nature; mind's own nature	sem nyi	sems nyid
mind-made	lö chay	blos byas
morally neutral	lung ma ten	lung ma bstan
naturally pure constituent or element	rang shin dakpa'i kham	rang bzhin dag pa'i khams
neither errs nor misleads	gol chuk maypa	gol 'phyugs med pa
nine means of bringing mind to rest	sem shiwa'i tap gu	sems zhi ba'i thabs dgu
nirmāṇakāya; body of emanation	trul ku	sprul sku
non-affirming negation; mere absence	may gak	med bgags
object of offering	chö dong	mchod sdong

English	Tibetan Phonetics	Transliterated Orthography
object of purification	jong cha	sbyong bya
objects of knowledge; knowable entities	shay ja	shes bya
oral instructions	men ngak	man ngag
path of juncture; path of connection	jor lam	sbyor lam
path of vision	thong lam	mthong lam
persistence and respectfulness	tak jor dang gu jor	rtag sbyor dang gus sbyor
person-to-person lineage	nyen gyu	snyan brgyud
personal endowments	rang jor	rang 'byor
phenomenal world; transitory realm	jik ten	'jig rten
polarity or poles of existence and nonexistence	tak chay kyi ta	rtag chad kyi mtha'
polemicists; pedants	togewa	rtog ge ba
position; assertion	shak	bzhag
positive qualities	yön ten	yon tan
possessing twofold purity	dakpa nyi den	dag pa gnyis ldan
preceptor; master of initiation	kenpo	mkhan po
preliminary; prerequisite	ngön dro	sngon 'gro
present wakefulness; attentive in the present moment	ta rang gi shaypa	da rang gi shes pa
primary operative condition	dak kyen	bdag rkyen
principal guru	tsawa'i lama	rtsa ba'i bla ma
pristine mind	dakpa'i sem	dag pa'i sems
proficiency	tsal jong	rtsal sbyong
profound sūtras	do de zabmo	mdo sde zab mo

English	Tibetan Phonetics	Transliterated Orthography
prophecy; prediction	lung ten	lung bstan
prove; establish; proof	drup	sgrup
provisional meaning; indicative meaning	drang dön	drangs don
reflective wisdom; mirror wisdom	melong yeshay	me long ye shes
refutation	gakpa	bgags pa
released from bondage	ching lay drol	'ching las sgrol
resolve conclusively	ten la bep	gtan la 'bebs
result of purification	jong dray	sbyong 'bras
reversal meditation	dok gom	ldog sgom
sacred, ultimate truth	dön dam denpa	don dam bden pa
saṃbhogakāya; kāya of perfected experience	long chö dzok ku	longs spyod rdzogs sku
scholars and realized masters	kay drup	mkhas grub
scripture	lung	lung
scripture and reasoning	lung rik	lung rig
secret preceptor	sang tön	gsang ston
secret; mysterious	sang wa	gsang ba
self-contradiction; paradox	gal du	'gal 'dus
self-disclosive awareness; apperception	rang rik	rang rig
self-identity of persons	kang zak gi dak	gang zag gi bdag
self-identity of phenomena	chö ki dak	chos kyi bdag
serene abiding	shi nay	zhi gnas
settle decisively	tak chö	thag bcod
seven conceptual engagements; seven engagements of mind	yid la chaypa dun	yid la byed pa bdun
seven dharmas of Vairocana	nam nang chö dun	rnam snang chos bdun

English	Tibetan Phonetics	Transliterated Orthography
sever the underlying root; undermine	shi tsa chöpa	gzhi rtsa bcod pa
siddha; accomplished or realized being	drup top	grub thob
simple; not elaborate	trö pa maypa	spros pa med pa
singleminded; one-pointed	tsay chik	rtse gcig
six branches of application	jorwa yenlak druk	sbyor ba yan lag drug
six limits	ta druk	mtha' drug
six paranormal cognitive powers	ngön shay druk	mngon shes drug
spiritual advisor	gewa'i shay nyen; ge shay	dge ba'i bshes gnyen
steady placement; resting steadily; remain in balance; equipoise; settling down	nyam par shak	mnyam par bzhag
study, reflection and meditation	tö sam gom	thos bsam bsgoms
sublime speech, precepts	sung rab	gsung rab
sugatas	dewar shekpa	bde bar gshegs pa
superior in all aspects	nam kun chok den	rnam kun mchog ldan
supplication prayer	sol dep	gsol 'debs
support	ten	rten
supramundane	jik ten lay daypa	'jig rten las 'das pa
supreme nirmāṇakāya	chok ki trulku	mchog gi sprul sku
supremely unchanging great bliss or mahāsukha	chok tu migyurwa'i dewa chenpo	mchog tu mi bsgyur ba'i bde ba chen po
svabhāvikakāya of abandonment	pang wa'i ngowo nyi ki ku	spangs ba'i ngo bo nyid kyi sku
svabhāvikakāya; essential kāya	ngo wo nyi ki ku	ngo bo nyid kyi sku

English	Tibetan Phonetics	Transliterated Orthography
tangible and intangible	ngö dang ngö may	dngos dang dngos med
tathāgata potential	de shek ki rik	bde gshegs kyi rigs
tendential imprints or impressions; ingrained predispositions	bak chak	bag chags
that alone; just that; just such	de ko na nyi	de kho na nyid
the view of the mantra system	ngak luk ki tawa	sngags lugs kyi lta ba
the view of Madhyamaka	uma'i tawa	dbus ma'i lta ba
the view of the sūtra system	do luk gi tawa	mdo lugs kyi lta ba
those who learn all at once	chik charwa	cig char ba
three concerns	kor sum	'khor gsum
three trainings	lap pa sum	slab pa gsum
torpor and agitation	ching gö	'bying rgod
totally pure intentions and actions	sam jor nam dak	bsam sbyor rnam dag
transference of primordial wisdom	yeshay powa	ye shes 'pho ba
treatises	ten chos	bstan bcos
twelve deeds	dzaypa chu nyi	mdzad pa bcu nyis
two-stage yoga	rim nyi naljor	rim gnyis rnal 'byor
ultimate empowerment	dön gyi wang	don gyi dbang
unified central course	zung jug uma'i lam	zung 'jug dbus ma'i lam
unified cognizance and emptiness	sal tong zung jug	gsal stong zung 'jug
universal ground	kun shi	kun gzhi
unrestricted and impartial or unpartitioned	ri may gya chay	ris med rgya chad
vajra posture	dorjay kyil trung	rdo rje skyil krung
valid inferential reasoning	jay pak gi tsayma	rjes dpag gi tshad ma

English	Tibetan Phonetics	Transliterated Orthography
venerable, learned, steadfast and benificent	kay tsun zang ten	mkhyas btsun bzang brtan
vibrant display	tsal nang	rtsal snang
victors	gyalwa	rgyal ba
vital or pertinent point of mind	sem nay	sems gnad
wisdom that knows all there is just as it is	ji ta ji nyay ki yeshay	ji lta ji snyed kyi ye shes
with faith, industry and prajñā	day tsön sherab den	dad brtson shes rab ldan
yoga of freedom from limiting constructs	trö dral gyi naljor	spros bral gyi rnal 'byor
yoga of nonmeditation	gom may kyi naljor	sgom med kyi rnal 'byor
yoga of one, single flavor	ro chik gi naljor	ro gcig gi rnal 'byor
yoga of undivided attention	tsay chik gi naljor	rtse gcig gi rnal 'byor
yoga without signs	tsen may kyi naljor	mtshan med kyi rnal 'byor

Appendix 2: Transliteration of Tibetan Names and Terms

Belu Tsewang Kunkyab	Be lu tshe dbang kun khyab
Changchub Dorje	Byang chub rdo rje
Chayulwa	Bya yul ba
Chen Ngawa	sPyan snga ba
Chenresig	sPyan ras gzigs
Chod Dong	mChod sdong
Chodrak Gyatso	Chos grags rgya mtsho
Choggi De	mChog gi sde
Chokyi Jungnay	Chos kyi byung gnas
Chokyi Jungnay Trinlay Kunkyab Yeshe Pal Zangpo	Chos kyi 'byung gnas 'phrin las kun khyab ye shes dpal bzang po
chungpo	gCung po
Dagpo Kagyu	Dwags po bka' brgyud
Dagpo Nyigom	Dwags po snyi sgom
Derge	sDe dge
Drogmi	'Brog mi
Dromton	'Brom ston
Dulwa'i De	Dul ba'i sde
Dusum Kyenpa	Dus gsum mhyen pa
Gakyong	dGa' bskyong
Gampo Naynang	sGam po gnas nang
Gampopa	sGam po pa
Geshe Ben	dGe bshes 'ban
Geshe Chagriwa	dGe bshes lcags ri ba

Geshe Tonpa	dGe bshes ston pa
Gyachakriwa	rGya lcags ri ba
Gyalwa Dampa	rGyal ba dam pa
Gyalwa Karmapa, Rangjung Dorje	rGyal ba karmapa rang byung rdo rje
Gyayon Dak	rGya yon bdag
Jamgon Lodro Tayay	'Jam mgon blo gros mtha' yas
Je Daö Shonnu	rJe zla 'od gzhon nu
Jigme Lingpa	'Jigs med gling pa
Jigme Shab	'Jigs med zhabs
Jowo Je	Jo bo rje
Kadampa	bKa' gdams pa
Kagyu	bKa' brgyud
Kagyu Thubten Choling	bKa' brgyud thub bstan chos gling
Kangyur	bKa' 'gyur
Karma Chagmay	Karma chags med
Karma Gon	Karma dgon
Karma Kamtsang	Karma kam tshang
Karma Pakshi	Karma pakshi
Karma Tenpa'i Nyinchay Tsuglag Chokyi Nangwa	Karma bstan pa'i nyin byed gtsug lag chos kyi snang ba
Karma'i Khenpo, Rinchen Darjay	Karma'i mkhan po rin chen dar rgyas
Khenpo Sonam Rinpoche	mKhan po bsod nams rin po che
Khenpo Tsultrim Gyatso	mKhan po tsul khrims rgya mtsho
Kusalipa	Ku sa li pa
Kyeu Rinchen Gyin	Khye'u rin chen byin
Lama Norlha	Bla ma nor lha
Lama Yeshe Gyatso	Bla ma ye shes rgya mtsho
Lekshay Maway Nyima	Legs bshad smra ba'i nyi ma
Lhen Kye Dorje	lHan cig skyes pa'i rdo rje
Lodrö Rinchen	Blo gros rin chen
Lodrö Yangpay	Blo gros yang pas

Loten	Blo brtan
Mapampa	Ma pham pa
Marpa Chokyi Lodros	Mar pa chos kyi blo gros
Mendong Tshampa	sMan sdong mtshams pa
Mikyo Dorje	Mi bskyod rdo rje
Milarepa	Mi la ras pa
Nangdzay Zangpo	sNang mdzad bzang po
Nezurwa	sNe zur ba
Nyingpo Tenpa'i Tencho	sNying po bstan pa'i bstan bcos
Nyugrumpa	sNyug rum pa
Orgyen Trinley	O rgyan 'phrin las
Pa'o Dorje	dPa' bo rdo rje
Padampa Sanjay	Pha dam pa sangs rgyas
Pagdrol	'Phags grol
Pagmo Drupa	Phag mo gru pa
Palpung	dPal spung
Rab Ga	Rab dga'
Rabtu Shiwa'i Shaynyen	Rab tu zhi ba'i gshes gnyen
Rangjung Dorje	Rang byung rdo rje
Rangjung Gyalwa	Rang byung rgyal ba
Rangjung Shab	Rang byung zhabs
Rigpa'i Kuchugs	Rig pa'i khu byug
Riwoche Khenpo Sonam Topgyal	Ri bo che mkhan po bsod nams stobs rgyal
Sanjay Yeshe	Sangs rgyas ye shes
Satsha Kukye Karma Ngelek Tendzin	Sats tsha sku skye karma nges legs bstan 'dzin
Senge Zangpo	Seng ge bzang po
Serkya	bSer skya
Serkyamo	Ser skya mo
Serlingpa	gSer gling pa
Shamar	Zhva dmar
Shamar Chokyi Dondrup	Zhva dmar chos kyi don 'grub
Shawalingpa	Sha ba gling pa

Shawaripa	Sha ba ri pa
Shenrab Miwo	gShen rab mi bo
Sherjung Baypa	Sher 'byung sbas pa
Shiwa'i Lodro	Zhi ba'i blo gros
Shiwatso	Zhi ba 'tsho
Situ Tenpa'i Nyinchay	Si tu bstan pa'i nyin byed
Tai Situpa	Ta'i si tu pa
Tangyur	bsTan 'gyur
Tenpa Tsering	bsTan pa tshe ring
Thubten Chokorling	Thub bstan chos 'khor gling
Togme	Thogs med
Tsundrol	bTsun grol
Tsurphu	mTshur phu
Tupa'i Wangpo	Thub pa'i dbang po
Wangchuk	dBang phyug
Wangpo'i Lo	dBang po'i blo
Yeshay Namshay Chaypa	Ye shes rnam shes 'byed pa
Yidam	Yi dam
Yignyen	dByig gnyen
Yung Drung Bon	gYung drung bon

Biblography of Works Cited

All references are to the Peking Edition (P) of the Kangyur and Tangyur, unless noted as (N) for the Narthang edition or (L) for the Lhasa edition. Text numbers and volume numbers refer to the standard redaction of the Peking Edition:

The Tibetan Tripitaka, Peking Edition. Tokyo-Kyoto: Tibetan Tripitaka Research Institute, 1957.

For other Tibetan works, (DNZ) refers to the collection by Jamgon Lodrö Tayay of teachings from all the major and minor dharma lineages of Tibet:

Treasury of Formal Instructions (gDams ngag mdzod). Delhi: 1971.

(R) refers to folio editions printed at Rumtek Monastery in Sikkim, India.

The words *Ārya* (Tib. *'Phags pa*) and *Mahāyāna* (Tib. *Theg chen*) have been deleted from the Sanskrit and Tibetan titles of sūtras.

"Kālacakra"
Parama-ādibuddhoddhrita-śri-kālacakra-tantrarāja
mChog gi dang po'i sangs rgyas las phyung ba rgyud kyi rgyal po spal dus kyi 'khor lo
P4, Vol. 1

"Guhyasamāja"
Sarvatathāgata-kāya-vāk-citta-rahasyo guhyasmāja-mahākalparāja
De bzhin gshegs pa thams cad kyi sku gsung thugs kyi gsang chen gsang ba 'dus pa brtag pa'i rgyal po chen po
P81, Vol. 3

"Abhidharma Treasury"
Abhidharma-koṣa-kārikā
Chos mngon pa'i mdzod kyi tshig le'ur byas pa
by Vasubandhu (dByig gnyen)
P5590, Vol. 115

"Abode of Mañjuśri"
Mañjuśri-vihāra-sūtra
'Jam dpal gnas pa'i mdo
P863, Vol. 34

"Abridged Vehicle"
Mahāyāna-saṃgraha
Theg pa chen po bsdus pa
by Asaṅga (Thogs med)
P5549, Vol. 112

"Absorption Gathering All Merit"
Sarvapuñya-samuccaya-samādhi-sūtra
bSod nams thams cad bsdus pa'i ting nge 'dzin mdo
P802, Vol. 32

"Absorptions of Four Youths"
Caturdāraka-samādhi-sūtra
Khye'u bzhi'i ting nge 'dzin mdo
P804, Vol. 32

"Accomplishment of Wisdom"
Jñāna-siddhi-sādhanopāyikā
Ye shes grub pa'i sgrub thabs
by Indrabhūti
P3063, Vol. 68

"Arrangement of Precious Ones"
Mahāratnakūṭa-dharmaparyāya-śatasāhasrika-grantha
dKon mchog brtsegs pa chen po'i chos kyi rnam grangs le'u stong phrag brgya pa
P760, Vol. 22

"Aspiration Prayer for Excellent Conduct"
Bhadracaryā-praṇidhāna-rāja
bZang po spyod pa'i smon lam gyi rgyal po
P716, Vol. 11

"Authoritative Commentary on 'Distinguishing the Two Truths'"
Satyadvaya-vibhaṅga-pañjikā
bDen pa gnyis rnam par 'byed pa'i dka' 'grel
by Śāntirakita (Zhi ba 'tsho)
P5283, Vol. 100

"Authoritative Commentary on 'Embarking on the Conduct'"
Bodhi-caryāvatāra-pañjikā
Byang chub kyi spyod pa la 'jug pa'i dka' 'grel
by Prajñākaramati (Shes rab 'byung gnas blo gros)
P5273, Vol. 100

"Autocommentary on 'Profound Inner Meaning'"
Zab mo nang don rang 'grel
(R)

"Binding the Network of Dākinis"
Śrī-ḍākinī-saṃbara-tantrarāja
dPal mkha' 'gro ma'i sdom pa'i rgyud kyi rgyal po
P51, Vol. 3

"Certain Liberation of Mind"
Saṃdhi-nirmocana-sūtra
dGongs pa nges par 'grol pa'i mdo
P774, Vol. 29

"Clarifying the Meaning of the Words of 'Ubiquitous Conduct of Yoginīs'"
[Yoginī-saṃcārya-nibandha-padārtha-prakāśa]
rNal 'byor ma kun tu spyod ma'i bshad sbyar tshig don rab tu gsal ba
by Vīravajra (dPa' bo rdo rje)
P2140, Vol. 51

"Close Attention Through Mindfulness"
Saddharmānusmṛty-upasthāna
Dam pa'i chos dran pa nye bar gzhag pa
P953, Vol. 37

"Commentary on 'Entrance to Mantra'"
Mantrāvatāra-vṛtti
gSang sngags la 'jug pa'i 'grel pa
by Jñānakara
P4542, Vol. 81

"Commentary on Bodhicitta"
Bodhicitta-vivaraṇa
Byang chub sems kyi 'grel pa
by Nāgārjuna (Klu sgrub)
P2666, Vol. 61

"Commentary on the Intention of the Five Stages"
Pañcakrama-mata-ṭīkā-candraprabhā
Rim pa lnga'i dgongs 'grel zla ba'i 'od zer
by Abhayākaragupta ('Jigs med 'byung gnas sbas pa)
P2700, Vol. 62

"Compendium of Abhidharma"
Abhidharma-samuccaya
Chos mngon pa kun las btus pa
by Asaṅga (Thogs med)
P5550, Vol. 112

"Complete Commentary on Validity"
Pramāṇa-vārttika-kārikā
Tshad ma rnam 'grel gyi tshig le'ur byas pa
by Dharmakīrti (Chos kyi grags pa)
P5709, Vol. 130

"Concise Versified Prajñāpāramitā"
Prajñāpāramitā-sañcaya-gāthā
Shes rab kyi pha rol tu phyin pa sdud pa tshigs su bcad pa
P735, Vol. 21

"Connate Accomplishment"
Śrī-sahaja-siddhi
dPal lhan cig skyes pa grub pa
by Dombi Heruka
P3067, Vol. 68

"Densely Arrayed Ornaments"
Ghanavyūha-sūtra
rGyan stug po bkod pa'i mdo
P778, Vol. 29

"Departed for Laṅka"
Laṅkāvatāra-sūtra
Lang kar gshegs pa'i mdo
P775, Vol. 29

"Dhāraṇi for Entering into Nonconceptuality"
Avikalpa-praveśa-dhāraṇi
rNam par mi rtog par 'jug pa'i gzungs
P810, Vol. 32

"Distinguishing the Two Truths"
Satyadvaya-vibhaṅga-kārikā
bDen pa gnyis rnam par 'byed pa'i tshig le'ur byas pa
(L) 3881

"Distinguishing the Center from the Extremes"
Madhyānta-vighaṅga
dBus dang mtha' rnam par 'byed pa
by Maitreyanātha (Byams pa mgon po)
P5522, Vol. 108

"Drop of Liberation"
Mukti-tilaka
Grol ba'i thig le
by Buddhaśrijñānapāda (Sangs rgyas dpal ye shes zhabs)
P2722, Vol. 65

"Eight-Thousand-Verse Prajñāpāramitā"
Aṣṭasāhasrikā-prajñāpāramitā
Shes rab kyi pha rol tu phyin pa brgyad stong pa
P734, Vol. 21

"Embarking on the Central Course"
Madhyamakāvatāra-kārikā
dBu ma la 'jug pa'i tshig le'ur byas pa
by Candrakīrti (Zla ba grags pa)
P5261, Vol. 98

"Embarking on the Course of Bodhisattva Conduct"
Bodhisattva-caryāvatāra
Byang chubs sems pa'i spyod la 'jugs pa
by Śāntideva (Zhi ba'i lha)
P5272, Vol. 99

"Entrance to Mantra"
Mantrāvatāra
gSang sngags la 'jug pa
by Jñānākara
P4541, Vol. 81

"Entry to the Two Truths"
Satyadvayāvatāra
bDen pa gnyis la 'jug pa
by Śrī Dīpaṃkarajñāna (dPal Mar me mdzad ye shes)
P5298, Vol. 101; P5380, Vol. 103; L4467, L3902

"Excellent Qualities"
Bhadrakarātri-sūtra
mTshan mo bzang po'i mdo
P979, Vol. 39

"Excerpts from Validity"
Pramāña-samuccaya
Tshad ma kun las btus pa
by Dignāga (Phyogs kyi glang po)
P5700, Vol. 130

"Explanation of 'The One of Thirty'"
Triṃśikā-bhāṣya
Sum cu pa'i bshad pa
by Sthiramati (Blo brtan)
P5565, Vol. 113

"Expounded by Lodrö Mizaypa"
Akṣayamati-nirdeśa-sūtra
Blo gros mi zad pas bstan pa'i mdo
P842, Vol. 34

"Expounded by the Renowned, Noble Drima Maypa"
Vimalkīrti-nirdeśa-sūtra
Dri ma med par grags pas bstan pa'i mdo
P843, Vol. 34

"Four Mudrā Stages"
[Catur-mudrā-krama]
Phyag rgya bzhi rim
by Vīravajra (dPa' bo rdo rje)

"Great Acclaim"
Mahābherī-hāraka-parivarta-sūtra
rNga bo che chen po'i le'u mdo
P888, Vol. 35

"Guidance Manual on Connate Conjunction"
lHan cig skyes 'byor 'khrid yig
DNZ, Vol. 6, p. 1

"Hevajra"
He-vajra-tantrarāja-nāma
Kye'i rdo rje zhes bya ba rgyud kyi rgyal po
P10, Vol. 1

"Higher Continuum"
Mahāyānottaratantra-śāstra
Theg pa chen po'i rgyud bla ma'i bstan bcos
by Maitreyanātha (Byams pa mgon po)
P5525, Vol. 108

"Indication of Emptiness"
Śūnyatā-nāma-mahāsūtra
mDo chen po stong pa nyid ces bya ba
P956, Vol. 38

"Jewelry Case"
Ratnakaraṇḍa-sūtra
dKon mchog gi za ma tog pa'i mdo
P785, Vol. 30

"King of Absorptions"
Sarvadharma-svabhāva-samatā-vipañcita-samādhirāja-sūtra
Chos thams cad kyi rang bzhin mnyam pa nyid rnam par spros pa ting nge 'dzin gyi rgyal po'i mdo
P795, Vol. 31

"Lamp for the Path of Awakening"
Bodhipatha-pradīpa
Byang chub lam gyi sgron ma
by Śrī Dīpaṃkarajñāna (dPal Mar me mdzad ye shes)
P5343, Vol. 103

"Lengthy Commentary on 'The Tenth Tattva'"
Tattva-daśaka-ṭīkā
De kho na nyid bcu pa'i rgya cher 'grel pa
by Sahajavajra (lHan cig skyes pa'i rdo rje)
P3099, Vol. 68

"Letter of Friendly Advice"
Suhṛllekha
bShes pa'i phrin yig
by Nāgārjuna (Klu sgrub)
P5682, Vol. 129

"Lotus-Laden Authoritative Commentary"
Padmani-nāma-pañjikā
Padma can zhes bya ba'i dka' 'grel
P2067, Vol. 47

"Mahāmudrā Drop"
Śrī-mahāmudrā-tilakaṃ-nāma-yoginī-tantrarāja-adhipati
dPal phyag rgya chen po'i thig le zhes bya ba rnal 'byor ma chen mo'i rgyud kyi rgyal po'i mnga' bdag
P12, Vol. 1

"Manifest Awakening of Vairocana"
Mahāvairocanābhisaṃbodhi-vikurvatī-adhiṣṭhāna-vaipulya-sūtra-indrarājā-nāma-dharmaparyāya
rNam par snang mdzad chen po mngon par rdzogs par byang chub pa rnam par sprul ba byin gyis rlob pa shin tu rgyas pa mdo sde'i dbang po rgyal po zhes bya ba'i chos kyi rnam grangs
P126, Vol. 5

"Mother of Victors"
Eka-akṣarī mātā-nāma-sarvatathāgata-prajñāpāramitā
De bzhin gshegs pa thams cad kyi yum shes rab kyi pha rol tu phyin pa yi ge gcig ma zhes bya ba
P741, Vol. 21

"One Hundred Essences Creating Understanding"
Pratipattisāra-śataka
Go bar byed pa snying po brgya pa
by Āryadeva ('Phags pa lha)
P4695, Vol. 82

"Oral Instructions of the Succession of Lineage Masters"
Guru-parampara-kramopadeśa
Bla ma brgyud pa'i rim pa'i man ngag
by Vajrapāṇi (Phyag na rdo rje)
P4539, Vol. 81

"Oral Instructions on Glorious Kālacakra"
Kālacakropadeśa
Dus kyi 'khor lo'i man ngag
by Kālacakramahāpāda (Dus 'khor zhabs chen po)
P2082, Vol. 47

"Oral Instructions on the Six Branches of Application"
[Ārya-kālacakrapāda-sampradāya-nāma-ṣaḍaṅgayogopadeśa]
sByor ba yan lag drug gi man ngag rje dus 'khor zhabs kyis mdzad pa'i snyan rgyud shal gyi gdams pa
by Ārya Kālacakrapāda (rJe Dus 'khor zhabs)
P2088, Vol. 47

"Origin of Saṃvara"
Śrī-mahāsaṃvarodaya-tantrarāja
dPal bde mchog 'byung ba zhes bya ba'i rgyud kyi rgyal po chen po
P20, Vol. 2

"Ornament for Clear Realization"
Abhisamayālaṃkāra-nāma-prajñāpāramitopadeśa-śāstra-vṛtti-durbodhāloka-nāma-ṭīkā
Shes rab kyi pha rol tu phyin pa'i man ngag gi bstan bcos mngon par rtogs pa'i rgyan ces bya ba'i 'grel pa rtogs par dka' ba'i snang ba shes bya ba'i 'grel bshad
by Dharmakīrtiśrī (Chos kyi grags dpal)
P5192, Vol. 91

"Ornament for the Central Course"
Madhyamakālaṃkāra-kārikā
dBu ma'i rgyan gyi tshig le'ur byas pa
by Śāntirakṣita (Zhi ba 'tsho)
P5284, Vol. 101

"Ornament for the Sūtras"
Mahāyāna-sūtrālaṃkāra-kārikā
Theg pa chen po'i mdo sde'i rgyan gyi tshig le'ur byas pa
by Maitreyanātha (Byams pa mgon po)
P5521, Vol. 108

"Ornament for the Thought of the Muni"
Muni-matālaṃkāra
Thub pa'i dgongs pa'i rgyan
by Abhayākaraguptapāda ('Jigs med 'byung gnas sbas pa'i zhabs)
P5299, Vol. 101

"Perfect Declaration of the Names of Mañjuśrī"
Mañjuśrī-jñānasattvasya-paramārtha-nāmasaṃgīti
'Jam dpal ye shes sems dpa'i don dam pa'i mtshan yang dag par brjod pa
P2, Vol. 1

"Praise to the Dharmadhātu"
Dharmadhātu-stotra
Chos kyi dbyings su bstod pa
by Nāgārjuna (Klu sgrub)
P2010, Vol. 46

"Precious Garland"
Rāja-parikathā-ratnāvali
rGyal po la gtam bya ba rin po che'i phreng ba
by Nāgārjuna (Klu sgrub)
P5658, Vol. 129

"Precious Sky"
Nam mkha' rinpoche'i mdo

"Principal Exposition of the Central Course"
Prajñā-nāma-mūlamadhyamaka-kārikā
dBu ma tsa ba'i tshig le'ur byas pa shes rab ces bya ba
by Nāgārjuna (Klu sgrub)
P5224, Vol. 95

"Proceeding to 'Just That Alone'"
Tattvāvatārākhya-sakala-sugata-vacas-tātparya-vyākhyā-prakaraṇa
De kho na nyid la 'jug pa zhes bya ba bde bar gshegs pa'i bka' ma lus pa mdor bsdus te bshad pa'i rab tu byed pa
by Śrī Jñānakīrti (dPal ye shes grags pa)
P4532, Vol. 81

"Profound Inner Meaning"
Zab mo nang don
(R)

"Requested by Gyatso, King of Nāgas"
Sāgaranāgarāja-paripṛcchā-sūtra
Klu'i rgyal po rgya mtshos zhus pa'i mdo
P820, Vol. 33

"Requested by Lodrö Gyatso"
Sāgaramati-paripṛcchā-sūtra
Blo gros rgya mtshos zhus pa'i mdo
P819, Vol. 33

"Requested by Madröpa"
Anavataptanāgarāja-paripṛcchā-sūtra
Klu'i rgyal po ma dros pas zhus pa'i mdo
P823, Vol. 33

"Requested by Noble Shiwa Lodrö"
'Phags pa zhi ba blo gros kyis 'dri pa

"Requested by Ösung"
Kāśyapa-parivarta-sūtra
'Od srung gi le'u mdo
P760.43, Vol. 24

"Saṃvara"
Śrī-cakrasaṃbaraguhya-acinta-tantrarāja
dPal 'khor lo sdom pa'i gsang ba bsam gyis mi khyab pa'i rgyud kyi rgyal po
P30, Vol. 3

"Secret Charnel Ground"
gSang ba dur khrod

"Segments of Oral Instruction"
Upadeśa-mañjari-nāma-sarvatantrotpannopapanna-sāmānya-bhāṣya
Man ngag gi snye ma zhes bya ba rgyud thams cad kyi skyed rdzogs thun mong du bstan pa
by Śrī Abhayākaraguptapāda ('Jigs med 'byung gnas sbas pa'i zhabs)
P5024, Vol. 87

"Sequence of Lives"
Jātaka-nidāna
sKyes pa rabs kyi gleng gzhi
P748, Vol. 21

"Sequence of Lives"
Jātaka-mālā
sKyes pa'i rabs kyi rgyud
by Āryaśūra ('Phags pa dpa' bo)
P5650, Vol. 128

"Seven-Hundred-Verse Prajñāpāramitā"
Saptaśatika-nāma-prajñāpāramitā-sūtra
Shes rab kyi pha rol tu phyin pa bdun brgya pa'i mdo
P737, Vol. 2

"Sky Treasury"
Gaganagañja-paripṛcchā-sūtra
Nam mkha'i mdzod kyis zhus pa'i mdo
P815, Vol. 33

"Stages of Meditation"
Bhāvana-krama
sGom pa'i rim pa
by Kamalaśīla
P5310, Vol. 102

"Stainless Light: The Great Kālacakra Commentary"
Vimalaprabhā-nāma-mūlatantrānusāriṇī-dvādaśasāhasrikā-laghukālacakra-tantrarāja-ṭikā
bsDus pa'i rgyud kyi rgyal po dus kyi 'khor lo'i 'grel bshad rtsa ba'i rgyud kyi rjes su 'jug pa stong phrag bcu gnyis pa dri ma med pa'i 'od ces bya ba
P2064, Vol. 109

"Summary of Words on Mahāmudrā"
Phyag chen tshig bsdus
DNZ, Vol. 5, p.47

"Sūtra of the Tenth Level"
Buddhāvataṃsaka-nāma-mahāvaipulya-sūtra—Daśabhūmika
Sangs rgyas phal po che zhes bya ba shin tu rgyas pa chen po'i mdo—Sa bcu pa
P761.31, Vol. 25

"Teaching the Conduct of Bodhisattvas"
Bodhisattva-carya-nirdeśa-sūtra
Byang chub sems dpa'i spyod pa bstan pa'i mdo
P851, Vol. 34

"Ten Dharmas"
Daśadharmaka-sūtra
Chos bcu pa'i mdo
P760.9, Vol. 22

"The Common Group"
Buddhāvatasaṃka-nāma-mahāvaipulya-sūtra
Sangs rgyas phal po che zhes bya ba shin tu rgyas pa chen po'i mdo
P761, Vol. 25

"The One of Thirty"
Triṃśikā-kārikā
Sum cu pa'i tshig le'ur byas pa
by Vasubandhu (dByig gnyen)
P5556, Vol. 113

"The Tenth Tattva"
Tattvadaśaka
De kho na nyid bcu pa
by Advayavajra [Maitrīpa] (gNyis su med pa'i rdo rje)
P3080, Vol. 68; DNZ, Vol. 5, p. 62

"Training"
Vinaya-vastu
'Dul ba gzhi
P1030, Vol. 41

"Twenty Pledges"
Saṃvara-viṃśaka-vṛtti
sDom pa nyi shu pa'i 'grel pa
by Śāntirakṣita (Zhi ba 'tsho)
P5583, Vol. 114

"Two Examinations"
He-vajra-tantrarāja
Kye'i rdo rje zhes bya ba rgyud kyi rgyal po
P10, Vol. 1

"Ubiquitous Conduct of Yoginis"
Yoginīsañcārya
rNal 'byor ma'i kun tu spyod pa
P23, Vol. 2

"Vajra Canopy"
Ḍākinī-vajrapañjara-mahātantrarāja-kalpa-nāma
mKha' 'gro ma rdo rje gur zhes bya ba'i rgyud kyi rgyal po chen po'i brtag pa
P11, Vol. 1

"Vajra Heart Commentary"
Vajrapadagarbha-saṃgraha-nāma-pañjikā
rDo rje tshig gi snying po bsdus pa zhes bya ba'i dka' 'grel
by Kaśmir Mahāpaṇḍita Śitakyaśrita
P2107, Vol. 48; L2515

"Vajra Pinnacle"
Vajra-śikhara-mahā-guhya-yoga-tantra
gSang ba rnal 'byor chen po'i rgyud rdo rje rtse mo
P113, Vol. 5

"Vajra Rosary"
Śrī-vajramāla-abhidhāna-mahāyogatantra-sarvatantrahṛdaya-rahasya-vibhaṅga-iti
rNal 'byor chen po'i rgyud dpal rdo rje phreng ba mngon par brjod pa rgyud thams cad kyi snying po gsang ba rnam par phye ba zhes bya ba
P82, Vol. 3

"Whence Fearlessness"
Mūlamadhyamaka-vṛtti-akutobhāya
dBu ma rtsa ba'i 'grel pa ga las 'jigs med
by Nāgārjuna (Klu sgrub)
P5229, Vol. 95

THE TIBETAN TEXT
of
Teachings of the Supreme Siddhas

by The Eighth Situpa Tenpa'i Nyinchay

1

༄། །ངེས་དོན་ཕྱག་རྒྱ་ཆེན་པོའི་སྨོན་ལམ་གྱི་འགྲེལ་པ་གྲུབ་པ་མཆོག་གི་ཞལ་ལུང་ཞེས་བྱ་བ་བཞུགས་སོ།།

2

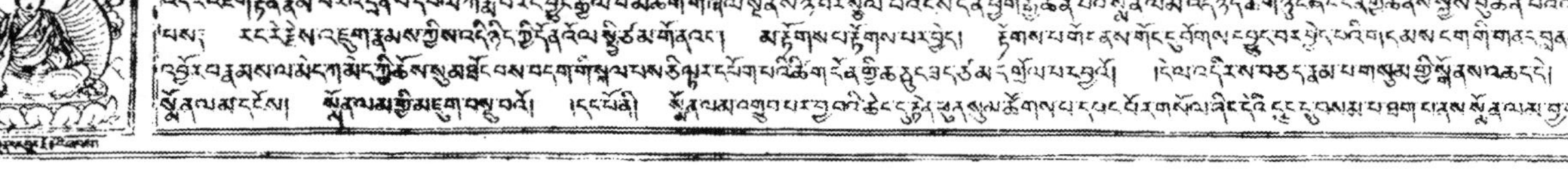

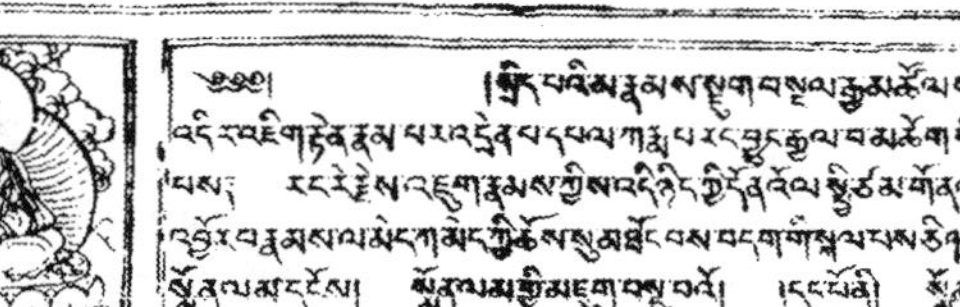

3

4

5

[illegible]
[illegible]
[illegible]
[illegible]
[illegible]
[illegible]
[illegible]

6

[illegible]
[illegible]
[illegible]
[illegible]
[illegible]
[illegible]

7

[illegible]
[illegible]
[illegible]
[illegible]
[illegible]
[illegible]
[illegible]

8

[illegible]
[illegible]
[illegible]
[illegible]
[illegible]
[illegible]
[illegible]

9

[illegible]

10

[illegible]

11

[illegible]

12

[illegible]

13 [illegible]

14 [illegible]

15 [illegible]

16 [illegible]

7 [illegible]

18 [illegible]

[illegible]

20 [illegible]

21 [illegible]

22 [illegible]

23 [illegible]

24 [illegible]

25

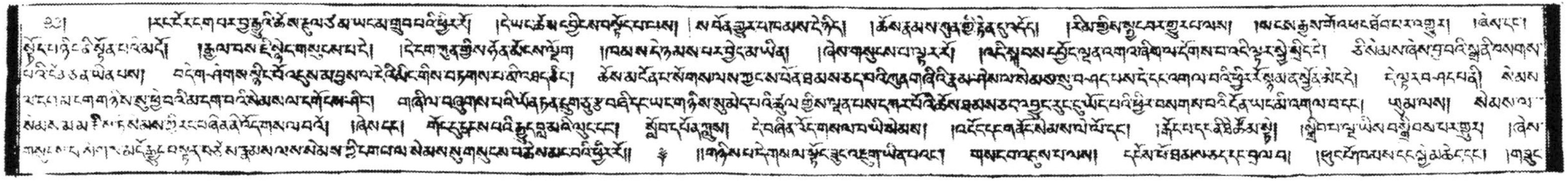

༄༅། །ངང་ངོ་རང་དག་པར་བྱ་རྒྱུ་རི་ཆེ་ས་རྡུལ་ཙམ་ཡང་མ་གྲུབ་པའི་ཕྱིར་རོ། །དེ་ཡང་ཆོས་ཉིད་ལས་བརྗོད་པ་ལས། །ས་བོན་ལྷུར་པ་ཁམས་དེ་ཉིད། །ཆོས་རྣམས་ཀུན་གྱི་རྟེན་དུ་འདོད། །རིམ་གྱིས་སྦྱང་བར་བྱ་བ་ལས། །སངས་རྒྱས་གོ་འཕང་ཐོབ་པར་འགྱུར། །ཞེས་དང་།
སྙིང་པོ་ཉིད་ནི་སྟོན་པ་འི་མདོ། །རྒྱལ་བས་རྡོ་རྗེ་གསུངས་པ་དེ། །དེ་དག་ཀུན་གྱིས་ཉོན་མོངས་སྐྱེ། །ཁམས་ནི་དེ་ཉམས་པར་བྱེད་མ་ཡིན། །ཞེས་གསུངས་པ་ལྟ་རོ། །འདི་སྐབས་རྟོགས་ལྡན་འབྲང་གཞི་ཡ་དག་ས་བ་འདི་ལྟར་སྒྲུབ་སྟེ། ཅི་སེམས་མ་ཞེས་བྱ་བའི་སྙིང་པོ་ལས་གསུངས་
པའི་དོན་ཅན་ཡིན་པས། བདག་ཞེས་གསུང་རབ་ལྟར་རྒྱུ་མཐུན་པ་དེའི་ཚིག་གིས་བཏགས་པ་ཞིག་ཡིན་ནོ། ཆོས་མ་དོན་པ་སོགས་ལས་བྱུང་བ་ཡོན་ཏན་ཐམས་ཅད་པའི་ཞུགས་གཞི་འདི་རྣམས་ཤེས་ལ་སེམས་ཀྱི་བ་ཤད་པས་དེ་དང་འགལ་བའི་ཕྱིར་རོ་སྐུ་མ་ནུས་སྤྱོད་མེད་དེ། དེ་ལྟར་བ་ཤད་པ་ནི། སེམས
རང་ལ་ངག་གཉིས་སུ་བྱེ་བ་འི་མ་དག་པ་འི་སེམས་ལ་དགོས་མེད། གཞིས་བཞུགས་པ་འི་ཡོན་ཏན་རྣམ་རྒྱུ་བཞི་དང་ཡང་དག་ཉིད་སུ་མེད་པ་འི་རྩལ་གྱིས་སྣང་བ་དག་པ་འི་ཚོས་རྣམ་ཅད་ལ་ཁྱབ་རུང་དུ་ཡོད་པ་འི་ཕྱིར་བས་ཁམས་པ་འི་དོན་ཡང་མི་འགལ་བ་དང་། ཕྱག་ལས། སེམས་ལ
སེམས་མ་མེད་ཀྱང་སེམས་ཀྱི་རང་བཞིན་འོད་གསལ་བ་འོ། །ཞེས་དང་། གཞི་དོན་རྣམ་པ་འི་ཆུ་ཀླུ་མི་ཞུང་དང་། ཤྭེ་ཏ་དབོན་ཀླུས། དེ་བཞིན་འོད་གསལ་བ་ཡི་སེམས། །འདོད་ཆགས་ཞེ་སྡང་མ་ཡོད་ཅིང་། །རྣོ་བ་དང་ནི་ཚིག་མི་སྐྱེ། །སྐྱིང་བ་ལྷ་ཡིས་བསྒྲིབས་པར་གྱུར། །ཞེས
གསུངས་པ་དང་། མེ་ལོང་ཉི་དང་སེམས་རང་བཞིན་ནི་འོད་གསལ་བར་བཏགས་པ་ཙམ་ལས་སེམས་ཀྱི་སྐབས་སུ་ཡང་ལྡན་འགྱུར་བའི་ཕྱིར་རོ། ༈ །གཉིས་པ་དེ་ཉིད་ལ་སྟོང་ཉིད་འབྲས་ཡིན་པ་དང་། གསང་བ་འབྲུལ་པ་ལས། དངོས་པོ་ཐམས་ཅད་རང་བཞིན་པ། །ཁྱད་པར་བ་དང་སྐྱེ་མཆེད་དང་། །གཟུང

26

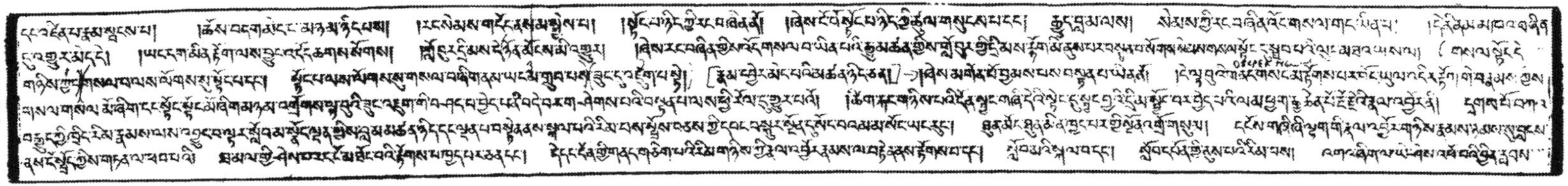

དང་འཛིན་པ་རྣམ་སྤངས་པ། །ཆོས་བདག་མེད་དང་མཉམ་ཉིད་པས། །རང་སེམས་གདོད་ནས་མ་སྐྱེས་པ། །སྟོང་པ་ཉིད་ཀྱི་རང་བཞིན་ནོ། །ཞེས་དོན་ལ་སྟོང་པ་ཉིད་ཀྱི་ཚུལ་གསུངས་པ་དང་། ཀྱེ་རྡོ་རྗེ་ལས། སེམས་ཀྱི་རང་བཞིན་འོད་གསལ་བ་གང་ཡིན་པ། །དེ་ནི་མ་ཁ་ལྟ་བུ་ཞིན
དུ་འགྱུར་མེད་དེ། །ཡང་དག་ཀུན་རྟོག་ལས་བྱུང་འདོད་ཆགས་སོགས། །གློ་བུར་དྲི་མས་དེ་ཉིད་མ་སོས་མི་འགྱུར། །ཞེས་རང་བཞིན་གྱིས་འོད་གསལ་བ་ཡིན་པར་རྒྱུ་མཚན་གྱིས་གློ་བུར་གྱི་དྲི་མས་དག་མི་ནུས་པར་འདུས་པ་སོགས་ལ་ཡང་སེམས་ལ་སྨོང་དམིགས་པ་འི་ལྟ་མཐའ་ལ་སོགས། (གསལ་སྟོང་དེ
གཉིས་ཀྱི་གནས་ལུགས་ལ་ལོངས་སུ་སྤྱོད་པ་དང་། སྟོང་པ་ལས་ལོགས་སུ་གསལ་བ་ཞིག་ནམ་ཡང་མ་གྲུབ་པས་ཟུང་དུ་འཇུག་པ་སྟེ། [རྣམ་པར་མི་རྟོག་པ་འི་མཚན་ཉིད་ཅན།] ཞེས་མགོན་པོ་ཀླུ་ལས་པ་ལ་བསྟན་པ་ཡིན་ནོ། །དེ་ལྟ་བུ་འི་ཀུན་གཞི་མ་རྟོགས་པར་བཅོས་ཡུལ་འདི་རྟོག་གི་ཐ་སྙད་ཐམས་ཅད་ཀྱིས
གསལ་བ་གསལ་མ་ཞིག་དང་སྟོང་སྟོང་མ་ཞིག་མ་ཉམ་འགྲོ་ཀུན་ལྷ་སྣུ་རྟེན་འབྲུགས་བའི་ཁ་ཤད་པ་ཕྱེད་པ་འི་བདེ་བ་རྣམ་ཞིགས་པ་འི་ཕུང་པ་ལ་རྗེ་རོལ་དུ་གྱུར་པ་འོ། །ཚིག་རྣམ་གཉིས་པ་འི་དོན་སྒྲུང་གཞི་དེ་འི་ལྷུང་དུ་སྒྲུང་གི་འི་དྲི་མ་སྤོང་བར་བྱེད་པ་འི་ལམ་ཕྱག་རྒྱ་ཆེན་པོ་རྡོ་རྗེ་འི་རྣལ་འབྱོར་ནོ། །དགག་པ་ལ་ཡར
བརྒྱུད་ཀྱི་གྲིང་རིམ་རྣམ་པ་ལས་འབྱུང་བ་ལྟར་སྤྲུལ་མ་སྟོང་ལྡན་གྱིས་རྣམ་མཚན་ཉིད་དང་ལྡན་པ་བསྟན་ནས་སྐལ་བ་འི་རིམ་པ་སྒྲུབ་ཚད་ཀྱི་དབང་བསྐུར་སྟོན་དུ་སོང་བ་བཞམ་མཐོང་ཡང་རུང་། ཐུན་མོང་སྦྱུ་ཚོགས་བྱུང་བ་ཀྱི་སྒྲོན་འགྲོ་ཀ་ལུ་པ། དངོས་གཞི་ཕྱག་གི་རྣལ་འབྱོར་གཉིས་རྣམ་པ་རྣམ་སྤྲུལ
བྱས་དགོས་ཀྱིས་གཏན་ལ་ཕབ་པ་འི། ཐམས་ཅད་ཤེས་པ་རང་དུས་མཐོང་བ་འི་རྟོགས་པ་བྱུང་པ་ར་ཅན་དང་། དེ་དང་དོན་གྱི་གནད་གཅིག་པ་འི་རིམ་གཉིས་ཀྱི་རྣལ་འབྱོར་རྣམས་ལ་བརྟེན་ནས་རྟོགས་པ་དང་། ལྷུག་མ་འི་སྤྱ་ལ་བ་དང་། སྤྱོད་པ་འི་ཆེ་རྣམ་པ་འི་རིམ་པས། འཁོར་ཞིག་ལ་ཡེ་ཤེས་འབབ་པ་འི་ཕྱིར་རྣམས

27

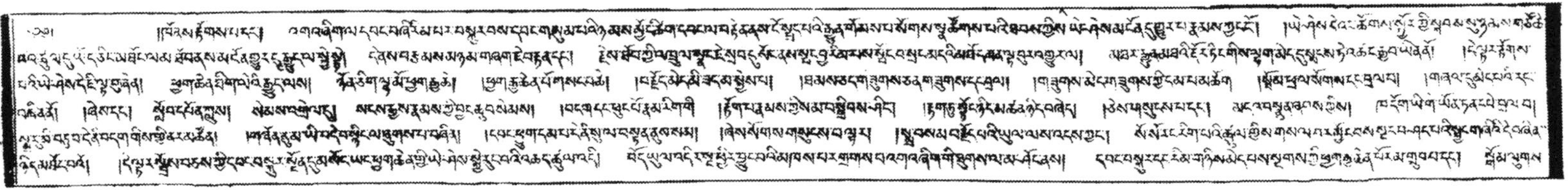

༄༅། །ཡོན་མ་རྟོགས་པ་དང་། འཁག་བཞི་གས་དབང་པ་འཁོར་མ་པ་ར་བསྐུར་བས་དབང་གསུམ་པ་འི་མས་ཀྱི་ཅིག་དང་ལམ་བརྡེ་ཆེན་པོ་འི་སྤྲུང་བ་འི་རྒྱུ་ན་མ་པ་སོགས་སྤྱ་རྟོགས་པ་འི་ཐབས་ཀྱིས་ཡེ་ཤེས་མངོན་དུ་འགྱུར་པ་རྣམས་ཀྱི་ཞང་ངོ། །ཡེ་ཤེས་དེ་འང་ཚིག་སྐྱོར་ཀྱི་སྐབས་སུ་ཉེས་པ་གཅིག
བ་དེ་བུ་བདུ་པོ་དུ་ཅིང་མཐོང་ལམ་ཆོས་ཉན་མ་མཐོང་རྒྱུར་དུ་རྒྱུད་ལ་སྐྱེས་སྐྱེ། དེ་ནས་བརྗོམ་མེས་ཀུན་མཁའ་ཁྲབ་རྟེན་དང་། རྡོ་རྗེ་ཐེག་པ་ཀྱི་ལམ་རྒྱུ་སྐྱུང་དེ་ལྡང་རྡོ་རྗེ་བུམ་སྐྱུང་དུ་རིམ་པས་སྐྱོང་བསྐྱང་མང་འཇིགས་རྩ་མེད་ཀུན་བུ་རྒྱུ་ར་འགྱུར་བ། མཐར་རྒྱུ་མ་ཁའི་རྡོ་རྗེ་ཏིང་ངེ་འཛིན་མངོན་གྱི་ཐག་མེད་དུ་སྐྱུང་ངས་དེ་འི་ཚང་རྒྱུ་བ་ཡིན་ནོ། །དེ་ལྟར་རྟོགས
པ་འི་ཡེ་ཤེས་དེ་རྡོ་རྗེ་ལྟ་བུ་ཞེན། །ཕྱག་ཆེན་ཐིག་ལེ་ཡི་རྒྱུད་ལས། །རྣམ་རིག་སྣ་མི་ཕྱུག་རྒྱ་ཆེ། །ཕྱག་རྒྱ་ཆེན་པོ་ཀླས་ལམ་ཆེ། །བརྗོད་མེད་མི་ཟད་ངས་སྐྱེས་པ། །ཐམས་ཅད་དག་ཏུ་གཉུག་ཅན་ཀུན་གཉུག་དང་བྲལ་བ། །གཉུག་མ་མེད་པ་ཀྱུག་མ་སྤྱོད་མ་པ་མ་མཆོག །སྒྲིབ་པ་ལ་སོགས་དང་བྲལ་བ། །གཞན་འདུ་སྣ་མེད་པ་འི་རང
འཆིན་ནོ། །ཞེས་དང་། སྒྲོན་པ་ཡོན་བྱས། སེམས་པ་སྤྲོས་བུ། སངས་རྒྱས་རྣམས་ཀྱི་བྱང་ཆུབ་སེམས། །བདག་དང་ཕུང་པོ་རྣམས་མ་ལོག་གི། །རྟོག་པ་རྣམས་ཀྱིས་མ་བསྒྲིབས་ཞེན། །རྟག་ཏུ་སྟོང་ཉིད་མཚན་ཉིད་བཞེད། །ཅེས་ཕ་གསུངས་པ་དང་། མདང་བ་སྐྱེ་མ་ཁས་ཀྱིས། ཀ་དག་ཡེ་ནི་ཡོན་ཏན་ཀུན་བུ་ལྡན་པ།
སྣ་ཚོགས་སྡུ་བ་བདེ་ཆེན་དག་གིས་ཀྱི་ཅན་རང་ཚན། །མཐོན་རྣམ་ཡེ་ནི་བརྗོད་ལ་ལྷུན་གྱིས་གྲུབ་པ་བཞིན། །དང་ཐུག་དམ་པ་རང་ཉིད་ལ་བསྐྱེད་ཏུ་ལས་ཀྱིམ། །ཞེས་སོགས་གསུངས་པ་ལྟར། །སྣ་ཚོགས་མ་བརྗོད་པ་འི་ཡུལ་ལ་ལས་འདས་ཀྱང་། སོ་སོར་རང་རིག་པ་འི་ཚུལ་གྱིས་གསལ་ལ་ཀར་སྒྲུབ་ངས་སྟོང་པ་ཤད་པ་འི་ཡུལ་གཞི་དེ་ལ་ཞེ
ཉིད་མཐོང་བ་འོ། །དེ་ལྟར་སྣུང་བ་རྣམ་ཀྱི་དང་ང་བཞུ་ར་སྟོན་དུ་མཁའ་ལ་ཡང་ཕྱག་གཞི་ཅན་ཀྱི་ཡེ་ཤེས་སྐྱེ་རྟུང་བ་འི་འཆད་ཚུལ་ལ་ནི། བོད་ཡུལ་བ་དེ་རང་སྟོང་རྒྱུ་ངང་བ་འི་མ་བས་པ་ར་གྲགས་པ་བའགའ་ཞིག་གི་སྒྲུབ་སྐབས་ལ་མི་འདོད་ཅིང་། དབང་བསྐུར་དང་རིམ་གཉིས་མེད་པ་ས་ཕྱག་གས་ཀྱི་ཕྱག་རྒྱ་ཆེན་པོ་ར་མ་གྲུབ་པ་དང་། སྟོང་ལྡན་གས

28

ཤེས་རབ་ལྟ་བུ་ཡི་ལྷ་བཅས་མ་རྟོགས་པ་སྒྲིད་དུ་ཤར་ལྟ་བུ་འི་སྒྲོ་འདོགས་གི་རིམ་པ་སོགས་དབྱིངས་ཀྱི་གསུང་ལས་འབབ་ཤིང་དང་པ་ལྟར་མེད་པ་ས་དེ་ར་ཡང་ཐམས་ཅད་པ་ར་སོགས་སྐྱེན་དུ་ས་མཇུག་པ་ར་མཛད་དོ། །དེ་ལྟ་དུ་རྡོ་འཚམ་ལྷ་ག་དགས་ཀྱིས་གདང་ལུ་གུ་ཡི་མས་སྤྱོ་ཚོགས་པ་གང་ལ་བ་འི་ཕྱིར་འདུ་གྱིས་ཀྱི་ཤད་ཀ་ཐ་ཐ་བ་ལས་པ་ར་གཏུལ་ལ་ཤང
ཡུལ་ས་རྒྱུད་རྣམས་ཀྱིས་སོ་སོར་ཚ་རིགས་པ་ར་འ་ཀུན་ནས་བ་ཤད་པ་འི་ལུང་ལ་པ་རྒྱན་ནི་ར་བུ་གི་ཤེས་ཉིད་དེ་ཕྱོགས་པ་དེ་ཉི་གཞན་ཞིག་ཡིན་ནོ། །ས་རྒྱུ་པ་འདི་ལས་པ་ར་སྤྱང་འོང་། བཀའ་བརྒྱུད་མཆོག་གི་གྲུབ་ཐོབ་ལ་འདི་ར་རྒྱ་བ་ལས་ལྟ་མ་དེ་དག་ཡོད་པ་ས་ཡིན་ཏེ། ‖ ཀ་ཤམ་དུ་ར་ཚད་པ་ལྟ་ར་འབྲི་སྤྱོ་ལ་ཞང་དང་བ་རྣམས་པ་ལས
ཀ་ལ་ལ་བུ་ཆེན་དབང་རྗེན་ལ་སྐྱོང་བ་ཆས་ཀྱི་དབང་བསྐུར་མེད་མི་སྲུང་བ་འི་ལམ་ལ་གཏུ་ཐོབ་བཞེད་ཀྱང་། རྡོ་རྗེ་སྦྱིན་པ་ཚ་མ་ཕྱི་ཡི། རྡོ་རྗེ་ཡེ་ཤེས་ཀྱི་དབང་བསྐུར་ཅིན་ཅིག་ལ་བཟླས་པ་གཞིག་ནི་དེ་ལ་པ་ར་སྒོམ་དུ་རྒྱུད་དགོས་པ་འི་ཕྱིར་དང་། དེ་ལ་བརྟེན་པ་འི་ལམ་པ་གཉིས་ཀྱང་དགོས་དེ་ལ་རང་ང་ཡོད་པ་འི་ཕྱིར་རོ། །ཡང་འདི་ལ་ཁ
ཅིག་ཉིད་སྣང་བ་འབོ་ངང་འི་དང་བ་གིས། དང་གི་གོ་མི་ཆོད་པ་དང་། ལྷ་མི་ཉིན་ལ་བསྒྱུར་བསྒོམས་པས་རིམ་གཉིས་ཀྱི་གོ་མི་ཆོད་པ་ར་བཞེད་མོད། དེ་ལྟ་ན། རྟུལ་ཆེན་སོགས་ཀྱི་དཀྱིལ་འཁོར་དུ་དབང་བསྐུར་བ་ས་དེ་པ་ས་ཀྱང་དབང་གི་གོ་མི་ཆོད་པ་ར་འགྱུར་ཏེ། དབང་ཞེས་པ་དང་དོན་གྱི་རྟོགས་པ་རྒྱུད་ལ་བསྐྱེད་ནུས
ཤིག་དགོས་པ་གང་ཞིག །དེ་བསྐྱེད་པ་ལ་ལྷས་མེ་ཀྱི་དབང་ལ་ས་སྒོམ་པ་ཅན་ཀྱི་དབང་བཟུ་ས་པ་ང་མཇལ་བ་འི་ཕྱིར། ལྷ་འི་རྣལ་འབྱོར་བསྒོམས་པ་ས་ཀྱང་རིམ་གཉིས་ཀྱི་གོ་མི་ཆོད་པ་ར་འགྱུར་ཏེ། ལྷ་ག་ས་ཀྱི་སྣང་བ་འདི་ར་སྣམ་དང་ཡི་དམ་གཉིས་སུ་མེད་པ་ར་བསྒོམ་དགོས་ཤིང་ཡི་དམ་ལྷ་མ་ལ་རྒྱས་འདེབས་པ་གང་ཞིག
རྒྱས་འདེབས་པ་པོ་དང་བྱ་ལ་བཞིན་ངས་བུ་གུ་བདེ་བ་ས་ཀྱི་ལྷ་ཡེ་ནི་མས་མཆོག་བཞི་ཁང་ངོ་ས་ཀུན་སྤྱིན་པ་ས་མི་བྱེད་པ་འི་ཕྱིར་རོ། །དེ་ས་ན་ར་ལུགས་ཉིད་ང་བ་འདིར་ཐེན་ཀྱི་དབང་ངམ། རྡོ་རྗེ་ཡེ་ཤེས་ཀྱི་དབང་ངོ་ནི་དཀའ་རུ་ས་མ་ཆད་ཀྱི་མཆོག་ཏུ་གྱུར་པ་ཡིན་པ་ས་དབང་གི་གོ་ཆོད་པ་ལྟ་ཅི་སྨོས། རྟོགས་ལྡན་ཀྱི་རྣམ་ས་ཕྱག་རྒྱ་ཆེན་པོ་ཀླ་ལ་འཛིན

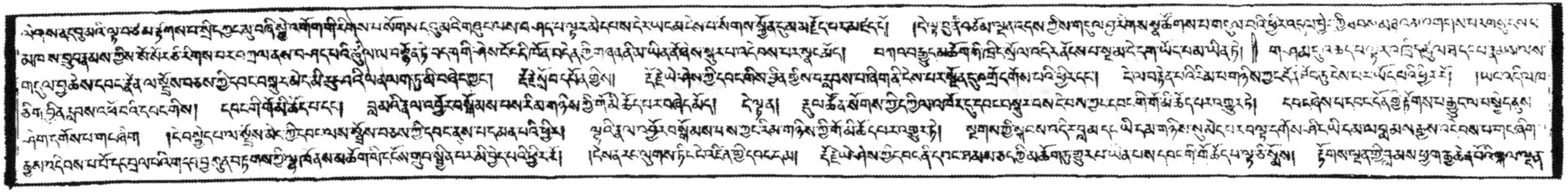

29

[illegible]

30

[illegible]

31

[illegible]

32

[illegible]

33

༄༅། །རང་རིག་བདག་ཏུ་བཟུང་བ། །གཉིས་འཛིན་དབང་གིས་སྲིད་པའི་གྲོང་དུ་འཁྱམས། །མ་རིག་འཁྲུལ་པའི་རྒྱུ་དང་རྐྱེན་དབང་ཞེ་ན། །ཅེས་གསུངས་ཏེ། འདི་ར་དངོས་བསྟན་རགས་པ་གཞོན་འཁོར་བའི་ཚོས་སེམས་ཀྱི་སྣང་བ་དུ་གནས་པ་ཡས་པས། ཕྱ་བ་ཏུ་ལ་ཁྱད་ཀྱི་ཚོས
སེམས་ཀྱི་ཕྲུག་དང་ཤུགས་ཀྱིས་གཞན་གོ་བ་ར་བཀོད་པའི་ཕྱིར་དངོས་སྟོབས་ཀྱི་དོན་ཉམས་ལས། དང་པོ་དངོས་བསྟན་པ། ཡུལ་ཡུལ་ཅན་གཉིས་སུ་འཁྲུལ་ཚུལ། དེས་འཁོར་བར་འཁོར་ཚུལ། འཁྲུལ་པ་དེ་ཞི་མཚང་...... རིགས་ཤེས་པར་སྟོན་པའི་རྩལ་གྱིས་གདམས་པའོ།། ༈ །།དང་
པོ་ནི། རྗེ་ཉིད་ཀྱི་ཟབ་མོ་རང་གི་དོན་ལས། །རྒྱུ་དེ་ཡང་ཉེ་སྨིག་མེད་པ། །རྒྱུ་ཆད་ཕྱོགས་སུ་ལྟུང་མ་ཆེས་ཀྱང་། །དེ་ཉིད་ནམ་འགགས་པའི་ཡུལ་པས། །དོ་བོ་སྟོང་པ་རང་བཞིན་གསལ་བ། །རྣམ་པ་འགག་མེད་ཅིར་ཡང་འཆར། །དེ་ཉིད་རང་རིག་རང་མ་རིག །འདུ་བྱེད་ཡིད་ཀྱི་ཡོ་བ་ནི། །འཁྲུ
ལ་སྣང་བ་ཡོས་པ་ལས། །དོན་དང་འཛིན་པ་གཉིས་སུ་སྣང་བ། །རང་གིས་རང་ལ་གདང་ཅི་ཡང་ཐུང་། །ཡིད་དེ་ཕྱིར་འཁྲུལ་སྣང་ཆགས་ལས། །ཡུལ་ལ་དོན་བཟུང་རྣམ་ཤེས་སྐྱེས། །བླང་དོར་སྐྱེད་ལས་ཚོར་བ་སྐྱེ། །དེ་ལ་མཚན་འཛིན་འདུ་ཤེས་ཏེ། །འདུ་བྱེད་ཡུལ་སྣང་གཞན་དུ་ཁྲུང་།
ང་བ་ལས་གཟུགས་ཀྱི་ཕུང་པོ་འགྲུབ། །ཅེས་གསུངས་ཤིང་། རང་བཞིན་རྒྱུ་ལ་དུ་རྣམ་པ་བཅས་བཅད་པར་ཀུན་སྣང་། །གཞི་རིག་རྣམ་གྲུབ་པ་ར་བཞིན་ཀྱིས་དག་པའི་ངོ་བོ་ལ་སེམས་ཀྱི་རྡོ་རྗེ་དེ་ཉིད་རང་གི་ངོ་བོ་རང་གིས་མ་རིག་ཅིང་། དེའི་རྩལ་ཡང་འདུ་བྱེད་པའི་ཡིད་ཀྱི་ཡོ་བ་ལས་རྒྱུ་དང་རྐྱེན་སྣང་རྐྱེན་བྱེད། དེ་ཉི
ར་བརྟེན་ནས་ཉོན་མོངས་པ་ཅན་དང་བྱེད་ལས་མ་རིག་པ་བསྐྱེད་དོ། །ཡིད་དེ་ལ་བརྟེན་རྣམ་པ་གཉིས་ཏེ་དེས་ཟིན་པ་ཡིད་ཀྱིས་རྣམ་ཤེས་ཚོགས་དྲུག་སྐྱེ་བ་ག་ལྟེ་བ་འཛིན་ཆོད་ཉག་ཅིག་ཀུན་གཞི་ལས་སྐྱེད་ཅིང་ཉོན་ཡིད་ཀྱིས་ཀུན་གཞི་ལ་བདག་ཏུ་བཟུང་ནས་འཁོར་བའི་ཕྱིར། སྣང་བས་ཉིད་ཀྱི་ཕ་རོལ་སྐྱེད་ཅིང་ཆོས་ཡི

34 བཀའ་འབུམ།

མ་ལས་དེ་དོན་མོངས་པ་ཅན་དུ་གྱུར་དོ། །ཀུན་གཞི་ནི་ཡིད་དེ་གཉིས་ཀྱི་རྟེན་དུ་རྒྱུར་གྱུར་ཉོན་མོངས་པའི་བག་ཆགས་རྣམས་ཅན་འཛིན་པ་ལས་མཐོན་ཐམས་ཅད་པར་བརྗོད་པས་སོ། །ཡིད་དང་ཀུན་གཞི་ལ་ཡང་ཉེ་རྒྱུ་ཆེན་དུ་སྣང་བ། དེ་ཉིད་ཉོན་ཡིད་དང་སྣ་ཚོགས་སྣང་རྒྱུ་ཡིད་ལ་ཡོད་པ་བཞིན་འཁྲུལ་པ་ཐམས་ཅད་ཀྱི་ཡིན་ཕྱིར་བའི་དེ་ལྟ་བུ་ནི་ཡིད་ཡིན་ནོ།
དེ་ལྟ་ར་ཡང་སློབ་དཔོན་ཀླུ་གཉིས་ཀྱིས། དེས་ཀུན་གཞི་རྣམ་ཤེས་ནི། །རྣམ་སྨིན་ཡང་དག་ཐམས་ཅད་པ། །རྟག་ཏུ་རེག་དང་ཡིད་བྱེད་དང་། །ཚོར་དང་འདུ་ཤེས་སེམས་པར་ལྡན། །དེ་ལ་ཚོར་བ་བཏང་སྙོམས་ཏེ། །དེ་ནི་ཟག་མེད་ལུང་མ་བསྟན། །དེ་ནི་རྒྱུན་འབབ་ཆུ་བོ་བཞིན། །དགྲ་བཅོམ
ཉིད་ན་ལྡོག་གོ། །ཞེས་དང་། དེ་ལ་གནས་ཏེ་རབ་འབྱུང་ཞིང་། །དེ་ལ་དམིགས་པས་ཡིད་ཅེས་བྱ། །ཉོན་མོངས་ང་ར་སེམས་པ་བདག་ཉིད་ཅན། །ཉོན་མོངས་པ་བཞི་དང་རྟག་ཏུ་འགྲོགས། །ཞེས་གསུངས་པ་ལྟར། སེམས་པ་བསྐྱེས་སོགས་ཀྱི་རྣམ་པ་ར་འབྱུང་བ་ཞིག་བར་དེ་ལྟར་བཤད་པས་སོ། །དེ་
ལྟར་ཀུན་གཞི་ལས་ཡིད་ཀྱི་ཡོ་བ་འི་མཐུས། ཕྱི་རོལ་ཁྱང་བ་ཡུལ་དུ་བཏགས་པ་ནང་དུ་རྣམ་པར་ཤེས་པ་དཀྲུགས་རྣམ་ཀ། དོན་ལ་ཐ་དད་དུ་གྲུབ་པ་མེད་པ་བཞིན་དུ་སྣང་བར་འགྱུར་ཏེ། དེ་ང་ཡུལ་དང་དབང་པོ་དང་རྣམ་པར་ཤེས་པ་གསུམ་ཚོགས་པ་འི་རྟེན་འབྲེལ་ལས་ཡིན་ཞིང་། དེ་ལས་སྣང་བ་མཚོད་པ་ར་ཀྱིས་
དེས་རྟོག་པ་འི་ཡིད་དུ་འབྲེལ་བ་ར་འགྱུར་བ། དེས་དོན་དུ་མཐོང་བ་ར་སྐྱེད་པ་ལ་སྣང་མཆེད་ཐོབ་གསུམ་དུ་གནས་སོ། །དེ་ལྟར་སྣང་བ་དེ་ནང་ཀུན་གཞི་ལ་ཡུལ་དབང་རྣམ་ཤེས་གསུམ་ཀྱིས་བོན་རྒྱུན་ཐམས་ཅད་པར་ཡོད་པ་འི་ཚུལ་གཞོན་གྱི་རྟེན་འབྲེལ་ལས་འབྱུང་བ་ཡིན་ཏེ། རྡོ་རྗེ་ཚེ་མོ་ལས། ས་བོན་ཀུན་གྱི་སྐྱན་ཀུན་
གཞི་ནི། །ཕྱི་ང་ནང་གི་འདུག་ཉིད་འདོད། །ཅེས་གསུངས་སོ། །སྣང་བ་འི་ངོ་མི་ཤེས་པ་ང་། །སེམས་ཀྱི་བྱུང་དང་བྱེད་ཀྱིས་བཅུལ་བ་འི་ཡིད་དེས་ཡུལ་དུ་སྣག་སྟག་པས་དེ་དག་དོན་དུ་མཐོང་བ་ར་ཞེན་པ་འབྱུང་། དེ་བྱུང་བས་བུང་དུ་རྟོག་པ་ཚོར་བ་འདི་པ་དང་། དོར་བྱུ་རྟོགས་པ་འི་ཚོར་བ་སྐྱུག་བསྔལ

35

༄༅། །དེ་གཉིས་གང་ཡང་མ་ཡིན་པ་འི་ཚོར་བ་བཏང་སྙོམས་རྣམས་སྐྱེ། དེ་སྐྱེས་པས་ཡུལ་ལ་མཚན་མ་ར་འཛིན་པ་འི་འདུ་ཤེས་བྱུང་། དེ་བྱུང་བས་ཡུལ་གཞན་དུ་བརྟགས་པ་འི་བག་ཆགས། འཕེལ་པ་གཟུགས་ཀྱི་ཕུང་པོ་འབྱུང་བ་འི་བར་དུ་ཞེས་པ་ར་བྱའོ། །དེ་ལྟ་ར་སེམས་ལ་ཉོན
ཀྱི་རང་རྣམ་པ་ལ་ཉེ་བར་སྣང་བ་འི་ཚོས་འདི་དག་མེ་ལོང་ལ་གཟུགས་བརྙན་ཤར་བ་ལྟ་བུ་ཞིག་ལ་གདོད་ནས་ཡོད་མཐོང་བ་ཞིང་ཡོད་པ་ར་འགྱུར་བ་མི་སྲིད་ཀྱང་། དེ་ལྟར་མ་རྟོགས་པ་ས་སེམས་ཉིད་རང་གིས་རང་ལ་ཡུལ་དུ་བཟུང་བ་ས་འཁྲུལ་ལོ། །མ་རིག་པ་ས་བསྐྱེད་པ་དེ་ཡིན་དང་གིས་རང་རིག་གཉིས་མེད་ཅུ་བྱ་ལ་དུ་མ་རྟོགས་ང་ཡུལ་
དབྱུ་འཛིན་པ་བདག་ཡིན་པ་ར་འཁྲུལ་ལོ། །རྒྱུ་མཚན་དེ་ས་གཟུང་འཛིན་གཉིས་བཟུང་ས་ཀྱི་ཚོས་ཐམས་ཅད་འཁྲུལ་པ་འི་བཞི་ཡིན་པ་འཁྲུལ་པ་འི་གཞི་དང་སེམས་ཡིན་པ་ས་སེམས་ལ་ཡས་ཞེས་ས་སྒྲུབ་ཅམ་ཡང་མ་གྲུབ་སྟོང་པ་ལ་སྣང་བ་ས་ཕྱི་རྒྱ་ཡས་རྡུལ་ཕྲ་དང་སྣང་བ་འི་སྟོང་པ་དེ་ཉིད་ལས་ལོག་ས་སྐུ
ཡིན་ང་མ་གྲུབ་པ་བཞིན་ནོ། །འོ་ན་སེམས་དེ་ཉམས་ཐམས་ཅད་ཀྱི་ཚོས་འཁྲུལ་པ་ས་སྐྱེད་པ་ཡིན་ཞིང་དེས་ས་སྒྲུབ་པ་ས་འཁྲུལ་པ་ས་སྐྱོ་བཏགས་པ་ཡིན་པ་ས་ཕྱི་རྒྱ་ཏུ་ནང་ས་ཐམས་ཀྱི་གྲུབ་པ་ས་ལ་འདི་ཞེས་མཚོན་དུ་མེད་ཀྱང་། མཐོང་མ་མེད་པ་འི་དུས་ཅན་ང་རང་གིས་རང་མ་རིག་པ་འི་ཉག་ཉིད་སྣང་བ་དེ་ཉིད་ངན་འཁྲུལ་པ་ར་བརྗོད་ལ།
དེ་ཙམ་ཉིད་དང་བདག་བཞི་སེམས་ཀྱི་ངོ་བོ་སྐྱོང་བ་ལ་ཀུན་གཞི་དང་། རང་བཞིན་གསལ་བ་ལ་འཁྲུལ་ཡིད་ཡོད་དང་། རྣམ་པ་འགག་མེད་ལ་རྣམ་ཤེས་སུ་བརྗོད་པ་ཡིན་ཏེ་མ་རིག་པ་ལ་བརྟེན་ནས་སྐྱེ་ཚོགས་དྲུག་སྐྱོང་བ་འི་ཕྱིར་རོ། །དེ་ལྟ་ར་སྒྲུབ་པ་རྣམས་ཀྱི་ལུང་ནི། ཡང་ཀ་རག་ཤེས་པ་དང་། རྒྱུན་སྤྱུག་པོ་བཀོད་
པ་སོགས་ལ་བཞི་ཡི་ཐམས་ཅད་འདི་ངོ་ཡིད་ཀྱི་རྣམ་པ་ས་འདི་བྱ་ཆེ་ར་བྱུང་ཡང་དེ་མ་སྒྲོས་སོ། །འཁྲུལ་པ་འི་ཚུལ་འདི་ལྟ་ར་སྔགས་ཀྱི་རྒྱུད་གྲོལ་རྣམས་སུ་བྱུང་དང་མ་ཉེ། དགོངས་ལ་གཞི་དང་དགོས་པ་ཞིང་དབང་ཡོངས་རྫོགས་ར་བས་ག་བཞི་ཡིན་ཚོང་ཀྱི་དོན་ཅི་ཕྱི་བ་གཅིག་པ་ར་འགྱུར་ངོ། །དེ་འདྲ

36 བཀའ་འབུམ།

ལས། །དབང་བའི་གྲོང་ཁྱེར་ཆད་ལ་ཅན་བྱུང་། །ང་ལས་ཀུན་གསུམ་པོ་ཡང་བྱུང་། །ང་ཡིས་འདི་ཀུན་སྤྲུལ་བ་སྟེ། །འགྲོ་བ་རིང་བཞིན་གཞན་མ་མཐོང་། །ཞེས་དང་། དུས་འཁོར་འགྲེལ་ཆེན་དུ། མཚོ་ནུ་མི་འགྱུར་བ་འི་འདོད་ཆགས་ཆེན་པོ་ནི་རིག་པ་སྟེ། མ་རིག་པ་ཡི་ཆ་སེམས་ཅན་རྣམས
ཀྱི་ཐིག་ལེ་མེད་པ་འི་འདོད་ཆགས་ཀྱི་བག་ཆགས་སོ། །ཞེས་སོགས་དང་། བདེ་ན་ཅེས་བྱ་བ་ནི་སེམས་ཅན་རྣམས་ཀྱི་འཁོར་བ་འི་སེམས་ཀྱི་བག་ཆགས་ཀྱི་རྒྱུ་མོ། །སངས་རྒྱས་ཉིད་ཅེས་བྱ་བ་ནི་ཐར་པ་འི་བག་ཆགས་དང་བྲལ་བ་འི་སེམས་སོ། །ཞེས་འབྱུང་བ་དང་། སེམས་ལ་འགྲེལ་ལས། ཀུན་
རྫོབ་ཏུ་ཉོན་མོངས་ལས་ལས་བྱུང་། །ལས་ནི་སེམས་ལས་བྱུང་བ་ཡིན། །སེམས་ནི་བག་ཆགས་དག་གིས་བསགས། །ཞེས་སོགས་གསུངས་པ་ལྟར་དུ་ཉེས། ༈ །།གཉིས་པ་དེས་འཁོར་བ་ར་འཁོར་ཚུལ་ནི། དེ་ལྟར་ཡུལ་དང་ཡུལ་ཅན་ཐ་དད་དུ་མེད་བཞིན་དུ། གཉིས་སུ་འཛིན་པ་འི་
འཁྲུལ་པ་དེ་ཉིད་ཀུན་གཞི་ཕྱོགས་པ་ར་མ་གྱུར་པ་འི་བར་དུ་རྒྱུ་མི་འཆད་པ་ར་སྣང་བ་འི་ཕྱིར། དེ་ལ་བ་ར་དུ་སྲིད་པ་འི་གྲོང་འདི་ར་ཐོ་རྒྱ་ལི་ཁྱུད་མོ་བཞིན་དུ་འཁོར་བ་ཞིང་འཁྱམས་པ་ར་འགྱུར་བ་ཡིན་ནོ། །དེ་ང་ཀུན་གཞི་ལས་ཡིད་དང་ཡིད་ལས་བཏགས་ཞེས་སྐྱེ་སྐྱེས་ནས་ཡུལ་སྐྱོང་བ་འི་བག་ཆགས་དེ། སྣང་བ་ཡང་ཡིད་ཀྱིས
ཀུན་གཞི་ལ་སོགས་པ་ར་བྱེད་པ་རྒྱུ་མི་འཆད་པ་ས་ཆོས་ཉིད་རྒྱུ་ཆེན་ཕྱིར་སྣང་བ་འི་རྟེན་འབྲེལ་ལས་ང་འབྱུང་བས་ལས་རྒྱུ་སྨིན་པ་འི་ཀུན་འབྱུང་ཉིད་ཀྱི་རྒྱུ་ཏུ་ཚུལ་པོ་བཞིན་དུ་འཁོར་བ་འི་ཀུན་གཞི་རྒྱུ་ཆད་པ་ར་མི་འགྱུར་བ་འི་ཕྱིར་པ། དེ་ནི་རྒྱུན་འབབ་ཆུ་བོ་བཞིན། །ང་ལྟ་བ་ཚམ་ཉིད་དུ་དེ་ལྡོག་གོ། །ཞེས་པ་ཡང་
དང་། འདག་ཤེས་ལས། སེམས་ཅན་ཉིད་ང་བཞིན་ཐང་ཞེས་པ་ཀྱི། །རྟོག་པ་ས་སྐྱེ་བ་ཡིན་ཡིན་ནོ། །རྣམ་པ་ར་ཞེས་དང་བཅས་པ་འི་ཡིད། །རྟག་ཏུ་བག་ཆགས་ལ་དེ་ཡིས་པ་ར་བྱེད། །ཅེས་དང་། རྣམ་པ་ར་ཤེས་པ་ཡིད་པ་ས་གྱུར། །ཡིད་ནི་ཀུན་གཞི་ལ་ས་བྱུང་སྟེ། །ཀུན་གཞི་ལ་ས་ཉི་ཚོས......

37

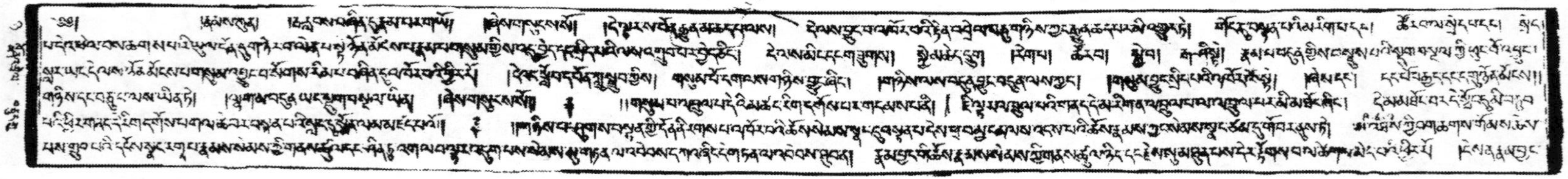

38

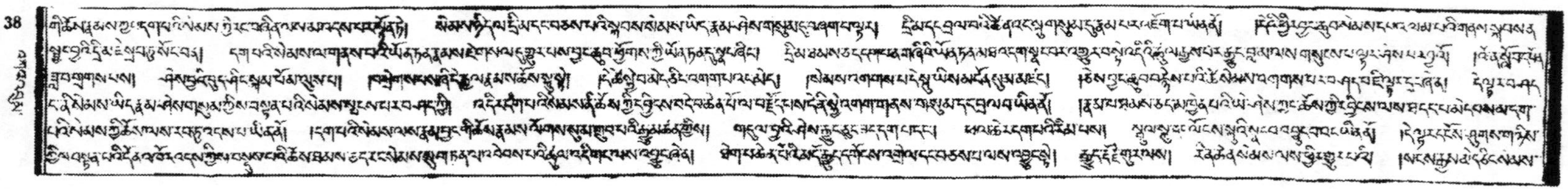

39

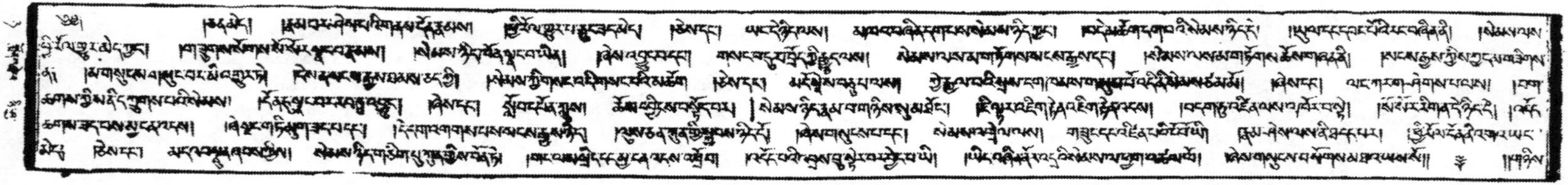

40

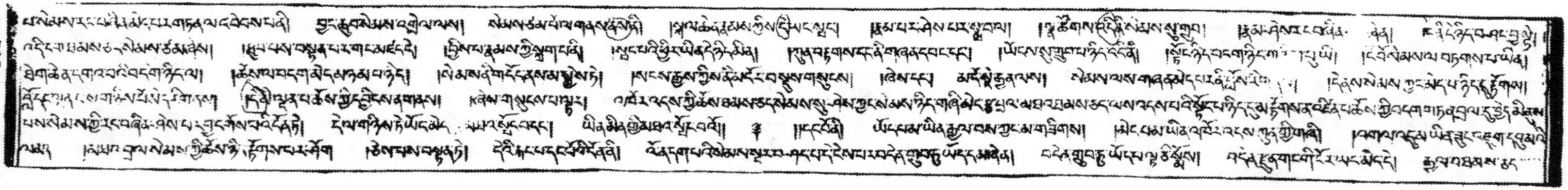

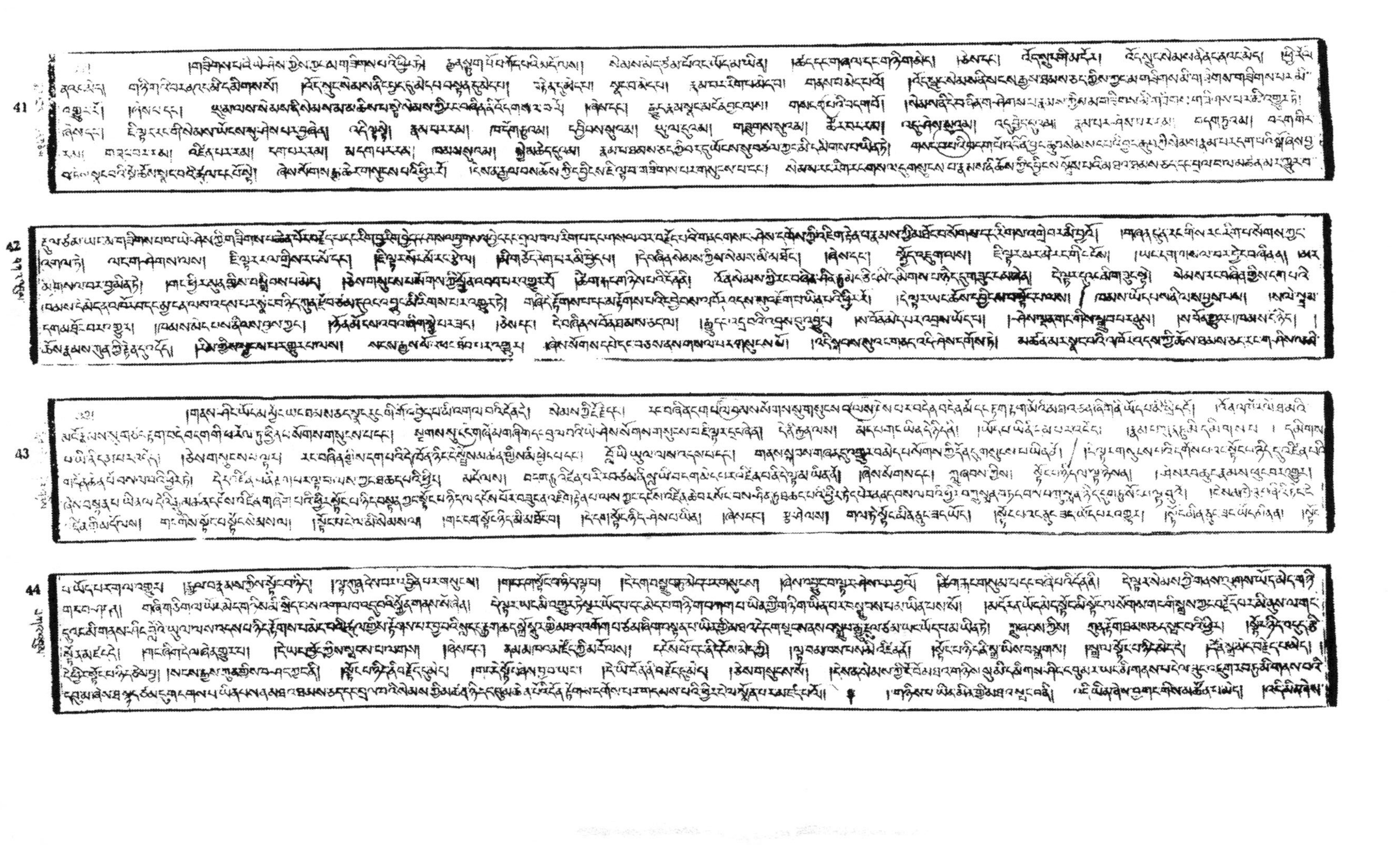

41

42

43

44

45

[illegible]

46

[illegible]

47

[illegible]

48

[illegible]

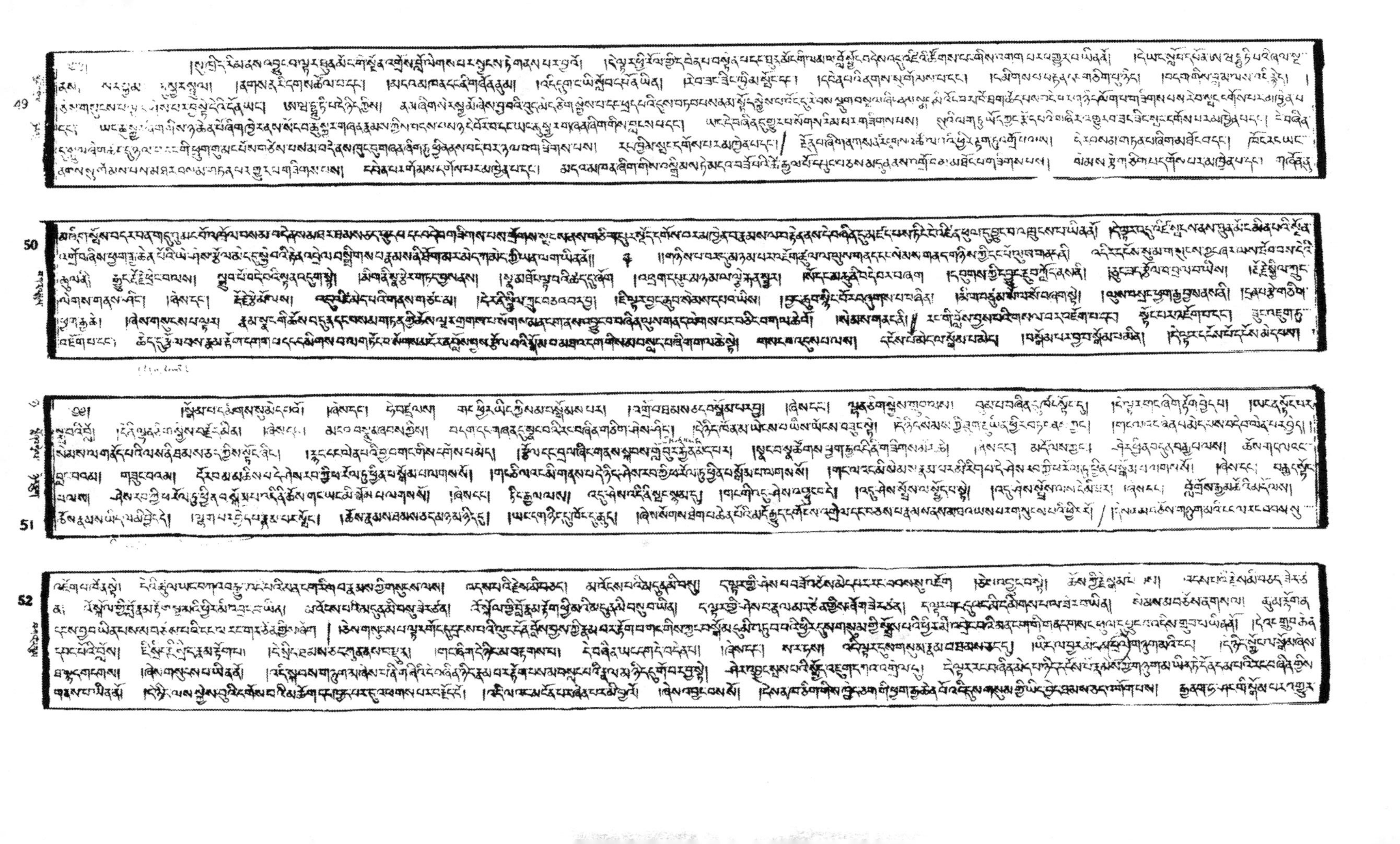

49

[illegible]

50

[illegible]

51

[illegible]

52

[illegible]

53

54

55

56

57 |ལྷུ་བའི་ང་གཟུགས་ཅན་གྱི་རྒྱུ་ཡིན་ནོ།| |འདིར་སྐབས་ཀྱི་ད་ལྟ་ཅེས་པས་མཚོན་ནས་ཞི་གནས་ཀྱི་གེགས་རྣམས་ལ་བསྟན་ཅིང་དེ་དག་ཐབས་ལ་དགོས་པ་ར་སྟོན་པ་སྟེ།| ལ་ཤེས་སྤྱོད་ལམ།| རྒོད་ཅིང་འགྱོད་དང་གནོད་སེམས་རྨུགས་པ་དང་། |གཉིད་དང་འདོད་ལ་འདུན་དང་ཐེ་ཚོམ་སྟེ།
ལྔ།| |ལྷག་མཐོང་གི་བསམ་གཏན་དགེ་བའི་ནོར།| |འཕྲོག་པ་ཡི་ཆོམ་རྐུན་ལྟ་བུར་གསུངས།| |ཞེས་འབྱུང་བ་ལྟར་གོགས་ཀྱི་རྒོད་འགྱོད་གནོད་སེམས། གཉིད་རྨུགས། འདོད་འདུན། ཐེ་ཚོམ་སྟེ་སྒྲིབ་པ་ལྔ་ཡིན་པ། དེ་ལ་རྒོད་པ་ནི་ཆོགས་ལ་རྣམ་ཕྲོག་པའི་ཚོར་བ་དང་། རྒྱུ་ང་ར།
མི་རིགས་པ་ལ་ཕྱོགས་པ་འགྱོད་པ་གཉིས་ཀྱིས་ནི་སེམས་ཞི་བར་གནས་པ་འགེགས་པར་བྱེད། གནོད་སེམས་ཀྱིས་བདེ་བར་གནས་པ་འགེགས་པར་བྱེད། སེམས་ལ་ཡ་གི་བས་འཕྲོ་བྱེད་པ་དང་། དེ་ལས་རྒྱུ་ཆེར་བྱེད་པའི་རྨུགས་པ་དང་གཉིད་ཀྱིས་ཀྱང་བསྒོམ་པ་ཐུམ་གྱིས་ཟིན་པ་ལ་ལས་འབར་གནས་པའི་གེགས་བྱེད། ཡིད་གཉིས་
དང་སེམས་ཅན་ལ་ཆགས་པའི་འདོད་པ་དག་གིས་ཡིད་ལ་ས་སྣ་ཚོགས་རྣམས་པ་ལ་གེགས་བྱེད། འཕྲོ་རྟེན་ཏེ་ཐེ་ཚོམ་ཀྱིས་ནི་ཡང་དག་པའི་ཆོས་ཀྱི་སྒོ་གཅིག་པར་གནས་པ་ལ་གེགས་བྱེད་པ་ཡིན་ནོ། |ལྔ་པོ་དེ་དག་ཀྱང་བསྐྱབ་གཉིས་སུ་འདུས་ཏེ། བྱིང་རྨུགས་ཀྱིས་ཉིད་གཉིས་སུ་མི་གྲིབ་པའི་རབ་འབྱུང་། གཞན
རྣམ་ཀུན་ལ་རྒོད་པ་ནི་འབྲས་ཡིན་ཉེས་སོ། |དེ་དག་སེལ་བ་ནི་གཉེན་པོ་ནི་ཡིད་ལ་བྱེད་པ་ཤེས་ལ་སྟོབས་ཀྱིས་ཟིན་པ་ན། ཇི་ལྟ་བ་ལ་བྱ་ཅི་ཡང་མེད། |གཞག་པ་ལ་རབ་ཏུ་ཆུང་ཟད་མེད། |ཡང་དག་ཉིད་ལ་ཡང་དག་ལྟ། |ཡང་དག་མཐོང་ན་རྣམ་པར་གྲོལ། |ཞེས་པ་ལྟར་གཅོད་པར་རྒྱུ་སྐྱོང་ཚོད་ཀྱི
ངང་ངོ་ལྟ་ཞིང་། དེའི་ངོ་བོར་མ་བཅོས་པ་ར་འཛོག་པ་ཉིད་ཐམས་ཅད། |དེ་ལྟག་མ་ཐོང་གི་ཉེན་དུ་ངེས་པ་པར་ཐོས་པ་དང་། ཞེས་བཤད། |ཞི་གནས་རབ་ཏུ་ལྡན་པའི་ལྷག་མཐོང་གིས། |ཉོན་མོངས་རྣམ་པར་འཇོམས་པར་ཤེས་བྱས་ནས། |ཐོག་མར་ཞི་གནས་བཙལ་བྱ་དེ་ཡང་ནི། |འཇིག་རྟེན་

58 ཆགས་པ་མེད་ལ་མངོན་དགའ་བསྒྲུབ།| |ཞེས་གསུངས་པ་ཡིན་ནོ།| |ཞི་གནས་ཀྱི་དབྱེ་བ་ལ་ལྔ་བོ་དག་ལས་གསུངས་པ་ལྟར་ན། ཞི་གནས་ལ་འཇུག་པའི་ཚུལ་ལ་ལྟ་བ་སེམས་ལ་གནས་པའི་ཐབས་དགུ་རུ་གྲགས་པ་དང་། |སེམས་གནས་ཀྱི་ངོ་བོ་ཞི་ཕྱོགས་པའི་ཕྱིར་ལ་བ་དེ་ཡིན་པས་དེ་ཡང་བསྡོགས
བསྒྲུབ་པ་ཡིད་བྱེད་བཞི་དང་། སེམས་གནས་ཀྱི་ངོ་བོ་གཞི་དང་སོ་སོར་བཞི་དང་། གཟུགས་མེད་ཀྱི་ཉིང་འཛིན་བཞི་དང་། འགོག་སྙོམས་རྣམས་ནི་དེ་ལས་ཐམས་གཟུགས་འགོག་སྙོམས་ལ་ཐབས་ཅན་ལ་སྙོམས་འཇུག་དགུ་རུ་གྲགས་པ་ཡིན་ནོ། |དེ་ལ་སེམས་གནས་པའི་ཐབས་དགུ་ནི།
ཡུམ་ལས། དེ་ལ་སེམས་འཇོག་པར་བྱེད། ཡང་དག་པར་འཇོག་པར་བྱེད། ཉེ་བར་འཇོག་པར་བྱེད། དུལ་བར་བྱེད། ཞི་བར་བྱེད། ཉེ་བར་ཞི་བར་བྱེད། རྩེ་གཅིག་ཏུ་བྱེད། མཉམ་པར་འཇོག་པར་བྱེད་དོ། |ཞེས་གསུངས་པ་རྣམས་སོ། |ཡང
བྱེད་བདུན་ནོ།| རྒྱན་ལས། དེ་ནས་དེ་དང་པོར་སྒོམ་བསྒོམ་ནས་ནི། |མདོ་ཡི་སྡེ་ལ་སོགས་པའི་ཆོས། |མི་གཉིས་དོན་ནི་ཉེ་བར་གནས་པ། |ཡང་སོ་སོར་མི་ལ་སེམས་འཇོག་གོ།| |དེ་ནས་དེ་ཡི་རིམ་བཞིན་དུ། |ཚིགས་སུ་ཉུལ་བར་བྱ་ཞེས་སོ། |སོ་སོར་རྟོགས་ལ་རྒྱུ་བ་གཉིས་དུ། |དེ་ཡི་དོན་ལ་ཡང་རྣམ་
པར་སྤྱོད། |དོན་དེ་དག་ནི་རིམ་བཞིན་ནས། |ཆོས་ལ་ཀུན་ནས་སྒོམ་པར་བྱེད། |དེ་ཡི་དོན་ནི་ལྷག་མཐོང་རྒྱུའི་ཕྱིར། |དེ་ནས་དེ་ནི་སྤྲོ་བར་བྱེད། |ཡིད་ཀྱི་བརྗོད་པ་མས་རྒྱུན་ཆགས་སུ། |མཚན་ཉིད་སོ་སོར་བརྟག་པར་བྱ། |ཡིད་ལ་བྱེད་པ་བརྗོད་མེད་པར། |ངོ་བོ་གཅིག་པས་ཀུན་དུ་བལྟ།
ཆོས་ཀྱི་ཚིག་ནི་བསྡུས་པ་བཤད་པ་དེ། |ཞི་གནས་ལམ་དང་ཞེས་བྱ་སྟེ། |ཞེས་འབྱུང་བ་ལྟར། སོ་སོར་རྟོག་པ་མེད་པ། རབ་ཞི་བ། དགའ་བ། སྤྲོད་པ། སྤྱོད་པ། སྦྱོར་བ་ཐབ་ལ། སྦྱོར་བ་ཐབ་ཡི་ལྷུག་ལུགས་སུ་ཡིན་བྱེད་དེ་བར་སྣང་ལས་ཀྱི་མ་རྟོག་ལ་ཉེར་བཤོག་ལ་མི་རྟོག་པ་མེད་ཅེས་བྱ་བོ། |ཐབས

59 ༄༅། |གཏན་བཞི་ནི། མཛོད་ལས། དངོས་ལ་རྟོག་དཔྱོད་དང་། |དགའ་བ་དང་བདེ་ཏེ་འཛིན་རྣམས་ལས། |གཉིས་པ་ལ་ནི་ཡན་ལག་བཞི། |རབ་དང་དང་ནི་དགའ་ལ་སོགས། |གསུམ་པ་ལ་ལྔ་བཏང་སྙོམས་དང་། |དྲན་པ་ཤེས་བཞིན་བདེ་དང་གནས། |མཐར
ཐ་བཞི་དྲན་དག་བཏང་སྙོམས་དག |བདེ་མིན་སྡུག་མིན་ཏིང་འཛིན་རྣམས། |ཞེས་འབྱུང་བ་ལྟར་རོ། |འདི་ནི་སྐབས་བསམ་གཏན་བཞི་པ་ལ་ཐ་ཉེ་ཉན་ཤེས་མངོན་ཤེས་ལྔ་ཀྱང་འབྱུང་སྟེ། དེ་ལྟར་ན། བསམ་གཏན་བཞི་པ་ཤིན་ཏུ་དག་པ་ཐོབ་ནས། |མི་རྟོག་ཡེ་ཤེས་ཡོངས་སུ་འབྱུང་བ་ཡིན། |དེ་ལྟར
གནས་རྣམས་ཡིད་ལ་བྱེད་པ་ལས། |མངོན་པར་ཤེས་པ་ཐོགས་མེད་འབྱུང་བར་འགྱུར། |ཞེས་སོ། |གཟུགས་མེད་པ་བཞི་ནི། ནམ་མཁའ་མཐའ་ཡས། རྣམ་ཤེས་མཐའ་ཡས། ཅི་ཡང་མེད། ཡོད་མིན་མེད་མིན་རྣམས་ཏེ་གཟུགས་ཀྱི་འདུ་ཤེས་ལ་བ་ཀུན་ནས་འགོག་ནས་ཐོག་ནས་སོང་དུ་སྤྱོད་པར་སྒོམ་པ་ཡིན་ནོ།|
འགོག་སྙོམས་ནི། ལུགས་བཞིན་ལྷུག་ལ་དང་ཚོར་བ་འགོག་པ་ལ་བསྒྲུབས་པ་སྟེ། ཉན་ཐོས་དང་རང་སངས་རྒྱས་ཀྱི་འདུ་ཤེས་དང་ཚོར་བ་འགོག་པའི་སྙོམས་པར་འཇུག་པ་ཞེས་བྱ་བའི་ཕྱིར་ཏེ་འདུ་ཤེས་མི་མངོན་པར་བཞག་པའི་ཏིང་ངེ་འཛིན་ནོ། |དེ་ལྟར་གནས་དབབ་ཀྱི་ཕྱིར་བརྟེན་པའི་སེམས་གནས་པའི་ཞི་གནས་སུ་ཕྱིན་པ་དང་། དེ་ཡང་ལྷག་མཐོང་དང་ཟུང་དུ་འབྲེལ་བ་ཉིད
དུ་ཤེས་པར་བྱའོ། |ཐེག་ཆུང་ཐུབ་སྙོམས་ཀྱི་ཡང་ཐེག་ཆེན་ལ་ས་འདུ་བའི་ཤེས་རབ་ཡིན་ལ། སྙོམས་འཇུག་འདི་དག་གི་འགོག་སྙོམས་པ་མ་གཏོགས་པ་ཐམས་ཅད་འཇིག་རྟེན་པ་དང་། ཐུན་མོང་བ་ཡིན་ལ། དེ་ལ་བཤད་པའི་གལ་བར་འགྱུར་ཞིང་ཉིན་སྨོན་མེད་དུ། འཇིག་རྟེན་པའི་ཤེས་རབ་ཚུལ་ལ་ལྟག་མཐོང་དུ་བཏགས་
པ་ནང་ཡོད་མོད་ཀྱི་མཚན་ཉིད་ཚང་བ་ཡིན་ ... ཞེས་པའི་ཕྱིར་དེ་ལ་ཞི་གནས་ཀྱི་རྣམ་གྲངས་སུ་བཤད་པ་ཡིན་པས་སོ། |དེ་ལྟར་སྙོམས་འཇུག་སོགས་པ་བཤད་པ་ནི། འདི་སྐབས་ཞི་གནས་ལ་གཅིག་ཏུ་མ་ཟད་པ་ཐོབ་པའི་ཐབས་སུ་ཐབས་ལམ་ལས་ནས་བའི་ཚིམ་པའི་ཡིན་པ་ཞིང་པར

60 ཀྱི་ཉམས་སུ་ཞེས་པར་བྱེད་ཅིག |འདི་སྐབས་བཀའ་བརྒྱུད་གོང་མ་དག་གི་ཕྱག་རྒྱ་ཆེན་པོ་ཡིན་པའི་ངོས་གཟུང་ལ། གནས་པ་དང་པོ་རིག་ནང་ཀྱི་རྒྱུ་སྟུག། གཉིས་པ་ཆུ་བོ་འབབ་པ་ལྟ་བུ། གསུམ་པ་མི་གཡོ་བ་རྒྱ་མཚོ་ལྟ་བུ་ཞེས་པའི་རྣམ་གཞག་ལ་བཤད་པ་ལྟར་ཞི་གནས་ལ་རྟེན་ལ་ཐོས་
པའོ།| |གཉིས་པ་ལྷག་མཐོང་བ་བཤད་པ་ལ་ངོས་དང་། གཞི་རྣམ་གཅོད་པ་གཉིས་ལས། |དང་པོ་ནི། བསྒྲུར་མེད་སེམས་ལ་ཡང་ཡང་བལྟས་པའི་ཚེ། |མཐོང་མེད་དོན་ནི་ཟབ་མོ་ལྷག་པར་མཐོང་། |ཡིན་མིན་དོན་ལ་ཐེ་ཚོམ་ཆོད་པ་ཉིད། ... ཉིད་ལ་ཀྱང་ལྟ་བུས་ཕྱག་ལས་གསལ་བར་འགོག
ཅེས་པ་སྟེ། བལྟ་བའི་ཡུལ་ལ་ས་འདས་ལས་བལྟ་བ་དར་བ་མེད་པའི་སེམས་ཀྱི་དོན་པོ་བགྲངས་ལུགས། དེ་ཉིད་ལ་མཉམ་པར་གཞག་ཅིང་ཐུགས་ལ་བཞིན་དགའ་དང་བསྒོམས་པ་ལ་སྟུང་བའི་ཤེས་རབ་ཀྱི་མིག་གིས་ཡང་དང་ཡང་དུ་བལྟས་པ་དེའི་ཚེ། མཐོང་བ་དང་། ཡིད་བཞིན་ལྟ་བུ་ལྷག་གིས་མཐོང་བ
གནས་ལུགས་ཀྱི་དོན་དེ་ལ་ཡིན་མིན་ཡོད་མེད་ལ་སོགས་པའི་སྒྲོ་འདོགས་དང་ཐེ་ཚོམ་ཐམས་ཅད་དེ་ཉིད་དུ་ཆོད་དོ། འཁྲུལ་པ་མེད་པའི་རང་ངོར་གསལ་ཞེས་པ་སྟེ་ལ་ཐུབ་པ་ལ་ཀླུང་བ་དེ་ལྟ་བུའི་ལྷག་མཐོང་སྟེ་ཀི་ཡེ་ཤེས་སྐྱེས་ཏེ། ཤར་སྐྱེས་ཕྱག་རྒྱ་ཆེན་པོ་ཉིད་ཕྱོར་ཟུང་ལྟར་ ... ཞེས་པ་ཡོ།|
དེའང་བསམ་པ་དང་། བསྒོམ་པ་དང་། ལྟ་བ་དང་། ཤེས་པ་དང་། མཐོང་བ་དང་། སྒོང་བ་ལ་སོགས་པ་རྣམས་ཀྱི་ཐམས་ཅད་དུ་ཤེས་པ་ལ་ཡིན་ནོ་ལུགས། ཞེས་པ་ཉིད་ལ་དེ་དང་དེར་བཏགས་པ་ཙམ་ལ་སྐྱེ་བ་ཅན་ཡོད་མེད་དང་གཉིས་ཙམ་ལ་ཡང་དག་པའི་དོན་དུ། ཟུང་འཇུག་ཡང་ཡོད་ ...
པའི་སྒྲིབ་གཡོགས་དང་བྲལ་བས། རང་རིག་པ་དང་། སྤྱོད་ཐོབ་པར་དང་ཡེ་ཤེས་ལ་སོགས་པ་བཅོད་པས་ངེས་པ་ཉིད་པ་དང་། མི་སྣང་དེ་བའི་རྣམ་པ་དག་པའི་རྒྱུ་དང་མཚན་མ་ལ་ཁྱུང་པ་... བཅད་བཅོས་དང་བཟོ་བ་ཆེན་པོར་ལ་རྟོག་པ་སོགས་ཞེས་དགོས་སོ། |དེ་ལྟར་ཡང་། བདེ་མཆོག་སྡོམ་འབྱུང་ལས། གཟུང་དང་

61 ༄༅། །འཛིན་པ་རྣམ་པར་གྲོལ། །རྟོག་གེའི་སྤྱོད་ལ་རྣམ་པར་སྤྱངས། །སེམས་དང་སེམས་བྱུང་བ་ནུབ་གྱུར་པ། །འགྲོ་བ་དེ་ཉིད་རང་བཞིན་ཉུལ། །ཇི་ལྟར་དག་མེ་ལོང་དྭངས་ཉིད་དང་། །མཁའ་བཞིན་སེམས་ཉིད་ཡང་དག་གནས། །ཚིག་ཤ་མཐའ་མེད་རང་བཞིན། །དཔང་པོ་དང་
བྲལ་སྤྲོས་པ་མེད། །ལྷུང་བ་མེད་ཅིང་རྣམ་འགྱུར་བྲལ། །ཐམས་ཅད་སྟོང་པ་ཉིད་མཚོན་མེད། །ཚིག་ཏུ་བརྗོད་དུ་བྲལ་བསྲེད་པ་ཡི། །ཀུན་ཏུ་བཟང་པོའི་གྲོལ་བའི་ཞིང་། །ཡིད་ཀྱི་ཡང་དག་སྤྱོད་ཡུལ་མིན། །ཆོས་ཉིད་སེམས་མེད་ཅིང་གཉིས་ལས་གྲོལ། །དོན་གྱི་དམ་པ་ཀློང་བ་སྦྱོལ། །འཕོ་མེད་དེ་ཡི་
ལ་ཕྱག་འཚལ། །གང་ཞིག་དེ་ཉིད་ལ་རེག་པ། །བསམ་པ་ཐམས་ཅད་བགས་དུ་མེད། །གང་ཆེ་བ་ལས་ཐམས་ཅད་ལས་པ། །དེ་ཆེ་བས་ན་མི་ཁྱབ་པར་འགྱུར། །སེམས་ཅན་ཇི་ལྟར་བསམ་མེད་དེ། །བསམ་མེད་ཇི་ལྟར་རྒྱལ་བ་དེ། །གང་ཕྱིར་འདས་ནས་ཐུབ་པ་ཡང་རྒྱལ་བ་ཡིས། །བསམ་པ་འདི་ནི
རང་ཕྱུག་པ་དང་། །ཐབས་སྣ་མེད་པའི་སེམས་དཔའ། །ཐབས་པ་ཀུན་གྱིས་བགྲོད་དང་བྲལ། །སྣ་ཚོགས་སྤྲུལ་པ་སྣང་བ་དེ། །ཆགས་མེད་བདེ་བ་ཆེན་པོ་སྟེ། །རྣམ་པ་ཐམས་ཅད་ཀྱི་ཉི་མ་ཆོག །དཔང་པོ་ཀུན་དང་མཉམ་པ་མེད། །དངོས་དང་དངོས་མེད་བདག་ཉིད་འབྱུང་། །ཆོས་དང་དངོས་
མེད་རྣམ་པར་ལྷུངས། །ཞི་མ་ཡི་ཤི་སྐྱེ་རང་རིག་པ། །ཞེ་ལ་བས་ཡིན་པ་མཐོང་བ་མིན། །གཟུགས་མེད་སྐྱེ་ནག་རང་གནས། །འགྱུར་བ་མེད་པས་དེ་རྟགས་པ། །ཞེས་དང་། རྒྱ་ཤིན་ལས། དམ་པའི་དོན་དུ་དབྱེ་རུ་མེད། །འཕྲུལ་སྣ་ཡིན་གཉིས་ཀ་ལ། །རང་གི་རིག་ཀྱང་མཚོན་གཞི
བ། །དངོས་དང་དངོས་མེད་བྲལ་བ་རུ་བྱེད། །དེ་ཉིད་ཆེན་པོ་མཆོག་བཞི། །དངོས་དང་དངོས་མེད་བཤད་ཉིད་ཞི། །ཞེས་དང་། ཆོས་བསྡུ་ལས། རང་རིག་བདག་ཉིད་དག་པ་ཉིད། །དགག་པ་གཞན་གྱིས་རྣམ་གྲོལ་མིན། །ཞེས་དང་། དུས་ཀྱི་འཁོར་ལོ་ལས། འདི་ལྟ་བ་འོད་གསལ་བ་རང་འགྱུར་བ

62 མེད། །ཉམས་པ་ཉམས་པ་ཉིད་ཀྱང་མེད། །རྒྱུ་བ་དང་ཡི་རྒྱུ་བ་མེད། །འཆར་བ་ཡི་ནི་འཆར་བ་མེད། །རབ་ཏུ་གསལ་བའི་རབ་གསལ་མེད། །བཀག་པ་ཡི་ནི་བཀག་པ་ཡང་མེད་དོ། །སྤྲུལ་པའི་སྤྲུལ་པར་འགྱུར་ཉིད་མེད། །འཆི་བ་ཡི་འཆི་བ་ཡང་མེད་དོ། །ཀུན་ནས་ཉོན་མོངས་པར་འགྱུར་བ་མེད།
མ་གནས་པ་ཡི་མི་གནས་མེད། །དངོས་པོ་མེད་པའི་དངོས་པོ་མེད། །དངོས་པོའི་དངོས་པོ་ཉིད་ཀྱང་མེད། །འགྱུར་བའི་འགྱུར་བར་འགྱུར་བ་ཡང་མེད། །མི་འགྱུར་བ་ཡི་མི་འགྱུར་མེད། །ཞེས་སོགས་མཐའ་ཡས་པ་གསུངས་ཤིང་། ཟབ་མོ་དེ་མ་ལྟོས་པ་ལས་ཀྱང་། ཤེས་བྱའི་སྒྲིབ་ལས།
ནམ་མཁའ་མཐོང་ཞེས་སེམས་ཅན་ཚིག་ཏུ་བརྗོད། །ནམ་མཁའ་ཇི་ལྟར་མཐོང་ཞེས་དོན་འདི་བརྟག་པར་གྱིས། །གང་ཞིག་དེ་ལྟར་མཐོང་བ་དེ་ཡི་ཆོས་རྣམས་མཐོང་། །མཐོང་བ་དཔེ་ཡི་གཞན་གྱིས་དེ་བསྟན་པར་ནུས་མ་ཡིན། །ཞེས་བཀྲ་ན་སོགས་དང་། བསྟན་བཅོས་རྣམས་ལས་ཀྱང་། སྲུ
ཤེས་ཅན་རྒྱུ་ལས། རྟོག་མེད་རྒྱུ་ལ་གཞིས་རྣམ་པར་ལས། །སྟོང་ཉིད་མཐོང་ཞེས་ཐ་སྙད་བཏགས། །མ་མཐོང་ཉིད་དེ་མཐོང་ངོ་ཡ། །ཤིན་ཏུ་ཟབ་པའི་མདོ་ལས་གསུངས། །ཞེས་སོགས་མཐའ་ཡས་པ་ལས་གསུངས་སོ།། ༈ །གཉིས་པ་གཞི་རྟག་ཅེ་ན། ལུས་ལ་ཕན་པ་ལ་སུ་
མེད་སེམས་སུ་མཐོང་། །སེམས་ལ་བལྟས་པས་སེམས་མེད་དོན་ཁོ་ཐོང་། །གཉིས་ལ་བལྟས་པས་གཉིས་འཛིན་རང་སར་གྲོལ། །འོད་གསལ་སེམས་ཀྱི་གནས་ལུགས་རྟོགས་པར་ཤོག །ཞེས་པའོ། །དེ་ལ་ཡུལ་ནི་གཟུགས་ [illegible]
བལྟས་ནས་མཉམ་པར་བཞག་པ་ [illegible] །དེ་བཞིན་དུ་སེམས་ཀྱི་ [illegible] སྣང་སེམས་ལ་གཉིས་ཀྱི་

63 ༄༅། །མཉམ་དུ་མཉམ་པར་བཞག་པའི་མཐུས་ཡུལ་ཡུལ་ཅན་གྱི་གཉིས་སུ་འཛིན་པ་གཞི་མེད་དུ་རང་སར་གྲོལ་བར་འགྱུར་བའི་ཕྱིར། ཐབས་དེ་ལྟ་བུ་ལ་བརྟེན་ནས། རང་བཞིན་གྱིས་སྒྲིབ་པ་དང་བྲལ་བ་གདོད་ནས་ལ་བབ་པའི་སེམས་ཀྱི་གནས་ལུགས་ཇི་ལྟ་བ་བཞིན་རྟོགས་
པའི་ལྷག་མཐོང་གི་ཡེ་ཤེས་སྐྱེ་བར་ངོ་ཤིག་པའོ། །འདི་སྐབས་ཕྱིད་ཀྱི་རྣམ་པ་ལས། སྣང་བ་སེམས། སེམས་སྟོང་པ། སྟོང་པ་ལྷུན་གྲུབ། ལྷུན་གྲུབ་རང་གྲོལ་དུ་ངོ་སྤྲོད་པའི་རྣམ་གཞག་མཛད་པ་ཡིན་ཏེ། ད་ར་ཡིད་ལ་བྱེད་པ་བརྟག་ཅིག་ལ་སོགས་པའི་མན་ངག་གིས་གནས་ལུགས་རྟོགས་
ཀྱང་ཕྱིན་གཞི་རྩ་གཅོད་པའི་མན་ངག་གིས་ངོ་མ་ཟིན་ནས་ཤེས་རྟོགས་པར་མི་འགྱུར་བའི་ཕྱིར་རོ། །དེ་ལྟར་གཏན་ལ་འབེབས་པའི་གདམས་ངག་གི་གཙོ་བོ་སེམས་འཚོལ་གྱི་སྐྱོན་སོགས་ལ་བོད་ཡུལ་ཚིག་བཤད་གང་གིས་གནས་སུ་ཕྱིན་མ་ཕྱིན་གྱི་རང་ཉིད་ཀྱི་ཆོས་པའི་དྲིན་ཐམས་ཅད་སྐྱེལ་བར་ཟད་དེ། རྣམ་སྣང་མངོན་བྱང་
ལས། བྱང་ཆུབ་དང་ཐམས་ཅད་མཁྱེན་པ་ཉིད་ནི་རང་གི་སེམས་ལས་ཡོངས་སུ་བཙལ་བར་བྱའོ། །དེ་ཅིའི་ཕྱིར་ཞེ་ན། སེམས་དེ་ནི་རང་བཞིན་གྱིས་ཡོངས་སུ་དག་པ་ཡིན་ཏེ། དེ་ནི་ནང་ན་ཡང་མེད། ཕྱི་རོལ་ན་ཡང་མེད། གཉིས་ཀའི་བར་ན་ཡང་མི་དམིགས་སོ། །ཞེས་དང་། སེམས་ཀྱི་ལུང་ལས་རིགས་ཀྱི་བུ་བྱ
ང་ཆུབ་ཡོངས་སུ་ཤེས་པར་འདོད་པས་རང་གི་སེམས་ཉིད་ཡོངས་སུ་བཙལ་བར་བྱའོ། །ཞེས་སོགས་སེམས་བཙལ་དགོས་པའི་རྒྱུ་མཚན་ཇི་ལྟར་བཙལ་བའི་ཐབས་སོགས་རྒྱ་ཆེར་གསུངས་ཤིང་། གསང་བ་བསམ་གྱིས་མི་ཁྱབ་པའི་མདོ་ལས། བྱང་ཆུབ་སེམས་དཔའི་བྱང་ཆུབ་ཀྱི་སེམས་རྣམ་པར་དག་པའི་སྒོ་ཞེས་བྱ་བ
ཆོས་སྣང་བའི་སྒོ་ཆོས་སྣང་བའི་ཚུལ་དང་པོ་སྟེ། གང་ལ་གནས་ན་བྱང་ཆུབ་སེམས་དཔའ་རྣམས་ཚོགས་ཀྱང་དུས་སྐྱེ་བ་ཐམས་ཅད་སྐྱོང་བའི་ཏིང་ངེ་འཛིན་འཐོབ་ཅིང་། དེ་ཐོབ་པས་བྱང་ཆུབ་སེམས་དཔའ་རྣམས་སངས་རྒྱས་ཐམས་ཅད་དང་ལྷན་ཅིག་འགྲོགས་པ་འཐོབ་པར་འགྱུར། །མངོན་པར་ཤེས་པ་ལྔ་དག

64 བྱང་འཐོབ་པར་འགྱུར། སྣང་དང་སྣ་དང་དབྱངས་ [illegible] འཐོབ་པར་འགྱུར། སེམས་ཅན་གྱི་བསམ་པ་རྗེས་སུ་ཤེས་པ་དང་། དེ་བཞིན་གཤེགས་པ་ཐམས་ཅད་ཀྱིས་བྱིན་གྱིས་བརླབས་པ་ [illegible]
ལ་ཡོངས་སུ་མི་སྐྱོ་བར་འགྱུར། འདུལ་བ་ [illegible] རབ་ཏུ་གནས་པ་དང་། ལོག་པར་ལྟ་བ་རྣམ་པར་སྤངས་པ་དང་། ཡང་དག་པའི་ལྟ་བ་ [illegible] ཡིན་ནོ། །ཞེས་སོགས་ཡོན་ཏན་དང་ཕན་ཡོན་ཤིན་ཏུ་མང་བ་གསུངས་ཤིང་། [illegible]
[illegible] །གཞན་ཡང་ཀ་མ་ལ་ཤཱི་ལའི་སྒོམ་རིམ་ [illegible] ཡིན་པར་སྣང་ངོ་། [illegible]
[illegible] ཞེས་རབ་ཀྱི་མིག་གིས་ [illegible] གསུམ་གྱིས་སོ། །དེ་ལས་ཀུན་ཆོས་ཉིད་ [illegible]
[illegible] ཞེས་ [illegible]
[illegible] ཡིད་ལ་ [illegible] ལམ་ལ་མཉམ་པར་བཞག་པ་ [illegible] ཅེས་པ་དང་། ལས་ཀྱི་མཐའ་དང་། ཆོས་ལ་བདེན་པར་ཞེན་པ་ [illegible] །ཞེས་ [illegible]

༄༅། །མི་སྲིད་པ་ར་བསྟན་པ་བཞིན་མདོ་རྒྱུད་ཐམས་ཅད་ནས་མགྲིན་གཅིག་པར་མི་རྟོག་པའི་ཡེ་ཤེས་ཀྱིས་མཉམ་པར་འཇོག་ཚུལ་གསུངས་པ་ལ་འདི་ངོས་སུ་བསྟན་པས་དོན་དུ་ཅི་ཞིག་འགྱུར་རང་ལས་མ་དགོས་སོ།། ༄ །།གསུམ་པ་ཞི་ལྷག་ཟུང་འཇུག་གི་ཉ་པ་ལ་གྱུར་དེ་ཡི་མཚན་ཉིད་ཀྱི
རྣམ་གྲངས་བསྟན་པ་ལ་དགོས་དང་། ཞི་ལྷག་ཟུང་དུ་འཇུག་ཚུལ་གྱི་འཕྲོས་དོན་ནོ། །དང་པོ་ནི། ཡིད་བྱེད་བྲལ་བ་འདི་ནི་ཕྱག་རྒྱ་ཆེ། །མཐའ་དང་བྲལ་བ་དབུ་མ་ཆེན་པོ་ཡིན། །འདི་ནི་ཀུན་འདུས་རྫོགས་ཆེན་ཞེས་ཀྱང་བྱ། །གཅིག་ཤེས་ཀུན་དོན་རྟོགས་པའི་གདེང་ཐོབ་ཤོག །ཅེས་པ་སྟེ།
། ཡང་རང་བཞིན་ལྷན་ཅིག་སྐྱེས་པ་ཇི་ལྟ་བ་རྟོགས་པ་ནི་ཡིད་ལ་བྱེད་པ་ཐམས་ཅད་དང་བྲལ་བས་ན་ཕྱག་རྒྱ་ཆེན་པོ་ཞེས་བྱ་བ་ཡིན་ལ། མཚན་གྱི་རྣམ་གྲངས་གཞན་ཡང་། མཐའ་ཐམས་ཅད་དང་བྲལ་བས་དབུ་མ་ཆེན་པོ་ཞེས་དང་། ཆོས་ཐམས་ཅད་རྫོགས་པ་འདི་ར་འདུས་པས་རྫོགས་པ་ཆེན་པོ་ཞེས་ཀྱང་བྱ
སྟེ། དེ་བཞིན་ཉིད་གཅིག་པུ་བདེ་བོར་ཤེས་པས་ཆོས་ཐམས་ཅད་ཀྱི་གནས་ལུགས་པ་རྟོགས་པའི་གདེངས་དང་ལྡན་པ་ཞིག་དགོས་སོ། །ཞེས་གདམས་པའི་ཕྱིར་སྨོན་པའོ། །རྒྱང་གི་སྒྲུལ་ཟླ་བ་དང་རྒྱ་ཆེ་བའི་ཆོས་རྣམས་ཀྱི་དོན་དང་མཚན་མཐའ་དག་འདིར་འདུས་པར་སྟོན་ཞིང་རྒྱ་མཚོ་དེས་གཅིག་ཤེས་ཀུན
གྲོལ་དུ་བསྒྲུབ་པར་མཛད་པའང་ཡིན་ནོ། །འདིའི་དགོངས་ནས། བདེ་གཤེགས་པས་གསོ་བ་ལས། རྣམ་རྟོག་དང་ནི་ཉོན་མོངས་པ། །ཐམས་ཅད་འདུལ་བས་འདུལ་བ་ཡིན། །རྣམ་པར་རྟོག་པ་ཆོས་སྐུ་སྟེ། །ངེས་པའི་ཤེས་པ་སྐྱེད་པའི་ཕྱིར། །སྒྲིབ་འདོགས་ནང་ནས་གཅོད་པ་ཡིན། །འདི་ནི
བུམ་རི་ཁ་ནས་ངག་ཡིན། །དུག་ཅན་སྦྲུལ་ལ་སོགས་པ་བཞིན། །མཐའ་དང་བྲལ་བས་དབུ་མ་ཡིན། །སྤྲོས་མ་བརྗོད་དུ་མེད་པའི་ཕྱིར། །ཕ་རོལ་ཕྱིན་པ་ཞིག་ངམ་ངག་ཡིན། །ཡ་ཆོར་དང་སྐྱུ་ངན་འདས་པའི་ཆོས། །སེམས་ལུས་རྫོགས་པས་རྫོགས་ཆེན་ཡིན། །འབྲང་རྟོག་འཁྲ་རྟོག་ཐམས

66

ཅད་ཀུན། །ཡིད་ལ་མི་བྱེད་ཕྱག་རྒྱ་ཆེ། །ཕྱུག་བརྟུལ་བཞི་པ་ལ་གྲེན་བྱེད་ཡིན། །ཉོན་མོངས་དང་ནི་རྣམ་རྟོག་ཀུན། །ལམ་དུ་སློང་བས་གསང་སྔགས་ཡིན། །སེམས་དང་རྣམ་རྟོག་ཆོས་སྐུ་གསུམ། །དང་པོ་ལྷན་ཅིག་སྐྱེས་པ་སྟེ། །གང་ཟག་ལས་པ་གཅིག་ཏུ་སྦྱོར་བའི་ཕྱིར། །ལྷན་ཅིག་སྐྱེས
སྦྱོར་ཞེས་སུ་བཤད། །འདུ་དང་འབྲལ་བ་སོགས་བ་ཡི། །ངར་གཅོད་ལ་ཡང་བསྡུགས་སོ་གསུངས། །ཞེས་གསུངས་པ་ཡིན་ནོ། །འོན་ཀྱང་རྒྱལ་ཀྱི་ཆོས་དགག་གི་དོན་དང་མཚན་རྣམས་ཕྱག་རྒྱ་ཆེན་པོ་ལ་འདུས་པའི་ཚུལ་ཇི་ལྟར་ཅེ་ན། མཚན་སོ་སོ་ཐ་དད་པ་དག་ཞེ་ར་རང་གི་མཚོན་བྱ་ཡི་གཞི་དེ་ལ་གནས
པ་མ་ཡིན་པས་གང་དུ་འང་བསྒྲུར་མི་གལ་ཏེ་ལྟར་འགྱེལ་ན་ཡང་བསྟན་པས་འདིར་བསྡུ་ནས་བསྟེ་ཕྱོགས་ཙམ་མཚོན་པའི་ཕྱིར་མཚན་གྱི་གཞི་གཞིག་སྤྱོད་ཚུལ་བསྟན་མ་ཐག་པ་དེས་ཤེས་པར་ནུས་ལ། དོན་རྣམས་ལས་ཟབ་མོ་རེ་དོན་ནི། ངོས་སུ་སྐྱོང་བ་ཉིད་དུ་རོ་གཅིག་པ་ཡིན་ཞིང་། རྒྱ་ཆེ་བའི་དོན་ལྟ་ཚོགས
པའི་ཕྱག་རྒྱ་ཆེན་པོར་དགོས་དང་བསྐྱེད་ནས་འཇུག་པ་ནི་ཐབས་ཙམ་དུ་གནས་པས་འདི་རྟོགས་པར་བྱེད་པའི་ཡན་ལག་ཏུ་འདུ་བ་ཡིན་ནོ། །རྒྱུད་བླ་མ་ལས། ཐུབ་སོ་ཐབ་མོའི་ཚུལ་བསྟན་ནི། །སྙིང་རྗེ་རོ་གཅིག་པ་བཞིན་ནོ། །རྒྱ་ཆེ་སྣ་ཚོགས་ཚུལ་བསྟན་པ་ང་། །རྣམ་གྲངས་སྣ་ཚོགས་བཞིན་ཤེས་བྱ། །ཞེས
གསུངས་པ་བཞིན་ནོ། །དེས་ན་བདེ་བར་གཤེགས་པའི་གསུང་རབ་སྣ་ཚོགས་ཀྱིས་བསྟན་དོན་མཐར་ཐུག་འདི་ཡིན་ཞིང་འདི་གཅིག་པུ་རྟོགས་པས་ཆོས་ཐམས་ཅད་ཀྱི་གནད་ཤེས་པར་འགྱུར་བ་དང་། ཡོན་ཏན་ཐམས་ཅད་རྫོགས་པ་དང་། སྒྲིབ་པ་ཐམས་ཅད་སྤོང་བར་འགྱུར་བས་ན་རྒྱལ་རིགས་གཉིས་ཀྱི་ཕྱག་ཏུ་འང
འཆད་ནས་ཀྱང་ཡང་ཡིན་ལ། དེ་རྟོགས་བྱེད་ཀྱི་སྒོ་བ་ལ་འང་མཚན་དེ་ལྟར་བཏགས་པ་མི་འགལ་ལོ། །ཕྱོགས་ཀྱི་གླང་པོས། ཤེས་རབ་ཕ་རོལ་ཕྱིན་གཉིས་མེད། །ཡེ་ཤེས་དེ་ནི་དེ་བཞིན་གཤེགས། །བསྒྲུབ་བྱ་དོན་དེ་དང་ལྡན་པས། །གཞུང་ལམ་དག་ལ་དེ་སྒྲ་བརྟེན། །ཞེས་པ་ལྟར་འཐད

67

༄༅། །བའི་ཕྱིར་རོ། །ཡིད་བྱེད་བྲལ་བ་འདི་ནི་ཕྱག་རྒྱ་ཆེ། །ཞེས་པ་དེའི་སྐབས་སུ་སྤྱོད་ལྡན་དུ་ཞག་གཅིག་ཏུ་ཚོས་པ་ཁ་ཅིག་ཡིད་བྱེད་དང་བྲལ་བ་ཕྱག་རྒྱ་ཆེན་པོར་འཆད་པ་ནི་ད་ཅང་ཐལ་ཆེས་སོ། སྒྲ་ཇི་བཞིན་རྟོགས་མ་ནུས་ཀྱི་སྐྱོན་མེད་དེ། ལེགས་སྦྱར་གྱི་སྐད་དུ་ཨ་མ་ན་སི་ཀཱ་ར་ཞེས་འབྱུང་བའི
ཨ་ཡིག་གིས་བདག་མེད་དང་སྐྱེ་མེད་ལ་སོགས་པ་སྤྲོས་པ་ཐམས་ཅད་ལས་འདས་པའི་སྟོང་པ་ཉིད་ཀྱི་དོན་སྟོན་ལ། ཡི་གེ་ལྷག་མ་རྣམས་ཀྱིས་སྟོང་པ་དེ་ཉིད་ལ་འང་ཞེན་པ་མེད་པར་ཡིད་བྱེད་དང་བྲལ་བའི་ཡིད་ལ་བྱེད་པ་སྟོན་པས་མཐའ་བྲལ་ཟུང་འཇུག་གི་ཕྱག་རྒྱ་ཆེན་པོར་གྲུབ་པ་ཡིན་ཏེ། མཚན་ཡང་དག
པར་བརྗོད་པ་ལས། ཨ་ནི་ཡིག་འབྲུ་ཀུན་གྱི་མཆོག །དོན་ཆེན་ཡི་གེ་དམ་པ་ཡིན། །ཁོང་ནས་འབྱུང་བ་སྐྱེ་བ་མེད། །ཚིག་ཏུ་བརྗོད་པ་སྤངས་པ་སྟེ། །ཞེས་དང་། བརྟག་གཉིས་ལས། དང་པོའི་དབྱངས་ཀྱི་ཡི་གེ་རང་བཞིན་ཏེ། །ཡི་ཞེས་པ་ནི་ཤེས་རབ་བདག །དེ་ཉིད་ཐབས་ཆེན་ལྡན་པས
ཤེས་རབ། །རྫོགས་པའི་རིམ་པའི་སྦྱོར་བ་ཉིད། །ཅེས་དང་། རྣམ་པར་མི་རྟོག་པ་ལ་འཇུག་པའི་གཟུངས་ལས། རིགས་ཀྱི་བུ་རྒྱུ་གང་གིས་རྣམ་པར་མི་རྟོག་པའི་དབྱིངས་ལ་ཡིད་ལ་བྱེད་པ་ཞེས་བརྗོད། རྣམ་པར་རྟོག་པ་ཐམས་ཅད་ཀྱི་མཚན་མ་ལས་ཡང་དག་པར་འདས་ཤིན་ཏུ་འདས་པའོ། །ཞེས་དང་།
བྱང་ཆུབ་སེམས་དཔའ་སེམས་དཔའ་ཆེན་པོ་རྣམ་པར་རྟོག་པ་ཐམས་ཅད་ཀྱི་མཚན་མ་ཉིད་ལྷུར་ལྷན་ལ་རྟོག་པ་སྤྱི་ཡིད་ལ་མི་བྱེད་པའི་ཡོངས་སུ་སྤོང་བ་ཡིའོ། །ཞེས་སོགས་ཀྱི་ལུང་དང་བཅས་ཏེ། སློབ་དཔོན་ནཱ་རོ་ཏ་པས། ཨ་ཡི་གེ་གཙོ་བོར་གྱུར་པའི་ཡིད་ལ་བྱེད་པ་ནི་ཡིད་ལ་མི་བྱེད་པ་སྟེ། ལོ་ཙཱ་བ་རྒྱལ་བ་ཐེག
ཚིག་དུ་མ་ཕྱིས་པའི་བསྡུ་བའོ། །ཞེས་དང་། ཡང་ན་ཨ་ཞེས་བྱ་བའི་དོན་ཤེས་པ་ལ་པའི་ཚིག་ལ། ཡིད་ལ་བྱེད་པ་བདེ་བ་དག་ལ་བྱིན་གྱིས་བརླབ་པའི་ཚིག་སྟེ། འདི་ལ་ཨ་ཡང་ཡིན་ལ་ཡིད་ལ་མི་བྱེད་པ་འང་ཡིན་པས་ཡིད་ལ་མི་བྱེད་པའོ། །འདིས་ནི་ཡིད་ལ་མི་བྱེད་པའི་གནས་པ་ལས་མ་ཐེ་བྱུང

68

པ་སྟེ་འོད་གསལ་བ་བདག་ལ་བྱིན་གྱིས་བརླབས་པའི་བདག་ཉིད་སྟོང་པ་ཉིད་དང་སྙིང་རྗེ་དབྱེར་མེད་པ་ཟུང་དུ་འཇུག་པ་གཉིས་སུ་མེད་པའི་རྒྱུར་ཡང་དག་པར་རིག་པ་སྐྱེད་པར་འགྱུར་རོ། །ཞེས་བསྟན་པ་རམ་མཛད་པའི་ཕྱིར་རོ། །འདིར་ཕྱག་རྒྱ་ཆེན་པོ་ཞེས་པའི་སྒྲ་དོན་ནི། ཕྱུ་ཤེས་པ་མི་འདའ་བར་བྱེད་པའི
རྒྱ་ནི་སྣང་དང་དོང་ཡིན་པ་ལ་བཀྲུལ་གཞིག་འབྲས་ལམ་ཕྱིར། མི་རྟག་བ་རྣམས་ཀྱིས་ཕྱག་གི་སྒྲ་ཐབས་སུ་བསྒྱུར་ནས་ཕྱག་རྒྱ་ཞེས་པར་བསྒྱུར་བ་སྟེ། འཁོར་བ་དང་མྱ་ངན་ལས་འདས་པའི་ཆོས་ཐམས་ཅད་འདི་ལས་མི་འདའ་བ་ནི་རྒྱ་དང་། ཆེན་པོ་ཞེས་པ་འདི་ལ་གོང་ན་ཆོས་གཞན་མེད་པ་འམ་ལས
ཆོས་དམ་ཚིག་གི་ཕྱག་རྒྱ་གསུམ་ལས་ཁྱད་པར་འཕགས་པའི་དོན་ནོ། །དེས་ན་ཕྱག་རྒྱ་འང་ཡིན་ལ་ཆེན་པོ་འང་ཡིན་པའི་ཕྱིར་གཞི་མཐུན་པའི་འབྲུ་བའོ། །དེ་ལྟར་ཡང་སློབ་དཔོན་བརྡ་ཏྲིས། ཕྱག་རྒྱ་ཆེན་པོ་ནི་རང་གི་ངོ་བོ་ཉིད་ལས་འདའ་བས་ན་ཕྱག་རྒྱ་སྟེ། དཔེར་ན་ཡུ་ཁང་ལ་ཐོགས་སྒྲུར་བའི་རྒྱལ་པོ་ཆེན
པོའི་བཀའ་རྟགས་ཀྱི་ཕྱག་རྒྱ་ལས། མཚན་འབའ་ཞིག་གི་ཀྱ་ལ་གྲུབ་དཔང་། བློན་པོ་སོགས་ལ་གང་གིས་ཀྱང་འདའ་མི་ནུས་པ་བཞིན་ཕྱི་ནང་གི་ཆོས་སྣ་ཚོགས་པ་རྣམས་ཕྱག་རྒྱ་ཆེན་པོ་ཕྱུད་ཀྱིས་ཟུང་བའི་ཡེ་ཤེས་ཟུང་དུ་འཇུག་པའི་ངོ་བོ་ལས་མི་འདའ་བས་ན་ཕྱག་རྒྱ་ཡིན་ལ། ཆེན་པོ་ནི་ལས་ཀྱི་ཕྱག་རྒྱ་དང་། ཆོས
ཀྱི་ཕྱག་རྒྱ་དང་། དམ་ཚིག་གི་ཕྱག་རྒྱ་གསུམ་གྱི་ངོ་བོ་ཡིན་པས་ན་ཆེན་པོའོ། །ཞེས་དང་། སློབ་དཔོན་དགའ་བ་སྐྱོང་གིས། ཕྱག་རྒྱ་ཞེས་པ་ལ་རྒྱས་བཏབ་པའི་ཕྱིར་འདི་ཆེན་པོ་འང་ཡིན་ལ་ཕྱག་རྒྱ་འང་ཡིན་ཏེ། ཞེས་དང་། དཀའ་འགྲེལ་པདྨ་ཅན་ལས། ཕྱག་རྒྱ་ཆེ་ཞེས་བྱ་བ་ནི། །ཞེས་པ་ང་དང་།
མཁྱེན་པ་དང་དཔྱར་བྱུང་བའི་དེ་ཁོ་ན་ཉིད། ཤེས་བྱ་ཐམས་ཅད་སྐྱེད་པར་མཛད་པ་ཤེས་རབ་ཀྱི་ཕ་རོལ་ཏུ་ཕྱིན་པ་ཡིན་ལ། ཐ་དད་མི་གནས་པའི་སྐུ་ང་ལ་འདས་བ་འམ། མི་འཕོ་བའི་བདེ་བ་ལ་རྒྱས་བཏབ་པ་ནི་ཕྱག་རྒྱ་སྟེ། ལས་ཀྱི་ཕྱག་རྒྱ་དང་ཡེ་ཤེས་ཀྱི་ཕྱག་རྒྱ་ལ་མི་སྲུང་བ་ར་འགྱུར་པ་དང་། འཁོར་བའི

69

༄༅། །ཚོགས་དང་བྲལ་བ་བར་རྒྱུ་རབས་ན་ཆེན་མོ་ཞེས་བྱ་བོ། །ཞེས་པ་ཤད་དོ། །ཅི་ཕྱིར་ངམ་གི་ཕྱག་རྒྱ་ཆེན་པོ་འདི་ཕྱག་རྒྱ་བཞི་འི་ཡ་རྒྱལ་ལ་ཡིན་ན་ཕྱག་རྒྱ་གཞན་གསུམ་པོ་ངེས་པར་སྔོན་དུ་འགྲོ་དགོས་པ་ལ... དེ་ལྟར་མ་བ་ཀད་པར་སོ། །ཞེན་སློབ་མེད་དེ་གདུལ་བྱ་དབང་པོ་རྣོན་པོ་འི་རྣོན
པོ་འདོད་དག་ཐུགས་ཀྱི་དགོས་གྲུབ་དོན་དུ་མི་གཞི་རབ་རྣམས་ནི་ཐོག་མ་ཉིད་ནས་ཕྱག་རྒྱ་ཆེན་པོ་ཉིད་ལ་འཇུག་པར་རྒྱུད་རྣམས་ལས་གསུངས་པ་ཡིན་ནོ། །དཔེ་རང་ཆོས་ན། དུས་ཀྱི་འཁོར་ལོ་ལས། ལས་ཀྱི་ཕྱག་རྒྱ་ཡོངས་ལ་དོར་ནས་ཀྱང་། །བརྟགས་པ་འི་ཡེ་ཤེས་ཕྱག་རྒྱ་སྤངས་ནས། །མཆོག་ཏུ་མི་འགྱུར་སྒྲུབ་པ
ཡིས། །ཕྱག་རྒྱ་ཆེན་མོ་རྣམ་པར་བསྒོམ། །ཞེས་དང་། འདོད་པར་སྤྱོད་པའི་དངོས་གྲུབ་ནི། །ལས་ཀྱི་ཕྱག་རྒྱ་ལ་བསྟེན་པར་བྱ། །འོག་མིན་མཐར་ཕྱུག་བར་དུ་ནི། །ཡེ་ཤེས་ཕྱག་རྒྱ་ལ་གཟུང་བ་ཞེས་བྱ་བོ། །རྣལ་འབྱོར་ཆེན་པོ་ཀུན་མཁྱེན་ཉིད། །གཅིག་ཕྱུར་སངས་རྒྱས་བདེ་བ་ཉིད། །ཕྱག
རྒྱ་ཆེན་མོ་འི་ཡན་ལག་གི །སྒོམ་པས་བསྒྲུབ་བྱ་འདི་ཉིད་དོ། །ཞེས་དང་། འགྲེལ་ཆེན་ལས། ལས་ཀྱི་ཕྱག་རྒྱ་ཡོངས་དོར་ནས་ཞེས། །ཡེ་ཤེས་ཕྱག་རྒྱ་རྣམ་པར་སྤངས་ནས། །ཕྱག་རྒྱ་ཆེ་ལས་ཡང་དག་སྐྱེས། །ལྷན་སྐྱེས་གཞན་དང་འགྲོགས་པ་མིན། །ཞེས་སྤྱད་པ་སྟེ། དུལ་བ་འོར་ཞབས
ཀྱི་སྤྱོད་རྡུལ་མཚན་དགུ། །རང་གིས་དང་པོ་ནས་རྟོགས་པ་སྟེ། །འཁོར་གྱིས་སྤྱོད་ཀྱི་སྤྱོད་པ་ལ་སོགས་ཡིན། །ཐམས་ཅད་བྱ་པོ་རིམ་བཞིན་བསྒོམ། །ཞེས་དཔང་པོ་ཡང་རབ་ཀྱིས་སྤྱོད་པ་ཡན་ལག་དྲུག་ལ་ལ་སོ་རབས་མ་བསྐྱེད་པ་འི་ཡན་ལག་པོ་དེ་ན་ཕྱག་རྒྱ་ཆེན་པོ་རྟོགས་པར་བ་ཤད་པ་ལྟ་རོ། །ཆེས་དབང
རྣོ་ན་ཉིད་དམ་ཡིན་ན་ལ་ཐོག་ཅར་ཕྱག་རྒྱ་ཆེན་པོ་སྒོམ་པ་འི་རྣལ་འབྱོར་པ་འཇུག་ངའི་ལེ་ལ་སྟེ། དེ་སྐད་དུ། མདོར་ན་རང་བཞིན་མ་ཡོ་བ་ཡ་ཕྲག །འཇིག་རྟེན་བྱ་བ་པོ་རྣམས་ནི། །གཉིས་མེད་ཡེ་ཤེས་བསྒོམ་པར་བྱ། །སྤྱོད་པ་ཞི་ང་ལས་མ་གཏོགས་པ། །རྟོག་མེད་ཉིད་དུ་མི་འགྱུར་བས། །དེ་ལ་ནི་སྨོན

70

དུ་སྨོན་པ་ཉིད། །རྣལ་འབྱོར་པས་ནི་རྟག་ཏུ་བསྒོམ། །དེ་ནས་ལྷ་ཚོགས་གཟུགས་མཐོང་ནས། །མཆོག་ཏུ་མི་འགྱུར་བདེ་བསྒྲུབ་ཕྱིར། །ལས་ཀྱི་ཕྱག་རྒྱ་ལ་སོགས་བསྟེན། །ཞེས་དང་། ཕྱག་རྒྱ་ཆེན་པོ་མི་ཤེས་པར། །ལས་ཀྱི་ཕྱག་རྒྱ་གཅིག་སྤུ་བས། །དེ་ཉིད་བརྒྱུད་པ་ལས་ཉམས
ནེ། །རྣལ་འབྱོར་པ་དེ་ནི་ཏུ་འཁོར་འགྲོ། །ཞེས་འབྱུང་བའི་ཕྱིར་རོ། །གཞན་ཡང་ཕྱག་རྒྱ་ཆེན་པོ་ཡིན་ན་ཕྱག་རྒྱ་གཞན་གསུམ་པོ་སྔོན་དུ་འགྲོ་དགོས་པ་འི་ཁྱབ་པ་དེ་ཤིན་ཏུ་འཐད་ལ་ཆེས་ཏེ་གྲུབ་པ་བརྙེས་པ་འི་སློབ་དཔོན་རྣམས་ཀྱིས་སློབ་མ་སྐལ་ལྡན་ལ་སྤྲུལ་པ་ཅན་གྱི་དབང་བསྐུར་བ་དང་། ལུང་འདོགས
པ་དང་། གདམས་ངག་དེ་ལས་བརྩོན་གསུང་ཡང་མི་དགོས་པར་བྱིན་རླབས་ལས་མ་བད་བསྟན་པ་ཙམ་ལ་ཡེ་ཤེས་རྟོགས་མེད་དུ་སྐྱེས་པ་འི་ལོ་རྒྱུས་ཚད་ལྡན་མང་དག་ཅིག་འཕགས་བོད་དུ་གྲགས་འདུག་པ་དང་། ཡེ་ཤེས་ཀ་འབབ་པ་འི་ཐབས་སུ་ཕྱག་ཆེན་གྱི་ཡེ་ཤེས་སྐྱེ་བར་གསུངས་པ་སོ་ནའ་ལ་འབང་དེ་ལྟ
ངེས་ཤིང་། དཔལ་འདུས་ཀྱི་འཁོར་ལོ་འི་མཐའ་དག་རྫུས་ཞབས་སྐྱབས་དབང་རྒྱུད་ཀྱི་ལུང་གོ་རྟེན་སྐལ་བ་སོགས་དབང་པོ་འི་རིམ་པས་ཕྱག་རྒྱ་གསུམ་ལས་གང་ཡང་རུང་བས་ཕྱག་རྒྱ་ཆེན་པོ་སྒྲུབ་པ་འི་ཚུལ་མཐའ་ཡས་པ་བ་ཀད་པ་འི་ཕྱིར་རོ། །དེས་ན་རང་ལུགས་ཕྱག་པོ་ཧཱུྃ་ཀྲི་ཐ་མཉེད་པ་ལྷན་ཅིག་སྐྱེས་སྦྱོར་གྱི་ཁྲིད་དོ
འདི་ཡིན་ལ། ཐོབ་དབང་ཅན་གྱི་རྒྱལ་པ་དང་། སྤྱོད་ཤིང་རྩེ་དབང་པོ་འི་རིམ་པ་ལས་འཆད་འཚེད་བསྙུ་པ་ཐད་དཔང་ཀ་ཤིག་ཏུ་འཚད་དབྱེ་རབ་སྐྱེར་ཡོད་པ་རྣམས་གཉིས་ཀ་ནས། གདུལ་བྱ་ཐུགས་ཀྱི་ཐུན་མོང་མ་ཡིན་པ་འི་སྤྱོད་དུ་མི་ལྡན་ཡང་སྒྱུར་བྲེག་ཆེན་ཅམ་གྱི་རིགས་སུ་ངེས་པ་འམ་མ་ངེས་པ་འི་རིགས་ཅན་རྣམས་ལ་ཐབ་བསྟུགས་ནི
འཆད་སྤྱོ་ལ་ཇི་འདོད་པ་དང་ཏུ་ཐལ་ན། ཕྱག་རྒྱ་གཞན་རྣམས་ཀྱི་རྣམ་གཞག་མི་མཛད་ཀྱང་ལམ་དེས་མཐར་ཕྱིན་བྱེད་པ་འི་ཟུང་འཇུག་གི་ཡེ་ཤེས་སྐྱེས་པ་ཐབས་ཀྱི་གདུ་བ་བྱེད་པ་ང་སྔོན་ལྷ་བཞའ་འཕོས་པ་སྐྱེན་སྒྱུར་དང་དེ་ལྟར་ཀྱི་ཁྱད་པར་རྒྱུས་ཕྱག་རྒྱ་ཆེན་པོ་འི་མཆོག་ཐོབ་པར་བཞེད་པ་ཡིན་ནོ། །ཡང་ལས་ཀགས

71

༄༅། །ཡུལ་གྱི་མཁས་པ་འགའ་ཞིག་ཕར་ཕྱིན་ཐེག་པ་འི་ཟུང་འཇུག་གི་ཡེ་ཤེས་དེ་ཉིད་ཕྱག་ཆེན་དུ་འཆད་པ་བར་ཡོད་པར་མངོན་ཏེ། ལྷན་སྐྱེས་རྡོ་རྗེ་འི་དེ་ཁོ་ན་ཉིད་བཅུ་པ་འི་འགྲེལ་པ་ལས། འདི་ཉིད་ལ་དེ་ཁོ་ན་ཉིད་ཀྱི་ཡེ་ཤེས་ཕྱག་རྒྱ་ཆེན་པོ་ཞེས་བཅིག་འཇོད་དེ། ཇི་སྐད་དུ། ཐབས
དང་ཤེས་རབ་མཉམ་སྦྱོར་བ། །སྒོམ་པ་ཉིད་ནི་རྣལ་འབྱོར་མཆོག །ཕྱག་རྒྱ་ཆེན་པོ་ར་མཉམ་སྦྱོར་བ། །སྒོམ་པ་རྣ་ནི་རྒྱལ་བས་བཤད། །ཅེས་པ་སོ། །ཐབས་དང་ཤེས་རབ་མཉམ་པར་སྦྱོར་བ་སྒོམ་པ་ཙམ་ནི་ཕྱག་རྒྱ་ཆེན་པོ་སྒོམ་པ་མ་ཡིན་ཏེ་ཕ་རོལ་ཏུ་ཕྱིན་པ་འི་ཚུལ་དང་སྔགས་ཀྱི་ཚུལ་ཐ་དད་མེད
པར་ཐལ་བར་འགྱུར་བ་འི་ཕྱིར་རོ། །ཞེས་བསྡུགས་བཀག་གོ། །ཞེས་ཕྱོགས་གཉིས་བཤད་པ་འི་ཕྱིར་རོ། །འདི་སྐབས་རང་ལུགས་གསལ་པར་མ་བཞག་ཀྱང་ལྷ་བ་འི་ཆ་ནས་དེ་གཉིས་ཐ་དད་མེད་པར་བཞེད་པ་གསལ་ལ་ཏེ་དེ་ཁོ་ན་ཉིད་བཅུ་པ་འི་གཞུང་འགྲེལ་ལ་ཞིབ་ཏུ་སྦྱོས་ཤིག་དང་ཤེས་པར་འགྱུར་རོ། །འདི
དག་ཡང་རིགས་དང་བཅས་པ་འི་རྒྱ་མཚན་མང་དུ་སྦྱོར་ནུས་མོད་ཀྱི་འཕྲོས་པས་ཆོག་གོ། ❀ །།གཉིས་པ་ནི། འོན་ཞི་ལྷག་ཟུང་འཇུག་ཅེས་མིང་དུ་བཏགས་པ་དེ་འི་ཟུང་དུ་འཇུག་ཚུལ་ཇི་ལྟ་བུ་ཞེ་ན། ཞི་གནས་ལ་བསམས་པ་དེ་འི་སྟེང་དུ་ལྷག་མཐོང་གི་ཡེ་ཤེས་སྐྱེས་པ་ན། ཡེ་ཤེས་དེ་ཉིད་ཀྱང་དེ་ངང་དེ་འི་ངོ་ན་དང་ར་
མཉམ་དུ་འགྱུར་བས་ཟུང་འཇུག་ཅེས་བྱ་སྟེ། དེ་ལྟར་རྟོགས་པ་འི་ཤར་ཟབ་དེ་འི་མཉམ་བཞག་གི་གནས་ལུགས་ལུ་ཞི་ལྷག་གི་རྣལ་འབྱོར་ཐ་དང་དུ་མི་དམིགས་པ་འི་ཕྱིར་རོ། །ལྷག་མཐོང་གི་ཡེ་ཤེས་མཚན་ཉིད་པ་དེ་འང་སྒྱུར་ལ་མཆེས་མཆོག་གི་སྐབས་སུ་ཐོག་མར་སྐྱེས་པ་ནས་བ་སྒོམས་ཏེ་གོང་ནས་གོང་དུ་རྟེགས་ལ་རྟེ
བརྟན་དུ་འགྱུར་བ་དེ་ནས་བཟུང་སྟེ་ཞི་ལྷག་ཟུང་འཇུག་དངོས་ཀྱང་འགྲུབ་པས་ཕར་ཕྱིན་ཐེག་པ་ལྟར་ན་ཇི་སྲིད་མཉམ་རྗེས་མ་འདྲེས་ཀྱི་བར་དུ་རྗེས་ཐོབ་ཏུ་ཤེས་རབ་ཀྱིས་དཔྱོད་ཅིང་མཉམ་གཞག་ཏུ་དཔྱད་དོན་ལ་མི་རྟོག་པར་རྩེ་གཅིག་ཏུ་གནས་པ་ཡིན་ཞིང་། མཉམ་རྗེས་འདྲེས་པ་ནས་བསྒོམས་པ་དཔྱོད་འཇོག་ཟུང་འཇུག་དུ་སྐྱོང་ཀྱི་སྒོམ་པ་ཞིག་ནས་ལྷུན

72

གྱིས་གྲུབ་པ་འི་ཤེས་རབ་དེས་ཆོས་རྣམས་ཀྱི་དེ་ཉིད་རྩོལ་མེད་དུ་མཐོང་བར་འགྱུར་བ་ཡིན་ནོ། །དེས་ན་རྟོག་དཔྱོད་བྱེད་པ་འི་ཤེས་རབ་ནི་ལྷག་མཐོང་རྟོགས་པར་བྱེད་པ་འི་ཡན་ལག་ཡིན་པ་འི་ཕྱིར་ལྷག་མཐོང་དུ་འཇོད་ཀྱི་ལྷག་མཐོང་དངོས་མ་ཡིན་པ་ཤེས་པར་བྱ་འོ། །རྒྱུ་མཚན་འདིས་ཟུང་འཇུག་གི་རྣལ་འབྱོར་དངོས་ཀྱི
མཐོང་བ..... གོང་གི་ཞི་ལྷག་ཟུང་འབྲེལ་དུ་བཤད་པ་རྣམས་ནི་ལྷག་མཐོང་གི་མ་འདྲེ་དང་འབྲེལ་བར་གོ་དགོས་སོ། །འདི་ལ་ཁ་ཅིག་ལྷག་མཐོང་ཆོས་རབ་རྣམ་འབྱེད་ཀྱི་ཤེས་རབ་ཡིན་པ་ས་རྟོག་དཔྱོད་ལས་མ་འདས་ཤིང་། ཞི་གནས་ནི་རྟོག་དཔྱོད་དང་བྲལ་བ་ཡིན་པ་ར་འཁས་པས་ན་དེ་གཉིས་ཟུང་དུ་འཇུག་པ་ར་ཁས་ལེན་
ན་རྒྱ་མི་ཤོང་བ་དང་། བག་ཞིག་ཟུང་འཇུག་གི་དོན་ཞིག་ནས་ཀྱི་རྩེ་དང་མི་འབྱུལ་བ་བཞིན་རྟོག་དཔྱོད་ཀྱང་སྐྱེད་རྒྱུ་ཡོད་པ་རྣམ་གྲགས་པ་བསྒྱུར་པ་འི་མཚོ་དང་ཉ་ཞིག་གི་ནང་ན་ཉ་རྒྱུ་ཞིང་འཕྱོ་བ་ལྟ་བུར་འདོད་མོད་ཀྱི། དེ་ལྟར་ཡུ་རབ་མི་ཤོང་བ་དང་འགལ་བ་བའི་རྗེ་བཙུན་ལྷག་མཐོང་གི་ཡེ་ཤེས་རྟོག་དཔྱོད་ཀྱི་ངོ་བོར་ཞེན་པ་དེས
བ་ནས། དེ་ཙེ་ཤིན་ཏུ་མི་རིགས་ཏེ། ལྷག་མཐོང་གི་དོན་ནི། མདོ་སྡེ་དགོངས་པ་ངེས་འགྲེལ་ལས། བཅོམ་ལྡན་འདས་ལ་ས། གང་གི་ཕྱིར་བྱང་ཆུབ་སེམས་དཔའ་དང་གི་སོ་སོར་ཤེས་པ་མི་མཐོང་ཞེས་པ་འི་རྣམ་པར་ཤེས་པ་བ་ཞ་ཅི་མཐོང་ལ་ཀུན་གཞི་དང་ཀུན་གཞི་འི་རྣམ་ཤེས་དང་། བཟང་གསལ
དང་། སེམས་པ་དང་། མིག་དང་། གཟུགས་དང་། མིག་གི་རྣམ་པར་ཤེས་པ་ནས་ལུས་ཀྱི་རྣམ་པར་ཤེས་པ་འི་བར་དང་ནང་གི་སོ་སོ་རང་གི་ཡེ་ཕྱང་ཀྱང་མི་མཐོང་ལ་དེ་ཡང་ཡང་དག་པ་ཇི་ལྟ་བ་བཞིན་དུ་ཡིན་པ་དེ་ནི་བྱང་ཆུབ་སེམས་དཔའ་དོན་དམ་ལ་མཁས་པ་ཞེས་བྱ་སྟེ། ཞེས་དང་། རྟེན་དེ་འི་འོད་ཀྱི་རྒྱལ
པོ་ལས། ཇི་ལྟར་བ་ར་སྣང་ནམ་མཁའ་བཞིན། །ཆོས་ཀྱི་མཚན་ཉིད་དེ་འདྲ་པར། །ཐོན་གྱི་མཐའ་དང་ཕྱི་མ་འི་མཐའ། །དེ་ལྟར་རྒྱུ་བ་ང་མཐོང་བ་ར་འགྱུར། །ནམ་མཁའ་གཟུང་བ་མེད་པ་ར་བཤད། །དེ་ལ་གཟུང་བ་མི་སྲིད་དེ། །ཆོས་ཀྱི་རང་བཞིན་དེ་ཉིད་ཡིན། །ག་ཟུང་བ་མེད་པ་ནས

73

༄། །མཁའ་འདྲ། །དེ་ལྟ་བུ་ཞི་ཆོག་ང་སྐྱ་ན་ནི། །དེ་ལ་གང་ཡང་མཐོང་བ་མེད། །སྣང་དག་ཆོས་འདི་མི་མཐོང་བ། །དེ་ཡི་ཆོས་རྣམས་བསམ་མི་ཁྱབ། །ཅེས་དང་། བསོད་ནམས་ཐམས་ཅད་བསྡུས་པའི་ཏིང་ངེ་འཛིན་གྱི་མདོ་ལས། གང་གི་ཚེ་ཆོས་ཐམས་ཅད་རང་བཞིན་
གྱིས་རྣམ་པར་ཞི་བ་དང་། རང་བཞིན་གྱིས་སྟོང་པར་རྟོགས་པ་དང་། གནས་དུས་སུ་སྐྱེས་པ་དང་། མཐུན་བ་དང་། གདན་དུ་ཡང་ལུས་སུ་ཉུང་ནམ་ལ་འདས་པར་མཐོང་བ་དང་། གང་མཐོང་བ་དེ་ལ་ང་མི་མཐོང་བ་དང་། ཇི་ལྟར་མི་མཐོང་བ་དང་། རྣམ་པར་མི་མཐོང་བ་དེ་ལྟར་མཐོང་ན་ཚུལ་བཞིན་དུ་མཐོང་
བ་ཞེས་བྱའོ། །ཞེས་སོགས་མཐའ་ཡས་པར་གསུངས་པའི་མདོ་སྡེ་རྣམས་པས་འབྱུང་བ་ལྟར། ཆོས་རྣམས་ལ་ཤེས་རབ་དང་རྟེན་འབྲེལ་དུ་གཏན་ལ་འབེབས་པའི་རྣམ་དཔྱོད་ཀྱིས་དཔྱད་པ་ན་ཅི་འང་མ་མཐོང་བར་ཤེས་པ་དེ་ཉིད་ཀྱང་དེ་ལྟ་བུའི་རིག་པ་ལས་འདས་པས་ཡུལ་ཡུལ་ཅན་གཉིས་སུ་མེད་པར་གྱུར་པ་ནི་རང་རིག་སོ་སོ་རང་གིས་རྟོགས་པ་ཡིན་པས། ཤེས་རབ་
ཀྱི་ཕ་རོལ་ཏུ་ཕྱིན་པ་དེ་ཉིད་ཡིན་པའི་ཕྱིར་ན་ཏེ། དེ་ལས་རིག་པའི་སྣང་ལ་ཕྱག་པ་ཐལ་བར་ནུས་ཤིང་། དེ་ཉིད་ལས་ཀུན་ཆེས་རྣམ་པར་ཐར་པ་ལ་འགྲོ་བ་ལ་ཞེས་པ་འབྱུང་བའི་ཕྱིར་རོ། །དེ་ལྟར་མ་ཡིན་པ་ཡུལ་མཐོང་ནི། ཡང་ཤེས་དེ་རྣམ་རྟོག་གི་ཕྱིང་བཞི་ག་ཡིན་པར་འགྱུར་ནམ་རིག་པའི་སྐྱེད་པ་ལེ་ལ་ཐུབ་པ་ལྟ་བ
སྲོལ་ཏེ། རྣམ་རྟོག་ཉིད་ཡང་རིག་པ་ཡིན་པ་དང་བཞིན་ཡིན་པའི་ཕྱིར་ཏེ། དེང་རྒྱལ་བས། རྣམ་རྟོག་ནི་མ་རིག་ཆེན་པོ་སྟེ། །འཁོར་བའི་རྒྱ་མཚོར་ལྟུང་བྱེད་ཡིན། །རྟོག་མེད་ཏིང་ངེ་འཛིན་ལ་གནས་ན། །ནམ་མཁའ་བཞིན་དུ་རྟོག་མེད་གསལ། །ཞེས་འབྱུང་བའི་ཕྱིར་རོ། །འདི་ལ་ཁ་ཅིག་དེ་ལྟར་ན་གལ་ཏེ
སྒྲུབ་པ་ལས་རིགས་འདུག་ཏེ་ཨ་ཕོར་ཚ་བའི་ཅ་རྒྱག་སྒོམ་གསུང་བ་ཅན་ལྡོག་ཏུ་འགྱུར་བ། ཁྱོད་རང་གི་ལུགས་ཀྱི་རྣམ་རྟོག་ཆོས་སྐུ་འི་རྣམ་བཞག་དེ་ནས་ཉམས་པར་འགྱུར་རོ་ཞེ་ན་སྐྱོན་མེད་དེ། བསྒོམ་སྒོམ་གསུང་བ་བཞི་སྟུག་ལ་ཀྱི་ཐབས་ཕྱུང་བར་ཅན་གྱིས་ཟིན་པའི་འདོད་ཆགས་ལ་སོགས་པས། ཐ

74

མལ་པའི་འདོད་ཆགས་ལ་སོགས་པ་ལས་ཁྱད་པར་སྐྱེས་ཤིང་། དེའི་ཚེ་ཐབས་དང་ལྡན་པའི་ཉོན་མོངས་པ་ལ་སོགས་པ་དེ་འདོད་ཆགས་ལ་སོགས་པ་མཚན་ཉིད་པར་མི་འགྱུར་ཏེ། འདོད་ཆགས་ལ་སོགས་པའི་ཡེ་ཤེས་ཡིན་པའི་ཕྱིར། འོད་དེ་བཟློག་སྒོམ་དུ་མི་འགྱུར་བའི་ཕྱིར་ན་བཟློག་སྒོམ་དུ་འགྱུར་ཏེ།
འདོད་ཆགས་ལ་མཚན་ཉིད་པ་རྒྱུ་ཞིག་པས་ལམ་དུ་སྤྱད་པ་དང་འབྲེལ་པ་དང་། ཀུན་ཏུ་ཅིར་བ་སོགས་འདོད་ཆགས་ཀྱི་ཆོ་ག་ལས་དང་རིགས་མཐུན་པ་བཞིན་དུ་ཐམས་ཅད་ཀྱང་རིགས་མཐུན་པའི་ཕྱིར་ཏེ། རིགས་འདུ་ཞེས་པའི་རྒྱུད་ལས། འདུག་པའི་ཕྱིར་ན་དངོས་མ་ཡིན། །ཤེས་རབ་ཐབས་ཀྱིས་རྒྱུན་བཅད་ཀྱི། །གཞན
དུ་ན་ཉོན་མོངས་པ་མཚན་ཉིད་པས་རང་གིས་རང་བཅིངས་པར་འགྱུར་ཏེ་མི་འགྱུར། ཁྱད་པར་དུ་གསང་སྔགས་ཀྱི་ཐབས་པའི་འདོད་ཆགས་ཀྱི་གཉེན་པོ་སྟེ་ཡང་དེ་ཉིད་སྐྱོད་ཅིག་དང་ཞེས་པ་ཡང་བསྒྱུར་རོ། །འོན་ཀྱང་ཐབས་ཀྱིས་མི་ལྡན་པ་སྟུག་ཆུང་འཛུགས་པ་ལས་ཉམས་པར་འགྱུར་བའི་ཚེ་ཚོགས་དང་སྤྱོད་རྒྱུད་པ་དང་དབང་ཀྱིས་ཟིན་པའི་རྟོག་སྤྱོད་ཡིན
པ་ལ་སྐྱོན་མེད་དོ་ཞེ་ན། དེ་འདང་མི་འཐད་དེ་དུས་ལ་བ་ལྟ་མ་རིམ་རྣམས་ལ་ལྷག་མཐོང་གི་ཡེ་ཤེས་མཐའ་བ་སོགས་པར་བྱེད་པའི་ཕྱིར་དང་སྒྲ་རྒྱུད་སྒོམ་གསུང་བ་ཡིན་གྱི་ཐབས་ཟིན་པའི་ཉམས་གཉུག་མ་ཡིད་ཅིང་འབྲུང་བ་དེ་བཞི་ཤིང་ད་རྒྱུ་བའི་ཕྱིར་དང་། ལུགས་ཀྱི་ཕྱག་ཆེན་སྒོམ་པ་ལ་ཐོག་མ་རང་ཡང་དག་པར་སྒོམ་བྱེད
པར་མ་བཅ་ཤད་པའི་ཕྱིར་དང་། སྐྱེད་རྫོགས་ཟུང་འཇུག་བསྒོམ་སྒྲུབ་པའི་ཐབས་ཀྱང་པར་ཅན་རྣམས་ལ་ཡི་ཕྱག་རྒྱ་ཆེན་པོ་སྒྲུབ་པའི་ཐབས་སུ་གསུངས་ཀྱི། ནང་འཛུག་གི་རྣལ་འབྱོར་ཕྱག་རྒྱ་ཆེན་པོ་དེ་མ་ཐོན་དུ་ཀྱང་ཕྱིན་དང་དུ་མཐོལ་བ་རམ་ཁ་བཤད་པའི་ཕྱིར་རོ། །འདི་ལ་རྣམ་རྟོག་ཆོས་སྐུ་ཞེས་པའི་ཆོས་སྐུ་ཉིད
ཅིག་གྲགས་པ་འདི་འི་དོན་ནི། རྣམ་པར་རྟོག་པ་ཙམ་ལ་སྐྱོང་བའི་ཆོས་འདི་མཐར་དགོས་ཀྱི་རྒྱུ་ཆེ་བས་འདི་བ་ཆེན་པོ་ལས་མ་འདས་པས་སྣང་ཙམ་ཉིད་ནས་ཆོས་ཀྱི་སྐུར་ཤར་བ། དཔེར་ན་རྒྱ་མཚོའི་རླབས་བ་རྣམས་ཆུ་ཡི་ངོ་བོ་ལས་མ་འདས་པ་དེ་སྣང་ཙམ་ཉིད་ནས་རྒྱ་མཚོ་ལ་བཞིན་དུ་ཐིམ་པ་སུ་འབྱུང་བའི་ལུང་ལ་སྐྱོལ་ཡིན་པར

75

༄། །སྣང་བ་ལ་དོན་དེ་ཉིད་དུ་ཅི་སྐྱེ་བ་མི་འགྱུར་བས། གཞན་དུ་རྣམ་རྟོག་ཉིད་ཆོས་ཀྱི་སྐུ་ཡིན་པས་རྟོག་སྤྱོད་ཀྱི་ཉེར་ཚེ་བ་སྤྱད་པ་ཚམ་ཀྱིས་གྲོལ་བར་སྐྱེ་བ་ཉིད་ཡང་ཡིན་པར་ཐལ་བར་རྟོགས་ཤིག །ཡང་ཁ་ཅིག་འདི་སྐད་ཅེས་པ་ཇི་སྙེད་བགྲངས་ལ་སོགས་པ་ཆགས་མེད་པར་ཐོབ
པ་དང་རྟེན་སོ། །དེ་ནི་གྲོལ་བ་རྒྱུ་ང་བར་ཟད་དེ། ལུགས་ཀྱི་རྒྱུ་ཤེལ་མདོང་ཅིག་ལས་ཞི་སྣག་གི་རྣམ་གཞག་མཛད་འཆུག་པ་དང་། ཕྱིད་པར་རྣལ་འབྱོར་ཀུན་སྐྱོད་ཀྱི་རྒྱུད་ལས་གསུངས་པའི་དོན་སྐྱོབ་པོ་དང་པ་པོའི་རྟེན་བཞུགས་པར། དང་པོ་རིམ་སུ་བསྟན་པ་ནི། ཕྱག་རྒྱ་ཆེན་པོ་ལ་ལ་སོགས
ལ་ས་བརྟན་ཏེ། ཕྱག་རྒྱ་ཆེན་པོ་ཆོས་ཀྱི་བྱིངས་སོ། །རྣལ་འབྱོར་ཀུན་ཞེས་པ་ཤེས་བྱེད་ནི་ཞི་གནས་དང་ལྷག་མཐོང་ངོ་། །ཞེས་དང་། རྣལ་འབྱོར་ཀུན་གྱི་དབང་ཕྱུག་རྒྱལ། །ཞེས་པ་ཉིད་ཡོད་གཅིག་གནས་ལུས་མཐོང་དེ་ཆེས་ཉུ་ཉེ་སྐྱེད་པ་མོ་མཆོག་ཏུ་གྱུར་པ་རང་ཤད་པའོ། །ཞེས་ཞི་ལྷག་གི་མང
འདུད་པ་ཙམ་དུ་མ་ཟད་དེ། ཕྱག་རྒྱ་ཆེན་པོ་སྒྲུབ་པར་བྱེད་པའི་རྣལ་འབྱོར་མཆོག་ཏུ་ཤར་ཤུང་བའི་ཕྱིར་རོ། ། ། །གཉིས་པ་དེ་ལ་ཉམས་རྟོགས་སྐྱེ་ཚུལ་ལ། ཉམས་དང་རྟོགས་པ་གཉིས་ལས། དང་པོ་ནི། ཞེན་པ་མེད་པའི་བདེ་ཆེ་ན་ཉམས་ཉོན་ཆད་མེད། །ས་ཚེ་ང་ཏེན་མེད་པའི་འོད་གསལ་ལ་སྐྱིབ
གཡོགས་བྲལ། །སྤྲོས་བ་འདས་པའི་མི་རྟོག་ལྷུན་གྱིས་གྲུབ། །རྩོལ་མེད་ཉམས་སྐྱོང་རྒྱུན་ཆད་མེད་པར་ཤོག །ཅེས་པ་སྟེ། དེ་ལྟར་བཞི་ལྟག་གི་རྣལ་འབྱོར་ལ་མཉམ་པར་བཞག་པ་ན་སྒོམ་ཉམས་འབྱུང་བའི་ཉམས་གསུམ་སྒྲུ་བར་འགྱུར་ཏེ། ཞེན་ཆགས་དང་བྲལ་བའི་བདེ་བ་ཞི་བ་ལྡོ་སྐྱེས་ཅིང་མེད་པའི་ཉམས
དང་། ཡུལ་ལ་མཚན་མ་རང་འཛིན་པ་དང་བྲལ་བའི་རང་རིག་འོད་གསལ་ལ་སྒྲིབ་གཡོགས་ལ་མེད་པའི་ཉམས་དང་། སྤྲོ་ཡི་སྒྲོ་ཡུལ་ལས་འདས་པའི་མི་རྟོག་པ་སྟོང་པ་ཉིད་ལྷུན་གྱིས་གྲུབ་པའི་ཉམས་སོ། །དེ་ལྟ་བའི་ཉམས་པ་མི་རྟོག་པའི་ཉམས་གསུམ་ཀ་རང་ལྷུང་ངང་དུ་ཤར་བ་ལ་སྤྲུ་གོལ་དུ་ཤར་ལ་ཞེན་པ་མེད་ཅིང་

76

གིས་ཀྱང་མི་དཔྱོད་པར་གཉུག་མའི་ངང་དུ་བཞག་པ་ཀུན་རྟོལ་སྐྱབ་མེད་པར་རང་གིས་རྒྱུན་མི་འཆད་དུ་འབྱུང་བ་ཆོས་ཉིད་དོ། །དེ་ལ་ཉམས་སྒྲོན་དང་བཅས་པ་ནི། ཆགས་ཞེན་དང་བཅས་པའི་བདེ་ཉམས། མཚན་འཛིན་དང་བཅས་པ་ཡི་གསལ་ཉམས། སྤྲོས་བཅས་བའི་མི་རྟོག་པ་ནམ་ཀ་དེ་དག་གི། དང
པོས་འདོད་ཁམས་སུ་གཏོལ། གཉིས་པས་གཟུགས་ཁམས་སུ་བཏོལ། གསུམ་པས་གཟུགས་མེད་ཁམས་སུ་གཏོལ་བའི་ཕྱིར་ཆགས་ཞེན་ལ་སོགས་པའི་སྐྱོན་དེ་དག་ནི་རྣམ་པ་ཀུན་ཏུ་སྤང་བར་བྱ་ཞིང་། ཁྱད་པར་ཉམས་ལ་ཞེན་པ་ལ་སྐྱོ་བའི་ཕྱིར་སྐྱོལ་བ་བྱེད་པ་དང་སྤྱོས་པ་ལ་ཚེ་དང་འཛིན་དང་གཉིས་ཀ་རང་སྟོན་པོ་ཉམས་པར
མཚུངས་ཏེ་ལྟ་མས་ཉམས་སྐྱོང་བའི་བཀག་ས་བྱེད་ཅིང་། སྤྱི་མས་སྦྱེས་པ་རྒྱུན་ཆད་པར་འགྱུར་བའི་ཕྱིར་དང་། མ་པ་ཀུན་ཏུ་རང་དགས་མཚན་འཛིན་མ་ལ་སྐྱབ་རྣམས་ཀྱི་རྟོག་པ་སྐྱོང་བ་ཉིད་གནད་དུ་ཆེ་བ་ཞེས་གདམས་པའི་ཕྱིར་སྐྱོན་ལ་མ་མཛད་པའོ། །འདི་སྐབས་ཀྱི་བདེ་ཉམས་ནི་ལུས་སེམས་ལ་གཉིས་ཀ་ནི་བདེ་བ་ཡིན་ལ།
གསལ་ཉམས་ནི་ཤེས་པ་བྱིང་རྨུགས་ལ་སོགས་པའི་སྐྱོན་གྱིས་མ་བསྒྲིབས་པར་ངང་རིག་རང་གསལ་ལ་དྭངས་སྙིང་བ་ཡིན་པ་ནས་རྩོལ་མེད་དུ་ཆོས་རྣམས་ཀྱི་དེ་ཉིད་ཤེས་པ་དང་། དྲགས་པ་བཅུ་ཆར་བ་སོགས་ཡིན་ཞིང་། མི་རྟོག་པའི་ཉམས་ནི་མི་རྟོག་པ་ཤས་ཆེ་བས་ཐམས་ཅད་སྟོང་པར་མཐོང་ང་སོགས་ཡིན་ནོ། །དེ་དག
འབོ་སོར་ཆེ་དབའི་ཚད་དང་ཞེན་པ་མེད་པར་གཉུག་མའི་ངང་དུ་སྐྱོང་བ་ནི་བསྒྲུབ་བ་ཡིན་ཏེ། སྒོང་ཆུང་འབྲུག་སོགས་དང་གསུམ་ཀར་ཞེན་མེད་པའི་རྣལ་འབྱོར་གྱི་ཚུལ་རྟོགས་པར་འགྱུར་ཞིང་དེས་ཡོན་ཏན་ཐམས་ཅད་ལྷུན་གྲུབ་ཏུ་འབྱུང་ངོ་། །ཉམས་དེ་ལྟར་སྐྱེ་པའི་རྒྱུ་ཆེ་ཡང་། མདང་ཁ་ནང་དུ་ཤེས་ལ་ཀྱིས། སེམས
བཀག་པ་དང་རྩེ་བ་བཀག་པ། །ངང་ལ་ལྷོད་ཀྱི་ལྷུམ་འ་ཟིན་བ་ཡིན། །ཤེས་གཏད་ཐངས་པ་ལྟར། སེམས་ཟིན་པས་རྩུང་ཞིག །དེས་དྲངས་སྐྱེ། །དེས་བདེ་བསྐྱེ། །དེ་ལ་བརྟེན་ནས་གསལ་བ་དང་མི་རྟོག་པ་ལ་སྐྱོང་བ་ཅན་བཅུ་བར་འགྱུར་ཞིང་གཙོ་བོར་སེམས་སྐྱིད་སྐྱོང་འདི་ལ་ཐབས་ལ་སོགས་ཆེ་དུ་མ་བསྒོམ་པ་དང་ང

77 ༄༅། །ཉམས་བརྒྱ་བ་སོགས་པ་གྲུབ་པ་ལས་ཀྱི་ངོ་རྟགས་ཐམས་ཅད་ཇི་ལྟ་བ་བཞིན་དུ་འབྱུང་བ་ཡང་ངོ་། །ཕྱིར་བ་དེ་གསལ་ལ་མི་རྟོག་པ་འི་ཉམས་གསུམ་ཀ་ཤར་ཡང་དོན་དུ་སྐྱེ་བ་ཆུང་ཀྱི་ལམ་ཡིན་པར་མངོན་ནོ་རྟོགས་པའི་ཚེ་ཉམས་རྟོགས་ཀྱི་ཁྱད་པར་འི་རྟོགས་པ་མ་འཛོམ་པ་གཉིས་པ་ལ་མ
ཡིན་ཏེ་སྒྲིབ་པ་བཀྲུབས་པར་གཞི་ལ་འཁྲུགས་པ་འི་དོན་སྣང་བ་ཡིན་པ་འི་ཕྱིར། དེས་ན་དེ་ལྟ་བས་ཀྱི་བདེ་བ་འང་མཚོན་ཏ་ཀྱི་འགྱུར་བའི་བདེ་བ་ནི་ལུས་སེམས་ཀྱི་འགྱུར་བའི་བདེ་བ་སྣང་བས་པས་འདི་ལྟ་བུ་མ་གཏོགས་ཡང་མི་གནས་པའི་ཕྱིར་རོ། །ངོ་བོ་འདི་ལ་དགོངས་ནས། ཉེ་བརྟན་ལས། དེ་བཞིན་ཉམས་དང་
མཐའ་མེད། །སྤྲོད་མེད་སྐྱང་ནང་འདས་པ་མེད། །འདི་ནི་མཆོག་ཏུ་བདེ་ཆེན་ཉིད། །བདག་མེད་གཞན་ཡང་མེད་པ་འོ། །ཞེས་གསུངས་སོ། །འདི་ལྟ་བུའི་བདེ་བ་ཆེན་པོ་ཉིད་ལ་ཀ་གསལ་བ་དང་མི་རྟོག་པ་འི་ཚོས་ཤིག་བུར་དུ་འབྱེད་ཅིང་གསལ་ཏེ་གསལ་ལ་[illegible]་འཛོམ་པ་ཡི་རྟེ་ལ་[illegible]་ཡང་དེ་ཉིད་མེད་པ་ཚ་རྣམ་པ
ཡིན་པ་འི་ཕྱིར་རོ། །དེ་ལྟར་ཡང་། སློབ་དཔོན་ཨཱརྻ་དེ་བས། ནམ་པར་རྟོག་པ་ཞུང་ལ་ཡིས། །ལྷག་པར་མོས་པ་མི་འགྱུར་བ། །གསལ་བ་རབ་སྣང་བ་འདི་དེ་ནི། རང་རིག་བདེ་བ་ཆེན་པོ་འོ། །ཞེས་བསྟན་བཅོས་སྙིང་པོ་བརྒྱ་བ་རྣམས་སུ་གསུངས་པ་ཡིན་ནོ།། ༈ །།ག་ཞིས་པ་རྟོགས་པ་སྐྱེ་ཚུལ་ནི། ནུ་བའ
ཞེན་ཉམས་ཀྱི་ངོ་བོ་ན་པར་དག་པར་གྲོལ། །ངན་རྟོག་འགྲུལ་པ་རང་བཞིན་དབྱིངས་སུ་དག །ཐམས་ཅད་ཤེས་པ་སྣང་སྤྱོད་བྲལ་ཐོབ་མེད། །སྒོམ་བྲལ་ཆོས་ཉིད་བདེ་ནི་རྟོགས་པར་ཤོག །ཅེས་པ་ལ་བཞི་ཏེ། ང་ཤར་ལ་ཐག་ང་ལྟ་ར་ཉམས་ཀྱིས་ལ་བཟ་དགོམ་གྱི་ཤེས་པ་རང་ལ་ར་གྲོལ་བ་ཞིག། །ཕྱུག་ཆོས་ཀྱི་རྟོགས
སུ་འདྲེང་བའི་རྟོགས་པ་ལ་ཞིག་གནས་ལུགས་ཀྱི་དོན་མཐོང་བ་ལ་སློབ་པ་ར་བྱེད་པས་ང་ཤར་འཛོག་པ་འི་ཕྱིར་རྟོག་པ་ངན་པ་ཡིན་ལ་དེ་ཚེ་དུས་ལྡུང་ཀྱང་མཉམ་པར་བཞག་པ་འི་མཐུ་ས་རང་བཞིན་གྱིས་ལ་ཡོད་ཉིད་ཀྱི་དབྱིངས་སུ་དག་པས། ཐམས་ཀྱི་ཤེས་པ་དེ་ལ་བ་གཏུག་མ་འདི་ལ་སྣང་ཉིད་དམ་དོན་དུ་ཐུ་བ་ཟ། ཟང་ཐལ་གྱི་བ་འི

78 ཆོས་ཀ་ཡང་སྤྲོས་པ་མེད་པ་འི་ཚུལ་ལོང་དུ་རྟུད་པ་དང་། དེ་བཞིན་དུ་ལྟ་ཏེ། སྣང་གྲགས་ཀྱི་ཆོས་དང་། སྣང་གྲགས་སྣང་བ་ལ་མ་བྱུང་བའི་བྲལ་བ་དང་། སྣང་གྲུབ་བྲལ་པས་ཐོབ་པ་འི་བྲལ་སྤུངས་ཅན་པ་དེ། དེ་འི་རང་བཞིན་དུ་ཡོད་ཅིང་ཨ་གནས་པ་ལ་འདི། སྣང་བ་ཤེ་ཀ་ང་ཉི་སུ་ས་རྩི་བ་གཏུ་ཀ་ད
འགྲོ་བ་ཀ་གཅིག་ཐ་དད་སོགས་སྤྲོས་པའི་མཐའ་ཐམས་ཅད་དང་བྲལ་བའི་ཆོས་ཉིད་ཀྱི་བདེན་པ་རྟོགས་པ་ཡིན་ནོ་ཞེས་སྟོན་པའི་ཕྱིར་དེ་ལ་སྟོན་པ་ར་མཛད་པ་འོ། །དེ་ལྟར་ཐ་མལ་གྱི་ཤེས་པ་ལ་སྤང་གྲུང་བྲལ་བའི་གྱི་མཚན་མ་མཐའ་དག་རང་ལ་ར་ཞི་བས་གནས་ལུགས་མཐོང་ང་ བཞག [illegible] ཡོད་དེ། ཉུང་ཏི
མདོ་ལས། དེ་ནི་སེམས་དང་བྱང་ཆུབ་དང་། །རྣམ་པ་གཉིས་སུ་མི་མཐོང་ངོ་། །བྱང་ཆུབ་ཀྱི་ནི་མཚན་ཉིད་གང་། །སེམས་ཀྱང་དེ་ཡི་མཚན་ཉིད་ཡིན། །ཞེས་དང་། ཏིང་རྒྱལ་ལས། གཟུགས་ཀྱི་རང་བཞིན་གཞན་ཡིན་ལ། །སྟོང་ཉིད་གཞན་དུ་མ་གསུངས་ཏེ། །[illegible]
དེས་ན་སྟོང་ཉིད་རང་རྒྱུ་ཤེས། །གང་གིས་སྟོང་ཉིད་རབ་ཤེས་པ། །དེས་ནི་སྤྱང་བ་འདས་པ་ཤེས། །རྣམ་པར་ཤེས་མི་ཤེས་པ། །དམིགས་པ་ཅན་རྣམས་ཐལ་དུ་བཏབ། །ཅེས་སོགས་ལྷུང་པོ་ལྔ་ག་ལ་སྦྱར་བ་དང་། དཀོན་མཆོག་ཟླ་མ་རྟོགས་ལས། ཉོན་མོངས་ལ་ང་རྣམས་དང་[illegible]་ཆོས་རྣམ་པ་པ་ཐ
དང་བ་རྒྱུ་བ་ཅི་རྒྱུ་ཟད་གྱུར་མེད་དོ། །ཞེས་དང་། དུས་ཀྱི་འཁོར་ལོ་ལས། རྒྱུ་ཏན་འདས་དང་གྲོལ་བ་འི་སེམས། །འཁོར་བ་ལས་འདས་བ་མི་འགྱུར་ལ། །རྟག་དང་ཆད་པས་དེས་པར་གྲོལ། །དེ་ཉིད་སྒྱུ་ར་བ་གཉིས་མེད་གཏན། །ཞེས་སོགས་མཐར་ཡང་པར་ག་[illegible]་བ་ཕྱུ་[illegible]་འཁོར་འདས་ལས་འདེ
པ་གཉིས་ཞེས་ཁྱབ་ནམ་དུ་དང་མེད་ཅིང་མི་དམིགས་པ་འི་གཉིས་སུ་མེད་པ་འི་ཚུལ་ནི་ཐམས་ལ་ཀྱི་སེམས་གནས་ལུགས་ཆོས་ཉིད་ཀྱི་བདེན་པ་ཡིན་ལ། དེ་དེ་ལྟ་ར་མཐོང་བ་ཞི་ཚེ་ལུང་བླང་ལ་སོགས་པ་འི་མཚན་མ་སྒྲོ་རང་ཇ་ལ་དུ་འགྲོ་སྟེ། སྒོམ་བདེ་པོ་རྒྱུས། གང་ལ་རྒྱུ་ང་ཞབ་ཀས་སྒྲུ་ང་མེད། །ཀ་ཕྱོ་ར་བགག

79 ༄༅། ། ངང་ཡོད་མིན་པ། །དེ་ལ་བསྒོམ་རྒྱ་ཅི་ཞིག་ཡིན། །སྒྲུང་ན་ངངས་པ་ཅི་ཞིག་བཏག །ཅེས་གསུངས་པ་ལྟར་ཡིན་ཞེ་རྒྱུ་མཚན་དེས་ན། གནས་ལུགས་ལ་མ་བཅོས་པར་དེ་ལ་སྣང་དང་རེ་ཆུ་མཚན་པ་རང་ཤེང་འགྱུར་ བ་མི་ཤེད་པ་འི་ཕྱིར་རོ། །དེ་ལྟར་གནས་ལུགས་སྣང་རྡོ་ར་མེད་ཅེ
དོན་འདི་ཉིད་ཇི་ལྟ་བ་ར་རྟོགས་ན། དགའ་པོ་བཀའ་འབྲུང་གྱི་མདུན་ལག་གཟིགས་པ་ས་རྣམས་ཀྱིས་གཏུག་མའི་སེམས་ངོ་མཐོང་བ་ཞེས་བ་འདིའི་སྐད་མཛད་པ་ཡིན་ཞིང་། སློབ་དཔོན་ཏོ་པི་པ་ས་ཀྱང་། བསྟན་པ་ལས་ནི་སློབ་པ་འི་ཁྱད་པར་སྐྱེས་པ་རྣམས་ལྡང་ས་ཏེ། གཉུག་མའི་རང་བཞིན་ཕྱུང་རྒྱུ་ཆེད་དོན་ཞེན་ཏུ་ག་ཏེ
ཟེ་ཏེ་དང་ལྡན་པ་འི་བློ་ཐོས་སུ་ཚོལ་ཏེ། གང་གི་ཚེ་ངེས་ཀུན་རྟུབ་ལྕུང་པ་ར་གྱུར་ན་དེའི་ཚེ་ནམ་མཁའ་དང་ནམ་མཁའ་བཞིན་དུ་འདྲེས་པར་གྱུར་ཏེ། སྦྱར་ཡུལ་ནམ་མཁའ་དག་པ་དང་ཆགས་པ་དང་ལྡན་པའི་རྣམ་པ་རག་ཡེ་ངན་འབྱུང་པ་ར་སྐྱེ་བ་ནམས་མེད་ཅིང་། ནམ་མཁའ་དང་མཉམ་པ་ར་རྟོགས་པ་དང་བྲལ་བས
ཕྱག་རྒྱ་ཐམས་ཅད་ཀྱི་མཆོག་གྱིས་བརྟག་པ་ཞིང་། དབང་པོ་ལས་འདས་པ་སྐྱེ་བ་མེད་པ་དང་ལྡན་པ་རང་རིག་ཤེས་བྱེད་ཀྱི་སྤྱོད་ཡུལ་ཅན་ཐ་སྙད་ལས་འདས་པ་སྤྱོར་མ་རང་དུ་མ་གྲུབ་པ་ཅན་ཁྲ་བ་དང་ཤེས་རབ་ཀྱི་རང་བཞིན་ཏེ་བཅིབ་དག་ཉིད་གཅིག་ཏོ་ཐོར་སྒྱུ་ར་པ་སྒྲུ་བ་ར་འགྱུར་རོ། །ཞེས་རྒྱུ་ལ་ལ་ཐེག་པ་ལ་ང་ར་བསྟན་པ་དང་།
ཟབ་མོ་འི་མདོ་སྡེ་རྣམས་ལས། འདི་ལ་ཡིད་ཆེས་པ་ཕྱིར་མི་ལྡོག་པ་འི་ས་ལ་གནས་པ་ཞེན་ཏུ་གསུངས་ཏེ། དཔེ་ན་མཆོག་ཏུ་ཀུན་དུ་བཟང་པོ་བ་སེམས་དཔའ་ འི་སྤྱོད་པ་བསྟན་པ་ འི་མདོ་ལས། ཕྱེ་དུ་དོན་ཆེན་ཕྱིར་ལ། འཇམ་དཔལ་གྱིས་བྱང་སེམས་ལ་ས་དང་པོ་ལ་ཆོས་ཇི་ལྟ་ར་སྟོན་ཕྱིར་ཞེས་འདྲ། འདོད་ཆགས་མ
སྤྱོད་ཅིག །ཞེ་སྡང་མ་གཞི་ལ་ཅིག །གཏི་མུག་མ་སེལ་ཅིག །འཇིག་ཚོགས་ལ་མ་ལ་ཀྱི་ནང་མ་སྤྱོད་ཅིག །སོ་སོ་ནས། སངས་རྒྱས་ཡིད་ལ་མ་བྱེད་ཅིག །ཆོས་མ་སེམས་ཤིག །དགེ་འདུན་ལ་མཆོད་པ་མ་བྱེད་ཅིག །བསླབ་པ་དག་ལ་མ་ལེན་ཅིག །སྤྲོད་པ་ཉེ་བར་ཞི་བ་དོན་དུ་མ་གཉེར་ཅིག །རྒྱ

80 ཆེ་བ་ས་ཅན་ལ་ཅིག །ཅེས་གདམས་ལ་ངག་འདི་ལྟ་བུ་འདོམས་ཤིང་དེ་དོ་པ་འི་བྱང་ཆུབ་སེམས་དཔའ་ལ་ཡ་གདམས་པ་ར་བསྒྲུ་ཧོར་ལ་སུ་བསྟན་པ་ར་བྱའོ། །དེ་ཅིའི་ཕྱིར་ཞེ་ན། ཆོས་ཐམས་ཅད་ཀྱི་ཆོས་ཉིད་ནི་བསྙུན་བ་ཡོད་ཡིན་པའི་ཕྱིར་རོ། །ཕྱིས་པ་དེ་དག་ནི་སྨྲ་བ་དང་འགག་པ་འི་ཆོས་ལ་སུ་ལྟུང་ལྡོན་པ་ར་བྱེད་དོ། །ཆེས
ཀྱི་བཙྱིད་ལ་འདོད་ནུ་ས་པ་ར་མི་རྟོག་པས་རབ་ཏུ་ཕྱེ་བ་ཡིན་ཏེ་ཆོས་འདི་རྣམས་ཀྱི་རང་བཞིན་དེ་ལྟར་རྗེས་སུ་རྟོགས་པ་ཀ་ང་ཡིན་པ་དེ་འི་བྱང་ཆུབ་པོ། །ཞེས་དེ་ལྟར་གདམས་ན་གལ་ཏེ་མི་སྐྲག་མི་དངང་པ་དེ་དང་དང་ ང་བ་ར་མི་འགྱུར་ན། ཡེ་མ་བྱང་ཆུབ་སེམས་དཔའ་འདི་ནི་ཕྱིར་མི་ལྡོག་པ་ལ་ཕྱིར་མི་ལྡོག་པ་འི་ས་ལ་གནས་པ་ཅན་ཡིན
ནོ། །མྱུར་དུ་ཤེས་པར་བྱ་སྟེ་གདམས་ལ་ངག་འདི་ལ་ཡང་ནས་ཡང་དུ་དགའ་བ་བསྐྱེད་པར་བྱ་འོ། །ཞེས་ལྟས་པ་ར་གསུངས་ལ་ལྟ་ར་རོ། །དེ་ལྟ་བུའི་བདེ་ཉམས་མཐོང་བ་ཉིད་ནི་ཕྱག་རྒྱ་ཆེན་པོ་ལ་ཡེ་ཤེས་ལྟེ་ས་པ་ཟང་ཡིན་ཏེ། བརྟག་གཉིས་ལས། རང་གིས་རིག་པ་འི་ཡེ་ཤེས་ནི། །ངག་གི་སྤྱོད་ཡུལ་ལས་འདས་ལ
ཏེ། །འདི་ནི་ཕྱིན་ སྤྱོད་ཡུལ་མིན། །ཀུན་ཀྱི་ཡེ་ཤེས་དེ་ལྟ་བུ། །ས་དང་ཆུ་དང་མེ་དང་ལ། །རླུང་དང་ནམ་མཁའ་ཉིད་དང་འདྲ། །རང་གཞན་རིག་པ་འི་ཚེ་རབ་ཡིན། །ཀུན་ཀྱི་སྙིང་ཅིག་མེད་དེ། །མཐོ་རིས་མི་ཡུལ་ལ་དགེ་ཀི །ལྷ་ཅིག་ལ་ལ་ནི་གཟུགས་ཅན་གཅིག་འགྱུར། །རང་གཞན
ཆ་ཡི་རྣམ་རྟོག་གིས། །གཉེན་པ་ཉིད་ནི་ཐུལ་པ་མེད། །ཞེས་ལམ་དུས་ཀྱི་ཕྱག་རྒྱ་ཆེན་པོ་འི་ཡེ་ཤེས་སྐྱེས་མ་ཐག་ཏུ་གཟུང་འཛིན་གཉིས་བལ་ཀྱི་ཆོས་ཐམས་ཅད་དེ་འི་རང་བཞིན་གཅིག་ཏུ་རྟོགས་པས་མཚན་མ་འི་སྤྲོས་པ་ཐམས་ཅད་ཀྱི་ཚུལ་བཞི་བར་མི་ནུས་ང་ང་བསྟན་པ་འི་ཕྱིར་རོ། །ཡང་འགག་འབྲེག་གིས
སེམས་ངོ་མཐོང་བའི་ཚད་ནུས་རྟོག་བརྟས་ཐེ་ཚོམ་ཟ་བ་ལ་ང་ཕྱིད་པ་ར་རྣལ་ཀྱང་ངེས་སེམས་ང་ར་མཐོང་བ་འི་གོ་ཚོད་ངེ། ངང་དང་རང་བཞིན་དོན་གཟིགས་པ་སྣང་ལ་རྟོག་སེམས་ཀྱི་རང་བཞིན་ནམ་དོན་ཉིད་མ་ཡིན་པ་འི་ཕྱིར་ཏེ། ཉམས་རྟོགས་གྲོལ་བ་ར་ཀྱིས་འཕྲུལ་བ་ཡིན་པ་འི་ཕྱིར་རོ།། ༈ །།གསུམ་པ་སྒོང་ཉེ་སྙིང་རྗེ་ཟུང་འཇུག

81

༄༅། །ཀྱི་ཉམས་ལེན་དཔོག་པར་སྟོན་པ་ལ། སྙིང་རྗེ་ངོས་གཟུང་བ། དེ་སྟོང་པ་ཉིད་དང་ཟུང་དུ་འཇུག་རྒྱུ་ལ་སོ།། ༈ །།དང་པོ་ནི། འགྲོ་བ་ཞི་རང་བཞིན་རྟག་ཏུ་སངས་རྒྱས་ཀྱང་། །མ་རྟོགས་པས་ནི་གཞི་མཐའ་མེད་འཁོར་བར་འཁྱམས། །སྡུག་བསྔལ་པ་མུ་མཐའ་མེད
པའི་སེམས་ཅན་ལ། །ཀ་དག་སྟོང་མེད་སྙིང་རྗེ་རྒྱུད་ལ་སྐྱེ་བར་ཤོག །ཅེས་པས་བསྟན་ཏེ། དེ་ཡང་ཕྱིར་སྙིང་རྗེ་ལ་སེམས་ཅན་དང་ཆོས་ལ་དམིགས་པའི་སྙིང་རྗེ་གཉིས། དམིགས་པ་མེད་པའི་སྙིང་རྗེ་དང་གསུམ་དུ་གསུངས་པ་ལས་དང་པོ་གཉིས་ནི། ཕྱིན་ཅི་ལོག་པ་འདི་རྣམས་འགྲོ་བ་ལ་དམིགས་པ་སྤྱི་ཉམས་སུ་ལེན་གྱི་ཡིན་ལ།
གནས་ལུགས་ཀྱི་དོན་མ་མཐོང་བས་ན། ཕྱོགས་མེད་ཀྱི་སྙིང་རྗེ་སྐྱེ་ཞེ། སྟོང་ཉིད་སྙིང་རྗེའི་སྙིང་པོ་ཅན། །ཞེས་བྱ་བ་དེ་འབྱུང་བ་ཡིན་པས་འདིར་བསྟན་གྱི་སྙིང་རྗེ་ལ་ཕྱིར་མ་ཡིན་ནོ། །བོན་ཉིད་ཀྱི་རྒྱལ་བ་ཞི་ལྷ་བཞེད། ཕོང་དུ་ལྷུང་བའི་དོན་ཆད་པའི་སྐྱབས་པ་ཞིང་ལ་ལྷ་ཚོགས་བསྐོར་བའི་ཉམས་ཀྱི་རང་བཞིན་ཞེ་སྡང་རྟག་ཏུ
སངས་རྒྱས་ཆོས་ཀྱི་སྐུ་ནི་ངོ་བོར་བཞུགས་པ་ཡིན་ཡང་། དེ་ལྟར་དུ་མ་རྟོགས་པ་ལ་བོན་ཉིད་དབང་གིས་མཐའ་མེད་པའི་འཁོར་བར་འཁྱམས་ནས་སྡུག་བསྔལ་གྱི་རྒྱ་མཚོ་མུ་མེད་པའི་ནང་དུ་བྱིང་བར་གྱུར་པ་རྣམས་སེམས་ཅན་རྣམས་ལ་བཟོད་བླག་མེད་པའི་སྙིང་རྗེ་དྲག་པོ་རྒྱུན་ཆད་པ་མེད་པར་སྐྱེ་བ་ཡིན་ཞེས། དེ་འང
གནས་ལུགས་ཀྱི་དོན་མ་མཐོང་བའི་དབང་གིས་འཁྱམས་ལྟ། ཇི་སྐད་དུ། ཐུང་ཆུབ་སེམས་དཔའ་ལ་ཉམས་གཞག་པས། །ཀོང་མ་པའི་སྟོབས་ཀྱིས་རྟོགས་པ་ན། །ངོ་བོ་འཛིན་གདོན་གྱིས་ཟིན་པ་ལ། །ཁྱད་པར་དུ་ཡང་སྙིང་རྗེ་སྐྱེ། །ཞེས་དང་། སྙིང་པོ་རྒྱན་ལས། དཔལ་དུ་རྟོགས་པ་ཉིད་ནི། །ཉེ་ལ་འབྱུང་
བ་ཡིས་བསྒོམས་གྱུར་ན། །གཞན་ཀྱི་དོན་ལ་ཆགས་པ་འབྱིན། །འདྲེ་བ་འཁྲུར་བ་ཟློག་མེད། །ཅེས་འབྱུང་བས་སོ། །བྱང་ཆུབ་སེམས་དཔའ་རྣམས་ཀྱིས་སྙིང་རྗེ་དེ་ལྟ་བུ་བསྐྱེད་ནས། གཞན་གྱི་དོན་བསོད་ནམས་ཀྱི་ལྷ་ཡིན་པར་མཛད་པས་རྒྱལ་བ་སྲས་དང་བཅས་པས་མཛད་པ་སྤྱོད་པའི་ཚུལ་བ་རྩ་བུ་ངུས་བསོར་བ

82

འདོར་བར་མི་མཛད་ཀྱང་ཉེས་པས་གོས་པར་མི་འགྱུར་ཏེ། ཇི་སྐད་དུ། གང་ཞིག་བསྒོམས་པས་བརྟེན་པ་ཡང་། །གཞན་གྱི་སྡུག་བསྔལ་གྱིས་གདུང་ནས། །བསམ་གཏན་བདེ་བ་དོར་ནས་ཀྱང་། །མནར་མེད་པར་ཡང་འཇུག་པར་བྱེད། །འདི་ནི་ངོ་མཚར་བ་དེ་བ་ལྟ་སུ་ཞིག །འདི་ཉིད་དམ་པའི་རྟོལ
ལུགས་ཡིན་ཏེ་ལོག །དེ་དག་རྣམས་ཀྱི་རང་ལུགས་དང་། །ཕོང་རྣམས་ཀྱི་ནི་དོན་མཚར་མེད། །ཆོས་རྣམས་སྟོང་པ་བདེ་ཞེས་སུ། །ལས་དང་འབྲས་བུ་བསྟན་པ་གང་། །དེ་ནི་ངོ་མཚར་བས་ངོ་མཚར། །རྨད་བྱུང་བས་ཀྱང་རྨད་དུ་བྱུང་། །སེམས་ཅན་སྐྱོབ་པའི་བསམ་པ་ཅན། །དེ་དག་གིས་
པའི་ནང་མ་སྐྱེས་ཀྱང་། །དེ་རྒྱུད་ཉེས་པས་མ་གོས་པ། །རྒྱུ་ཡི་པདྨ་ཡིན་དཔེར་བཞིན། །ཞེས་བཤད་པ་ལྟར་རོ། །གཞི་ཅེས་པ་དེ་ལྟ་སྟོང་པའི་ཚིག་གོ། ༈ །།གཉིས་པ་དེ་སྟོང་པ་ཉིད་དང་ཟུང་དུ་འཇུག་རྒྱུ་ལ་ནི། བཟོད་མེད་སྙིང་རྗེའི་ཚེ་ཡང་མཐའ་བཀག་པ་པའི། །བ་རྗེ་དུལ་ངོ་བོ་སྟོང
དོན་རྟེན་པར་ཤར། །ཟུང་འཇུག་གོལ་ལ་བྲལ་བའི་ལམ་མཆོག་འདི། །འབྲལ་མེད་ཉིན་མཚན་ཀུན་ཏུ་སྒོམ་པར་ཤོག །ཅེས་པ་སྟེ། དེ་ལྟ་བུའི་དམིགས་པ་མེད་པའི་སྙིང་རྗེའི་རྩལ་དེ་ཡང་མཐའ་གཉིས་པ་དང་ཆར་བཞིན་པ་ནས། བརྩེ་བའི་དུས་དེ་ཚེ་ཉིད་ན་སྟོང་པ་དང་བྲལ་པའི་གནས་ལུགས་ཀྱི་
ངོ་བོ་སྟོང་པ་ཉིད་ཀྱི་དོན་ཡང་དངོས་སུ་ཚམ་མ་ཡིན་པར་མངོན་སུམ་རྟེན་པར་ཤར་བས་སྟོང་པ་ཉིད་དང་སྙིང་རྗེ་ངོ་མཉམ་དུ་འབྱེལ་བའི་ཟུང་འཇུག་གི་ལམ་དེ་ནི་གོལ་ས་དང་བྲལ་བའི་ལམ་གྱི་མཆོག་ཡིན་ནོ། །དེ་ལྟར་ཡང་། མཁའ་འགྲོ་རྒྱ་མཚོ་ལས། སྟོང་ཉིད་སྙིང་རྗེར་བྱེར་མེད་པ། །སེམས
ཀྱི་ལ་ཞེན་ཞིག་ཏུ་སྟོན་པས་སྐྱེ་ངན། །གང་ཕྱིར་དེ་སྐད་རྒྱས་དང་ཆོས། །དགེ་འདུན་དུ་ཡང་ལྟར་པའོ། །ཞེས་གསུངས་པ་ཉིད། རྡོ་རྗེ་སེམས་དཔའ་ཀྱང་། སྟོང་ཉིད་སྙིང་རྗེ་འབྱེད་རྩེ་བ། །ཐར་མེད་དེ་ནི་ཕྱག་བབ་བཞིན། །སྟོང་ཉིད་སྙིང་རྗེ་གཅིག་པ་ཡང་། །ཐར་མ་སྟོང་བ་ཟ་བཞིན་ནོ། །ཞེས་གསུངས

83

༄༅། །སོ། །དེ་དོན་ལྟར་སེམས་དང་ཤེས་རབ་ཀྱི་ཟར་ཕྱིན་པ་ཡང་ཡིན་ཏེ། མདོ་སྡེ་ལས། འདི་ལྟར་སྟོང་པ་ཉིད་དང་སྙིང་རྗེ་དབྱེར་མེད་པར་བསྒོམ་པ་ནི་ཤེས་པ་ཞི་སེམས་ནི་བྱང་ཆུབ་ཀྱི་སེམས་དང་ཤེས་རབ་ཀྱི་ཕ་རོལ་ཏུ་ཕྱིན་པའོ། །ཞེས་པ་དང་དོ། །ཤེས་རབ་སྟོང་པ་ཉིད་དང་ཐབས་སྙིང་
རྗེ་ཆེན་པོ་གཉིས་ཟུང་དུ་མ་ཆུད་པས་གྲོལ་ལ་གཅིག་ཁོ་ན་ཉམས་སུ་བླངས་པས་ནི་བླ་ན་མེད་པའི་གོ་འཕང་ཐོབ་པར་མི་ནུས་ཤིང་དེ་མི་ནུས་པས་རྡོ་རྗེ་འི་ནུ་ལ་འཆིང་དུ་འང་ཡི་ཞ་རོ་ཏེ། གསང་བ་འདུས་པ་ལས། ཐབས་ལ་འཆིང་བ་ཐབས་ཀྱི་ཀྱང་འབྲེལ་ཞིང་། །ཤེས་རབ་ཅན་ཅིག་ཅེས་ཀྱང་མིན། །ཐབས་དང
ཤེས་རབ་སྦྱོམས་པ་འཇུག་པ། །ཐབ་ལ་འཆིང་སྟེ་བཞིན་ལ་ཤེས་རབ་བས་པ་ ཡང་། །ཞེས་དང་། གང་ཞིག་ཐབས་ནི་མེ་བསྒྲུབ་ཀྱི་ཉིད། །འཛིན་པ་ཤེས་རབ་ཀྱི་དམ་ཐར་བྱེད། །ཅེས་དང་། ལྷ་ཡི་རྒྱལ་པོ་རྒྱ་མཚོས་ཞུས་པ་ཡི་མདོ་ལས། ཐབས་ཀྱི་ལས་ཤེས་ཀྱི་ཉེས་ཏེ། ཤེས་རབ་དང་ཐབས
བའི་ཐབས་དང་། ཐབས་དང་བྲལ་བའི་ཤེས་རབ་ཆེ། །བདུད་ཀྱི་ལས་སུ་ཤིན་པས་ལྷུང་བར་བྱའོ། །ཞེས་དང་། རྡོ་རྗེ་ཡི་ཡེ་མགོན་དུ། །ཐབས་དང་བྲལ་བའི་ཤེས་རབ་དང་། །ཤེས་རབ་བྲལ་བའི་ཐབས་དག་ཀྱང་། །གང་ཕྱིར་འཆིང་བའི་ཞེས་གསུངས་པས། །དེ་བས་གཉིས་ཀ
སྤང་མི་བྱ། །ཞེས་དང་། མདོ་རྟོག་རྒྱན་ལས། ཤེས་པས་སྲིད་ལ་མི་གནས་དང་། །སྙིང་རྗེས་ཞི་ལ་མི་གནས་དང་། །ཞེས་སྲིད་ཞི་གཉིས་ལ་མི་གནས་པ་འདི་རྒྱུ་བ་འདས་པ་ཐོབ་པ་ལ། ཐབས་ཤེས་ཟུང་འཇུག་དགོས་པར་གསུངས་པ་ཡིན་པ་ཡི་ཕྱིར་རོ། །
དེ་རྣམ་ཟད་སྟོང་ཉིད་མ་རྟོགས་པ་ འདི་སྙིང་རྗེ་ལོ་ནུས་ལ་གཞན་དོན་དུ་ཕྱོགས་པར་སྙོམས་ཀྱང་གཞན་དོན་མི་ཐུབ་པ་འཁོར་བ་རང་ཉིད་ཀྱི་དགེ་སྦྱོར་རྒྱུན་ལ་བསྐུར་བས་ལྷུང་ནས་གཞན་དོན་བྱུང་འགྱུར་རམ་ལ་འབའ་ཞིག་གེ་གསུལ་ལུ་འགྱུར་བ་དང་། སྟོང་ཉིད་གཅིག་པུ་བསྒོམས་པས་ཉན་རང་གི་ལམ་དུ་གོལ་བར་འགྱུར་བས

84

གཞན་དོན་ལ་ཡུན་རིང་པོ་ཞིག་ལ་སུ་འགྱུར་བ། ཇི་སྐད་དུ། དབུ་མ་བ་རང་འགྲེལ་དུ་ང་རྒྱལ་ལ། །གཏན་ཚིགས་ལ་བྱེད་པ་ཡིན་ཏེ། །ཉན་ཐོས་དང་ནི་རང་རྒྱལ་དག །རྫུང་རྒྱལ་ཡོན་པ་འདི་ཀུན་ཏུ་གི་གོ་ས། །ཞེས་འབྱུང་བ་ལྟར་ངེས་པས་ཐེག་པ་ཆེན་པོའི་ལམ་ཀྱི་གོལ་ས་འདང་ཡིན་ནོ། །དེ་ལྟར་གོལ
ས་དང་བྲལ་བའི་ཟུང་འཇུག་གི་ལམ་འདི་ཟུང་འཇུག་རྡོ་རྗེ་འཆང་ཆེན་པོའི་གོ་འཕང་མཐོབ་ཀྱི་བར་དུ་འབྲལ་བ་མེད་པར་ཉིན་དང་མཚན་མོ་མ་ཆད་པའི་དུས་ཐམས་ཅད་དུ་བསྒོམས་དགོས་པར་སྟོན་པས་མཛད་པའི་ཚུལ་ཀྱིས་གདམས་པ་སྟེ། སེམས་འགྲེལ་ལས། སངས་རྒྱས་རྣམས་ཀྱི་བྱང་ཆུབ་སེམས། །ཁམས་
དང་སྐྱེ་མཆེད་རྣམ་རིག་གི། །རྟོག་པ་རྣམས་ཀྱིས་མ་བསྒྲིབས་ཤིང་། །རྟག་ཏུ་སྟོང་ཉིད་མཚན་ཉིད་བཞེད། །སྙིང་རྗེས་བརླན་པའི་སེམས་ཀྱིས་ནི། །འབད་པས་བསྒོམ་པར་བྱ་བ་ཡིན། །ཞེས་གསུངས་པ་ལྟར་རོ། །དེ་ནས་ལྷ་རྣམས་སྐྱེ་རྒྱུ་སྟོན་པའི་ཚིག་ལ་བཅད་གཅིག་གིས་ཚོགས་སྐོར་གྱི་ལམ
དང་། རྟོགས་པ་སྐྱེ་རྒྱུ་ཡི་ཚོགས་བཅད་གཅིག་དང་། དེ་ཕྱིན་ཚིགས་བཅད་གཉིས་དང་ངའི་ཆོས་པ་འདི་ཡི་མཐོང་བསྒོམ་ཀྱི་ལམ་བསྟན་པ་ལ་ཤེས་དགོས་སོ། །འོག་མ་འདི་ཡན་ཆད་དུ་སྦྱོང་པ་མ་བསྟན་པ་ཡིན་ནམ་ཞེ་ན། སྨོན་པ་བསྟན་པ་ཉིད་ཀྱིས་སྦྱོང་བ་བསྟན་པར་གྱུར་ཏོ། །སྦྱོར་ལུགས་ཀྱི་སྤྱོད
པ་ལ་སློབ་བཅས་སློབ་མེད་གཉིས་སུ་གསུངས་པའི་སྔ་མ་ལ་ཕྱི་ཞི་སྤྱོད་པ་དང་། ཕྱི་མ་ལ་ནང་གི་སྤྱོད་པ་ཟབ་ལྷུང་བྱེད་པ་ལ་སོགས་ཀྱི་སྤྱོད་པ་ཉིད་མ་ཚོགས་ཡིན་པས། དེའི་ཕྱག་རྒྱ་ཆེན་པོའི་རྣལ་འབྱོར་ཉམས་སུ་ལེན་པ་འདི་ཉིད་ལས་གཞན་དུ་མེད་པའི་ཕྱིར་དང་། དེ་ཡང་ཀུན་ཏུ་བཟང་པོའི་སྤྱོད་པ་ཞེས་བྱ་སྟེ།
དེ་ལ་གཞན་པས་དགོས་པ་ཐམས་ཅད་འགྲུབ་པར་འགྱུར་བ་ཡང་། གསང་བ་འདུས་པ་ལས། འདི་དེ་རྣལ་འབྱོར་མཆོག་དེ་འི་ཕྱིར། །དེ་བཞིན་གཤེགས་རྣམས་ཀྱིས་ཕྱག་འཚལ། །དཔལ་ས་ལྷུང་སྦྱོར་པའི། །མཐར་ཡས་པ་རྣམས་རབ་ཏུ་ཕྱུག །དེ་ཕྱིར་ལྷ་ཡི་དངོས་གྲུབ་ནི། །མཐར

85

86

87

88

89

90

91

92

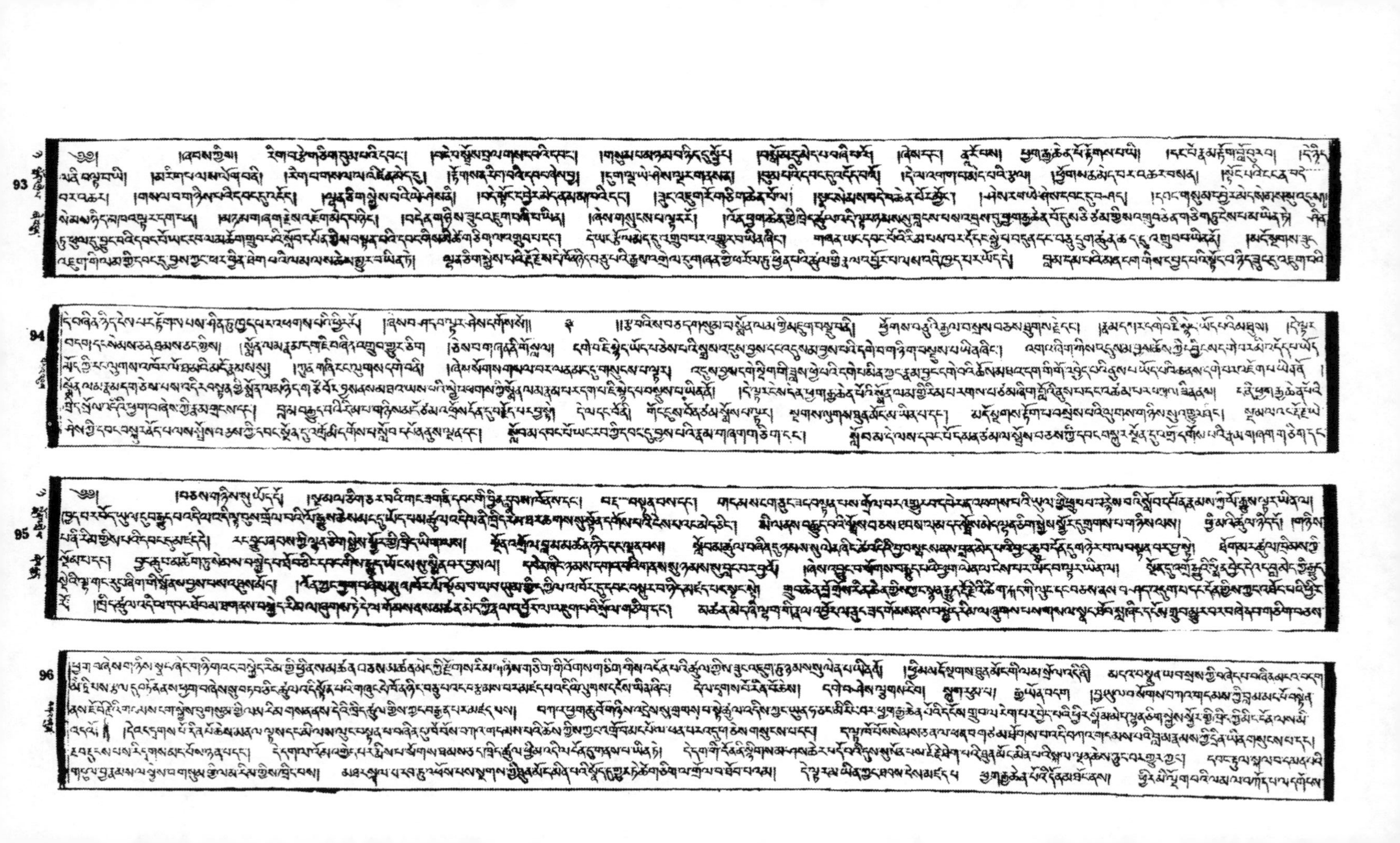

93

[illegible]

94

[illegible]

95

[illegible]

96

[illegible]

97 ༄༅། །པ་ཡི་ནི་པའི་ཕྱི་རོ། །དེ་ནས་རྗེ་རྗེ་འཛིན་པ་ཉིད་ནས་ཀྱེ་ཡཱ་ར་བརྒྱུད་སྤྱོད་ལྡན་ཡན་ལག་ཀྱི་རྩེ་ལ་བདེ་བས་བདུད་ལ་ཕྱག་ལ་པས་མཆོག་དམ་ཐམས་ཅད་མ་བརྟགས་པར་བཀྲི་བའི་ཕྱག་བཞེས་ཡོད་ཅིང་། དེ་བཞིན་དུ་ཡུམ་པ་ལྟར་ལ་སྤྲུགས་ཀྱི་ཐབས་ལམ་ཐབ་མོ་སྟོན་པའི་ཚེ་ན། འདི་འི་རྒྱུ་
དུས་ཀྱི་གདམས་ངག་ཡམ་ག་ཞི་ཕྱིད་ཀྱི་མིང་དུ་མཛད་པ་ཡིན་ནོ། །སྔོན་ས་ཏི་ཀྱུད་ཕྱག་མི་དགོས་ས་རང་ཟབ་མོའི་དོན་འདི་ལ་མོས་ནས་བརྟག་བ་ལྟ་ཏི་སློས། །ཟབ་ཆོས་སྤྱེལ་པས་ཀྱང་ཟབ་ཡོན་ཞེན་པ་ཐོབ་ནའི་ཕྱིར་ནི། རིན་ཆེན་ཕྲེང་བས། བསོད་ནམས་རྒྱུ་བས་ཆོས་འདི་ལ། །ཐེ་ཚོམ་ཙམ་ཡང་
མི་བྱེད་དེ། །འདི་ལ་ཐེ་ཚོམ་ཟ་བ་ཀྱང་། །སྲིད་པ་རྒྱལ་པོར་བྱེད་པ་ཡིན་པར་འགྱུར། །ཞེས་དང་། ལྷ་རྒྱལ་བ་སེམས་དཔའ་སྤྱོད་པ་བསྟན་པའི་མདོ་ལས། ཀྱེ་རྒྱལ་བའི་ཆེན་ཀྱི་ཀྱིས་འཇམ་དཔལ་ལ་གདུང་ས་ཀྱི་བཞིན་འབྱུང་དོན་མེད་པའི་དོན་སྒྲུབ་པ་འི་ཚེ། དམིགས་པ་ཅན་གྱི་དགེ་སྦྱོང་
བརྒྱ་དམ་སོས་པས། དེ་དག་ཐག་ཆོད་ཆོ་སྐུགས་ཏེ་ཤི་ནས་དམྱལ་བར་སྐྱེས་པ་ལ། བཅོམ་ལྡན་འདས་ཀྱིས། དགེ་སློང་དེ་དག་ཟབ་མོའི་ཆོས་སོ་མ་ཉིད་ཅེས་བཅས་པས་ཐོས་པའི་མཐུས་དེར། །ལོང་དུ་གྱུ་ལ་པ་ལས་ཐ་ར་ཏེ་དགའ་ལྡན་ཀྱི་ལྷར་སྐྱེས་ཞེ། བསྐལ་པ་དུ་ག་བརྒྱད་བརྒྱ་དུ་སངས་རྒྱས
ཕྱག་ཕྱི་ག་བརྩམ་ཉི་མ་པར་དུ་ནས་གདོན་ས་ངས་རྒྱ་བར་འགྱུར་བ་ལུང་བསྟན་པའི་ཞོལ་འབྱུང་བ་དང་། འཇམ་དཔལ་གནས་པའི་མདོ་ལས། ཟབ་མོའི་ཆོས་ལ་མོས་པ་བའི་དགེ་སློང་བརྒྱད་སྤྱལ་བར་འགྱུར་བའི་ཚེ་མ་དེ་ཐོས་པ་ཙམ་གྱི་མོ་དབང་ལས་འབྱུང་དང་ཀུ་ལ་ཚེམ་མཆོག
པར་ཡང་བསྟན་པས་ཡོག་ནམ་ལ་དེ་སྟོན་ས་བཟང་འདུ་ཏིང་ཤུ་ར་ངེས་པ་སོ། ༈ ། །གཉིས་པ་བྲམ་པ་བརྒྱུད་པའི་རིམ་པ་ལ། སྣགས་ལུགས་ཐུན་མོང་མིན་པའི་བརྒྱུད་རྩ་བ་ནི། རྡོ་རྗེ་འཆང་། ཏི་ལོ་པ། ན་རོ་པ། མར་པ་ལོ་ཙྩཱ་ཆེ་བརྒྱུད་རྒྱུད་ལ་གཏོ་ག་དང་། རྡོ་རྗེ་འཆང་། བློ་གྲོས

98 རིན་ཆེན། མདའ་བ་སྤྱན་སྔ་བ། ཞ་བ་རི་པ། མི་ཏྲི་པ། མར་པ་ཆོས་ཀྱི་བློ་གྲོས་ཏེ། དེ་ནས་བརྒྱུད་པ་ཉི་ས་འདོམ་ཀྱིས་དབང་ཕྱུག་མི་ལ་རས་པ། རྗེ་སྒམ་པོ་དགས་ཞོན་ནུ་སོགས་པ་ཀ་ཚང་གི་དོན་བརྒྱུད་བཞིན་དུ་བརྒྱུད་པ་ཡིན་ཞིང་། མདོ་ལུགས་རྣ་ག་པ་བགྲེལ་པའི་འཆད་རྒྱུ་ལ
འདི་ཡང་འབ་སྤྱན་ཞབས་ནས་བརྒྱུད་པའི་རྒྱ་བོ་ཕྱིམ་པ་བོན་ཡར་དང་། དེ་ལ་ཕྱེས་བུ་གསུམ་ཀྱི་པ་མ་རིམ་ཀྱིས་བརྒྱུད་པའི་དབང་གིས་རྒྱ་ཆེན་སྤྱོད་བརྒྱུད། ཟབ་མོ་ལྟ་བརྒྱུད། ཉམས་ལེན་བྱིན་རླབས་ཀྱི་བརྒྱུད་པ་གསུམ་གྱི་དང་པོ་ནི། །ཐུབ་པའི་དབང་པོ། རྒྱལ་ཚབ་བྱམས་པ།
ཐོགས་མེད། དབྱིག་གཉེན། འཕགས་པ་གྲོལ། བཙུན་གྲོལ། མཆོག་གི་སྡེ། དུལ་བ་འི་ལྷ། ཕྱོང་མཛད་འཆང་པོ། སེང་གེ་བཟང་པོ། ཀུ་ས་ལི་པ་ཆེ་རྒྱུད། གསེར་གླིང་པ། ཇོ་བོ་རྗེ་དཱི་པཾ་ཀ་ར་ཤྲཱི་ཛྙཱ་ན་རང་རྒྱུད། ༈ ། །གཉིས་པ་ནི། རྗེ་བཙུན་བའི་སངས་རྒྱས། འཇམ
དཔལ། ཀླུ་སྒྲུབ། ཙནྡྲ་ཀཱིརྟི། བྲམ་ཟེ་ས། རིག་པའི་ཁུ་བྱུག་གཉིས། རྗེ་བོ་རྗེ། ༈ ། །གསུམ་པ་ནི། རྡོ་རྗེ་འཆང་། ཏཻ་ལོ་ར། ནཱ་རོ། མཻ་ཏྲི་པ། རྗེ་བོ་རྗེ་བོ། །རྗེ་བོ་ནས་བརྒྱུད་པ་ལུགས་གཉིས་ཀ་འདྲེས་ཀྱིས། དགེ་བ་ཤེས་སྟོན་པ། སྤྱན་སྔ་བ། བྱ་ཡུལ་པ།
སྣམ་པོ་བ་རམ། དུ་ཡུལ་བས་ཕེབ་ནས་ཞིས་པ་ཆེད་ཀྱིས་ལྷག་མ་ཕུག་པ་དང་། འགྲོ་མགོན་མཉམ་ཆད་ལ་བསྟེན་པའི་སྐུ་ཞུ་ར་པ་དང་། སྒྲུབ་ཐུབ་པ་དང་། རྒྱ་ལྡུ་གས་རི་པ་དང་། ཤ་བ་སྒྲིང་པ་སོགས་ཐམས་ཅད་ལ་ཐུགས་པ་པ་སོ་ག་སྐྱེད་པ་སྙིང་ཕྱིན་དོན་བརྒྱུད་ལྡན་ནོ།། ༈ ||
འདར་སྤུངས་པ། བཅོམ་མའི་ཐུགས་བརྡ་གསེར་སྦྱང་ཅན་པ། །ཡབ་བུད་པར་བཞེད་ནས་ལྡན་ལྡོམ་ཕྱག་རྒྱ་ཆེ་ནི། །དཀའ་ཐུབ་མཆོག་འདི་ལ་ཕྱགས་ཡང་མཁས་གྲུབ་ཀྱི། །ཚང་ས་པ་ས་གྲུབ་ར་བྱེད་པའི་རིང་གཞན་ཕན་ཅན། །སྐྱ་བ་ལྡན་ཞིང་ཏུ་བོར་སྤྱར་བ་དེས། །ལམ་གསུམ

༄༅། །ཉིད་དགའ་ས་ལ་བར་བྱམས་མགོན་ཀྱིས། །ཕྱིར་ནས་རྟོག་གེ་ས་དཀྲུགས་པའི་དྲི་མ་ཀུན་ཅན། །མཁྱེན་པ་པ་ཐོ་ར་སྤྱར་བའི་ཡི་དྭགས་ཀྱི། །སྙོང་དང་མ་འཚམ་པ་ལ་ཅི་བྱ་ཡོད། །འོན་ཀྱང་ལྟུང་དང་བླ་མ་འི་མན་ངག་གིས། །ཡིད་ཆེས་བསྐྱེད་ཕྱིར་ཐུང་ཟད་བཤད་པ་ནི།
རང་ཉིད་ཕོན་འདི་དོན་དུ་སྦྱར་དོ་སྐུས། །ཞེས་ངེས་དོན་ཕྱག་རྒྱ་ཆེན་པོའི་སྒྲོན་ལ་མ་ཀྱི་འགྲེལ་བ་མདོར་བསྡུས་ཙམ་བཤད་པ་འདི་ནི། རང་ཉིད་ཀྱི་གདུང་པོས་གསུང་ས་བ་སྒྲུབ་སྣ་ཚོགས་ཀྱི་ངོར་ལེགས་བསྒྲུབ་པ་ཉེ་ཉིད་ཀྱིས་རྒྱུ་བཞིན་སྦྱར་བ་བཞིན་དུ་བསྒྲུབ་པའི་ཚེ་ཉིད་ཀྱི་རྒྱལ་ཁང་ལོར་བྲིས་
བརྒྱན་ཆོས་འཁོར་དུ་རྟོགས་པར་བྱེད་པ་དགེ་ལེགས་སུ་གྱུར་ཅིག || མངྒ་ལཾ་བྷ་ཝནྟུ། ཀུན་ས་ལན་གཅིག་ཞུས་སོ།།

Printed in the United States
By Bookmasters